C000215230

Bob McIntyre

THE FLYING SCOT

Drawing by David Boarer.

BOB McINTYRE

THE FLYING SCOT

MICK WALKER

breedon **books**
PUBLISHING

First published in Great Britain in 2006 by
The Breedon Books Publishing Company Limited
Breedon House, 3 The Parker Centre,
Derby, DE21 4SZ.

©MICK WALKER, 2006

All Rights Reserved. No part of this publication may be reproduced, stored in
a retrieval system, or transmitted in any form, or by any means, electronic,
mechanical, photocopying, recording or otherwise without the prior
permission in writing of the copyright holders, nor be otherwise circulated in
any form or binding or cover other than in which it is published and without a
similar condition being imposed on the subsequent publisher.

Dedication

This book is dedicated to all my countless loyal readers all over
the world, who by purchasing my books have allowed me to
write 100 titles since the first was published in 1985. And
especially Agnes and Bill Cadger, who have done so much over
the years to keep Bob Mac's memory alive.

ISBN 1 85983 500 7
UPC 8 262051 0012

Printed and bound by Biddles Ltd, King's Lynn, Norfolk

Contents

*"I am privileged to
have access to the
Mortons Motorcycle
Media Archive,
which I consider to
be the finest in the
world and a national
treasure."*
MICK WALKER

Every so often a unique snapshot of times gone by is discovered in a dusty vault or in shoeboxes in an attic by an enthusiastic amateur photographer. They are living history. Each and every one of us cannot resist the temptation as we marvel at the quality of the images, to let our mind drift back to the good old days and wonder what it was really like.

We at Mortons Motorcycle Media, market-leading publishers of classic and vintage titles, own one of the largest photographic archives of its kind in the world. It is a treasure trove of millions of motorcycle and related images, many of which have never seen the light of day since they were filed away in the dark-room almost 100 years ago.

Perhaps the biggest gem of all is our collection of glass plates – almost two tons of them to be precise! They represent a largely hitherto unseen look into our motorcycling heritage from the turn of the century. Many of the plates are priceless and capture an era long gone when the pace of life was much slower and traffic jams were unheard of.

We are delighted to be associated with well known author Mick Walker in the production of this book and hope you enjoy the images from our archive.

Terry Clark,
Managing Director,
Mortons Media Group Ltd

Preface

THIS, the fourth in a series intended to cover the careers of the world's greatest motorcycle racing champions, presents the man who never actually won a world championship – but certainly deserved to more than many who have actually achieved the feat.

Bob McIntyre – The Flying Scot tells the story of the man who was in many ways the two-wheel equivalent of that great car racing driver, Stirling Moss, who is seen as one of the real greats in his sport, but who, like Bob, never won an official world title.

Even today, well over four decades after his untimely death following an accident while racing his 500cc Manx Norton at Oulton Park, Cheshire in August 1962, Bob McIntyre's memory lives on. And every year (since 1985) there has been a Bob McIntyre Memorial race meeting. Currently held at East Fortune, it attracts racing enthusiasts from as far afield as Australia. The reason why his memory has survived the decades is evident. Not only was 'Bob Mac' a brilliantly gifted rider and self-taught mechanic, but he was also a man of the people, someone who would always help a fellow competitor or take the time to sign an autograph or chat to a fan. He was also honest, loyal and modest; his word was his bond.

Unlike the three riders already covered in this series, John Surtees, Mike Hailwood and Giacomo Agostini, Bob McIntyre did not come from a motorcycling family (Surtees) or a moneyed family (Hailwood and Agostini). Bob Mac was very much a self-made man; someone who started from the very bottom and reached the very top in his chosen profession.

Many good people helped me produce this tribute to Bob Mac, providing either information or photographs and often both. These include: Bill and Agnes Cadger, David Pike, Stan Wright, Hugh Ward, Eleanor Quigley, Jackie Campbell, members of the Scottish Classic Motorcycle Racing Club, Colin Dunbar, Dougie Muir, Jimmy Mitchell, David Boarer, Pamela and Ian Lawton, Geoff Leather, Peter Reeve, Rodney Turner, Denis Gallagher, George Plenderleith and Ian and Rita Welsh. Morton's Media Group Ltd, who house the archives of *The Motor Cycle* and *Motor Cycling* magazines of yesteryear, helped in their usual way.

Read on and discover just how great Bob McIntyre really was – the first man to lap the Isle of Man TT circuit, the most fearsome in the world, at over 100 mph. I'm sure you, the reader, will gain as much pleasure in following Bob's career as I have had in writing it; this is my 100th book.

Mick Walker, Wisbech, Cambridgeshire.

Chapter 1

A Glasgow Boy

ROBERT Macgregor (Bob) McIntyre was born on 28 November 1928, the eldest of two sons. The family home was at 28 Harefield Drive, Scotstoun, a suburb of Glasgow. Bob's father Robert worked as a riveter in the shipyards overlooking the Clyde, with his wife Elizabeth (also known in the family as Iza). Their second son, David Killow, was born in 1937.

It was a close-knit, working-class family, which knew the good times as well as the bad, certainly in the early 1930s when young Bob was an infant. The Great Depression that hit America and Europe meant that things were tough in the McIntyre family, with Bob's father out of work for long periods. But somehow they got by, thanks in no small part to the community spirit which existed at the time.

In the main, Bob and his younger brother attended local schools in the Scotstoun area, except for a period after the German bombing raids on Glasgow in 1940–41, when both boys were packed off to Alva in Clackmannanshire as evacuees. However, as Bob was to recall later 'we made ourselves unpopular and were soon home again'.

As Bob also admitted 'I cannot say that I was a good scholar – average I suppose'. But he was good at athletics, particularly running, and an excellent soccer player, generally as a centre-half. As proof of his leadership qualities he was captain of the Victoria Drive Senior Secondary School team.

In his teenage days, although he was interested in both cars and motorcycles, he admitted that 'I was not excited by race meetings... my reason for seeking a job in a garage when I left school at 14 was to learn a useful trade, not because of any passion for motors'. This statement was due to the realisation that his father had not had an easy working life. And McIntyre senior did not want his sons to follow in his footsteps in the Glasgow shipyards. As Bob said, 'he wanted to see me with an assured future in a trade less subject to alternate booms and depressions'. But in Bob's youth neither of them could have dreamed that the profession would be that of racing motorcyclist!

His future career could not have been further from young Bob's mind when he began his first job at the Robb Brothers garage in Byron Street, Partick, the next borough to Scotstoun. As Bob said in his booklet *Motor Cycling Today*, which was published in 1962, 'it was a fairly big garage, just off the main road, and employed 60 to 70 people in all, including six or seven mechanics and several apprentices. I could not be apprenticed until I was 16, so for two years I repaired punctures, washed and greased cars, sold petrol and did all the odd jobs one does when starting in a garage. I learned to drive cars, moving them around the garage.' But what Bob didn't learn anything about was motorcycles, as the Partick garage only dealt in cars and commercial vehicles.

On Bob's 16th birthday, he signed on as an apprentice. As he said later 'now I learned electrical wiring, welding, panel beating, engine overhaul... it was a good general training I received on both petrol and diesel-engined vehicles.'

His first motorcycle

Next Bob purchased his first motorcycle. This was a 1931 Norton Model 16H. Costing £12, it was, for the young Bob, a lot of money, as his wages were in the region of £1 per week at the time.

He got a good earbashing from his mother when he returned to Harefield Drive. Bob described the episode in the following words: 'when I came home with it I discovered quickly that my mother did not share my enthusiasm for the idea. She took one look at the Norton and raised all the objections about oil and noise and danger that mothers have been raising since youngsters started motorcycling. My bag was packed for me and I was invited to choose between my home and my motorcycle.'

However, eventually Mrs McIntyre relented, and Bob was allowed to keep the bike. He said, 'besides riding it to and from work I was soon using it for Sunday afternoon runs. There was no question of burning up the road on it; side-valve engined, it was a sturdy slogger but no high speed performer.'

Bob was to spend many happy hours with this machine and during his ownership the Norton was stripped down to the smallest component part and a rebuild undertaken. Bob remembered: 'I rebored the engine. I scraped every part until the metal gleamed. I repainted the machine and rechromed the brightwork.' When Bob sold the bike after some six months it was in showroom condition and raised a princely £50.

With the proceeds of the Norton sale and a loan from his parents for the balance, Bob's next acquisition was a 1935 Ariel Red Hunter single. The 497cc (81.8 x 95mm) ohv engine was much more powerful than the old side-

Bob on military service,
Suez, 1948.

valve 16H. And it was much faster – Bob was to fall off it several times, without injury, while making this discovery. But still Bob said, 'I had no competitive ambitions.'

A bike club was in the process of being formed locally, and just prior to his 18th birthday the young Bob McIntyre became one of the first half-dozen founder members. This organisation was the Mercury Motor Cycle Club – the emblem of which was to adorn Bob Mac's crash helmet throughout his future racing career. But at that time the youngster was purely a touring member.

National Service

Bob was called up for 19 months of National Service (this lasted in Great Britain until 1961) and the Ariel was put into storage. Following some six weeks of 'square bashing' with the Green Howards at Gallowgate Camp in Yorkshire, Bob was posted to Rhyl in North Wales, where he undertook a driver-mechanics course and passed a vehicle mechanics test.

Next he was sent to the Royal Artillery and Dispersal Centre in Plumstead, south-east London. Interestingly, Plumstead was where the AMC works were, manufacturers of Matchless and AJS. Bob later recalled, 'that did not interest me at the time.' In truth, he probably didn't even know how close he was to one of his future racing factories!

In January 1948 Bob was posted to Suez and the remainder of his military service was spent on the North African coast; this was the first time he had been outside the British Isles. At first the young Scot was in a light aid detachment, carrying out inspections of lorries. He also drove what he was to describe as a 'wreaker' – a truck equipped for rescuing broken-down vehicles.

Next Bob became a DR (Dispatch Rider). This was at Homs, 60 miles east of Tripoli. He got the job because he was the only man in the platoon who could ride a motorcycle! The job involved taking despatches between Homs and Tripoli. But as Bob was to relate 'I thought that as a job it was a bit overrated.' This was because, in Bob's words, 'the trouble was that there were not enough despatches!'. In fact, most of his time was spent 'loafing about' rather than riding. Finally tiring of looking for excuses to ride his motorcycle, Bob obtained a transfer back to repair work in the workshops.

He moved with the unit from Tripoli back to Benghazi, then as Bob said, 'we were disbanded and I came home for demobilization.'

And so Bob returned home in July 1949 and continued his apprenticeship in the Partick garage. Because he had been working at his trade in the army, 18 months of his service was counted as part of his apprenticeship – only the six weeks spent in primary training were wasted. This meant that Bob now only had 18 months of his five-year apprenticeship left.

Next, as Bob said, 'I cleaned up the Red Hunter. By now the Mercury Club had grown and two or three of the lads were taking part in scrambles and trials. With a pal I went along to a scramble at Airdrie, 12 miles from Glasgow, quite a good scramble centre in its day.' It was the first motorcycle sporting event Bob had witnessed and the day out was to change his life.

This is how he described it in his own words: '... all the big Scottish names of the time were there, but the rider I remember vividly – I believe he won the event – was a certain Bill Smith, who cut a very dashing figure on a brand new AJS.' At the time Bill Smith worked for Edinburgh dealers Alexanders; later he became sales manager of Norton in Birmingham before, in 1961, transferring to south-east London to become sales manager of AJS and Matchless. Bob recalled the day in 1962, saying, 'the bug bit me, I thought I'd like to have a go at this.'

Competition debut

And so, after watching another scrambling event shortly afterward, in late 1949 Bob entered a scramble at Craigend Farm, near his Scotstoun home.

Again Bob describes the scene:

... my preparation for the event was very simple; merely removed the Red Hunter's headlamp. I did no tuning. The result? I cannot remember. I doubt if I even finished; I probably fell off on every lap. I remember little about the event except that it was an appallingly wet

Bob got the job of DR (Dispatch Rider) as he was 'the only man in the platoon who could ride a motorcycle'. He is seen here at Homs, some 60 miles east of Tripoli.

The McIntyre family c.1950. Left to right: father Robert McGregor (a riveter in the Clyde shipyards), mother Elizabeth, younger brother David and Bob.

The Mercury Motor Cycle Club one Sunday morning, early in 1950, outside the Ascot cinema in Annesland in the west end of Glasgow. Bob's Ariel 500 is the fourth machine from the left and Bob is at the rear (seventh person from the left).

and dirty day and I got soaked to the skin. When I reached home my mother took one look at me and ordered me to go outside and strip before coming in. I do not blame her a bit. My waterproofs were holding the water in instead of keeping it out. I must have looked as though I had been wallowing in mud, and I suppose I had.

Even though Bob thought to himself that he must be mad, he continued racing off road. For two more meetings the bike was much as it had been on that first outing, but during the winter months he spent much time converting the Ariel into a more suitable machine. For starters there was a new frame, described by Bob as 'a shorter, higher one', with new wheels and a tuned engine. So by the following spring he was 'ready for serious scrambling. I competed in every event I could and did reasonably well, winning quite a few.'

As he was to recall later:

… only one still stands out in my mind. It was at Auchterader, near Perth. During the race the Ariel's back wheel collapsed. Now I was still using the same machine to get to and from meetings. Indeed, I rode it to and from work as well – knobbly tyres, small lights and

Beveridge Park

Bob McIntyre's road racing career really began on Saturday 1 July 1950, when he went to Beveridge Park, Kirkcaldy, to watch the annual Scottish Road Races. This was his first sight of the tarmac sport. And from then on he was to begin a love affair which was to stay with him for the rest of his life. In addition, Bob was to race at the Fife coastal venue every year from 1951 until 1962, except for 1954 (AJS works rider) and 1957, when the Kirkcaldy club was unable to run the event through fuel shortages caused by the Suez Crisis.

So what of Beveridge Park itself? It had first opened back in 1892, the 104 acres being created from Robbie's Park and land purchased from the local Raith Estate. This was thanks to Provost Michael Beveridge who had died two years earlier, leaving money in trust for the people of Kirkcaldy to create a park, a library and a hall.

As for Michael Beveridge himself, he had been born in Kirkcaldy in 1836, the youngest child and only son of a local bank agent. After schooling in Kirkcaldy and London, he had returned to the town of his birth, becoming a successful businessman; he was also involved in politics, finally becoming a Provost.

Beveridge Park, 1951. M.E. Patey (350 BSA) leads L. Currie (350 BSA) and Alastair King (500 Norton).

The opening ceremony for Beveridge Park was held on 24 September 1892; over 10,000 people attended. Features of the superb parkland included two lodges (Raith Gate and Southerton), two life-size lions and four cannon (these together with gates and railings vanished during World War Two). There was also an ornamental bandstand, which occupied a central position in the park and was a focal point for the Opening Day ceremony. This bandstand was finally scrapped in 1956. The other important feature of Beveridge Park was its large lake.

The first motorcycle race meeting held on the perimeter road, which ran just inside the park, was held in the summer of 1948, the circuit

THIS PARK WAS PROVIDED OUT OF MONEY BEQUEATHED FOR THE PURPOSE TO THE PROVOST MAGISTRATES AND TOWN COUNCIL OF KIRKCALDY BY MICHAEL BEVERIDGE Esq OF BEECHWOOD WHO DIED PROVOST OF KIRKCALDY 4TH MARCH 1890

Wall plaque at Beveridge Park for Michael Beveridge (1836–1890).

Beveridge Park, Kirkcaldy, held special memories for Bob; it was there, in 1950, that he first witnessed road-racing and over the years he would return as a competitor. In 1962 he brought the works 285 Honda four to the tiny tree-lined 1.375-mile circuit.

measuring 1.375 miles in length. Motorcycles ran anti-clockwise and important sections of the course included: The Railway Dip, Raith Road, The Brae and The Snake. For the most part trees lined the narrow circuit. Another feature was the severe cambers – the road surface dropping away quite sharply from its high point in the middle of the road; this being to assist drainage – but was also something of a hazard for the riders. Another problem was moss, which was prone to form on the road surface in the areas covered by trees. In fact, this had to be 'burned' off on several occasions before racing could take place!

During the early days of Beveridge Park as a motor-sport circuit, not only bikes, but also cars competed (the cars in the opposite direction, i.e. clockwise). In 1952 a combined bike/car meeting was staged – with Joe Potts driving one of his own JP Formula 3 cars.

Even though it was an extremely demanding course (due to the narrowness and awkward cambers of the road – and the potential danger caused by the myriad of trees) Beveridge Park continued to be a firm favourite with competitors

and spectators alike. But eventually in 1988 the final meeting – billed as the 40th Scottish Road Races – was staged on Saturday 18 June. The Kirkcaldy and District Motor Club were still the organisers, working, as they had done over the years, with the local Kirkcaldy District Council (the park owners). Quite simply the latest machines had become too fast. And having walked around the circuit I have to agree that this was the right decision. However, in the context of the Bob McIntyre story, Beveridge Park was to play an important role in his developing career. And, to the author's mind, taking the factory 285cc Honda four to the Fife circuit in spring 1962 was an act of faith to his many Scottish fans, which one cannot imagine being repeated in today's big money, hi-tech MotoGP world.

It said a lot for the real Bob McIntyre.

Bob (80) following Leslie Cooper, both mounted on AJS 7Rs, Beveridge Park, 1952.

scramble-tuned as it was; it was the only machine I had. The trouble now was that I had to get home on it and Glasgow was close on 50 miles away. I ripped off the tyre, removed all the spokes and started rebuilding the wheel. The race had long since finished. Time passed before I got the wheel to spin reasonably true. Then I realised everyone had gone, it was growing dark rapidly and I was alone in the middle of the moor. A grey, damp mist was rolling down with the night and there was not a soul about but me. It was silent and clammy and eerie. I got the tube and tyre on very quickly and departed at speed!

By now the Ariel had been converted to a two-fifty, since it was then possible to enter and win events in three capacity classes!

One of the famous Beveridge Park lions.

Bob scrambled an Ariel 500 Red Hunter of pre-war vintage similar to the bike shown, but modified with telescopic forks. Later still, it was changed to 250cc – so he could compete in more than one class!

Bob carried on scrambling until as late as mid-1951, by which time he was regularly winning at club events – and in some cases bigger meetings including the Scottish national scrambles championship series.

But by now, as Bob said:

I was infatuated with motorcycling. I wanted to work full-time on motorcycles, and when I reached my 21st birthday and finished my apprenticeship I found a job with a firm of Glasgow motorcycle dealers, Valenti Brothers. The job was servicing and repairing touring machines; the firm had little or no connection with the sport at that time.

Road racing

Up until 1950 Bob had never seen a road race. He then went with friends to spectate on Saturday 1 July. The venue? Beveridge Park, Kirkcaldy, Fife. This was a public park, owned by the local council – the perimeter track of which was used for an annual road race. As Bob was later to recall 'Tommy McEwan and the veteran Denis Parkinson were the stars but the general standard of riding in Scotland at that time was not high, and my chief impression was, well, I reckon I could do as well as half of those chaps. I'd like to have a go.' And that was what set the Bob McIntyre racing effort into gear.

Bob again:

I had not got a bike suitable for road racing, but I was friendly with another member of the Mercury Club named Alan McKenzie who had a BSA 350cc Gold Star. When I told him of my ambitions he offered to lend it to me to ride in a race at Ballado Airfield, Kincardine, three

*weeks later [on 21 July 1950]. Alan and I set off together on the Gold
Star. I got on first, Alan pushed until the engine started, then loaded
tools, spares and cans of petrol on top of the tank and against my
stomach. After he climbed on the pillion we did not dare stop until we
reached Ballado!*

At the airfield the two of them removed the silencer and the headlamp –
and, as Bob said later 'that was our preparation done. Our rivals included
KTT Velocettes and Manx Nortons, but I was lucky. The track was covered
with loose gravel and most of the lads – all amateur riders, no great names –
were nervous of the way the machines slid on it. With my scrambling
experience this did not bother me and, in fact, suited me.'

The above is in typical modest McIntyre prose. In fact he had entered four
events and won three of them – two in the 350cc class and one in the 500cc
division – and fell off in the fourth event (the 500cc final) after locking up the
rear wheel.

Bob left Ballado with £15 in his pocket (almost a month's wages for a
working man in those days) and, as he recalled later:

*… feeling a very rich young man. It seemed easy. Alan and I went to
more meetings and I won some more. Alan left most of the racing to
me. He realized I could go quicker than he could and he was keen to
see his machine win. We ploughed all our winnings back into buying
high compression pistons, a rev counter, megaphones. I even sold my
Red Hunter to buy more bits. We worked on the machine in a garage
behind my friend's house.*

As for Bob's riding gear when he made his racing debut at Ballado, he later
recalled 'I wore a leather lumber jacket, corduroy breeches and an old pair of
riding boots that were too big for me.' In fact, he was not to buy
professionally made leathers and boots until he was about to ride in the 1952
Clubman's TT in the Isle of Man (see Chapter 2), but all this was very much
in the future.

One of the very last dirt bike events which Bob took part in on the Ariel
was the Lanarkshire Grand National, the first round of the Scottish Scrambles
Championship at Faskine Farm, near Airdrie. Weather conditions were
described as 'perfect – too good', and the course, situated on the site of a
disused mine, rapidly became a dust bowl. *The Motor Cycle* dated 7 June
1951 reported: 'several thousand spectators witnessed fully 3½ hours of
exciting racing.' And 'J. Forster (Velocette) took the lead and was never really

The BSA Gold Star was one of the classic motorcycles of all time. It was capable of taking part in most forms of motorcycle sport, as well as providing daily transport.

BSA Gold Star

There is absolutely no doubt that the famous BSA Gold Star was the most versatile motorcycle ever built. Touring, fast road work, road racing, scrambling, trials, enduro, sand racing, grass track, sprinting – you name it, the 'Goldie' has done it!

The original M24 Gold Star was born out of success achieved by a specially prepared M23 Empire Star ridden at Brooklands in June 1937 by former TT rider Wal Handley, who won one of the coveted Brooklands Gold Stars for circulating the Surrey track at over 100mph.

BSA decided to capitalise on this success by introducing the new all-alloy-engined M24 Gold Star for the 1938 season. This displaced 496cc (82x94mm) running on a compression ratio of 7.75:1 petrol or the optional 12.5:1 for dope; BSA claimed 28 and 36bhp respectively.

Then came the war and during the immediate aftermath of the conflict no Gold Star models were built at BSA's Small Heath factory until 1949. However, development did not stop. First BSA introduced the 348cc (71x88mm) B31 in August 1945, and this became the basis of what was to become known as the pre-unit B range. The newcomer was quickly joined in January 1946 by the 348cc B32 competition mount to cater for the Clubman rider of the day. The three-fifty engine was then bored out to 85mm to become the 499cc B33 roadster early in 1947 and the B34 competition mount followed later that year. The B32 and B34 competition machines used iron cylinder heads and barrels of the standard roadster range. These machines used telescopic front forks (the pre-war bikes had girders), but the rigid frame was retained.

When an alloy top-end conversion became available for the B32 in 1947, many riders specified this fitment in order to lower the overall weight of the trials orientated machine. This did not go unnoticed among the road racers of the era, and much experimental work was carried out, both by the works and privateers, to gain additional horsepower.

After the inaugural Clubman TT races of 1947, a couple of customers approached Jack Amott at BSA with the idea of building racing machines using trials alloy top-ends, with a view to the following year's Clubman TT. This approach set great minds at Small Heath thinking.

And so, during late 1947 and much of 1948, secret development was set in motion at the BSA factory, resulting in the surprise announcement of a new plunger-framed, all-alloy B32 Gold Star on the eve of the London Earls Court Show in November 1948.

Coded the ZB32, this was basically a competition bike for the off-road rider, but it could also be quickly converted for track use. The ZB32 Gold

Star was capable of 25bhp as against 18bhp for the standard B31. A wide range of easily available factory options transformed the Gold Star from its primary role of either trials or roadster into a potent scrambler or fast Clubman's racer.

A year later the larger ZB34 arrived, offering even more performance. However, the smaller engined bike was to prove more successful in the early days, because it was not only more competitive in its class, but also more reliable.

The first major change to the Gold Star's specification occurred at the end of 1951, when a redesigned, die-cast cylinder head with separate rocker box was introduced. A continuous engine development programme ensured almost yearly changes to specification and performance.

For 1953, BSA introduced the BB model; essentially using the small fin alloy engine from the B32/34, but mounted in a swinging arm frame.

Small fin ZB32 of the type used by Bob McIntyre early in his career.

In spring 1954 a new Gold Star made its debut: the CB. The newcomer employed the BB cycle parts but the engine had been considerably altered. The most notable external difference was the much more comprehensive finning of the cylinder barrel and head. Besides the updated engine, there were a couple of other important innovations, which the power unit would retain as features of the Gold Star Clubmans until production finally ceased during the early 1960s. These were the now classic swept-back exhaust header pipe and the replacement of the BB's RN carburettor by the new Amal GP instrument. In addition, there were also separate clip-on handlebars for the first time. Coded CB32 and CB34, the new models retained the earlier bore and stroke dimensions. But even so there were numerous changes to the engine, such as a shorter con-rod and a correspondingly decreased cylinder barrel height, a new form of tappet

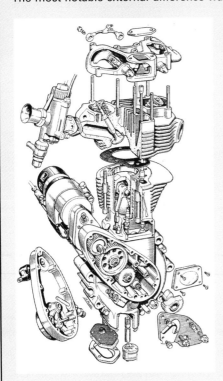

Exploded view of small fin ZB32 Gold Star engine, showing details such as valve gear, timing gears, oil pump, mad/dyno and carburettor.

Bob pictured in 1951 during his early racing days; note the use of two-piece leathers at this time.

adjustment and a slightly altered crank angle, while the 1953 flap-type breathing device had been superseded by a timed rotary breather.

The continual search for superior performance and reliability led the BSA development team to introduce the DB32 and DB34 for the 1955 season. But unlike the previous year, the majority of changes were minor, attention to detail being the key word.

1956 was the final year of the Clubman's TT, and it also saw the final development of the Gold Star, the DBD34, which was actually not that much different from the DB34. The 350 was effectively at the end of its development, as no DBD version was ever offered. There was also by now a pukka Gold Star Scrambler, known as the Catalina in the US. This, together with the DBD34, continued to be available until 1962, although a few bikes were built as late as 1964. In fact American dealers were largely responsible for the Gold Star remaining in production after the B31 and B33 roadsters had been axed in 1960 and 1961 respectively.

Today, well over four decades after its demise, the Gold Star has become an icon among classic bike enthusiasts, with prices rising ever higher for pristine examples.

worried. R. McIntyre (Ariel) and R. Pullar (Triumph) scrapped throughout the race for second place.' Which Bob eventually took.

Bob McIntyre now saw road racing, rather than off-road sport, as his sole objective. However, after his successful debut at Ballado the previous year, as he later recalled:

> …we did not clean up quite to the extent we had optimistically hoped for, but I did quite well and won most of the events in Scotland that we could reach. Alan and I still rode the Gold Star, two-up to the meetings, with our spares heaped around us, and other competitors arrived in much the same way. We were all ordinary working lads. None of us had money or wealthy backers. There was virtually no dealer sponsorship or trade support in Scotland at this time.

Kirkcaldy, July 1951

Probably the biggest road races in Scotland during the early 1950s were those staged at Beveridge Park, Kirkcaldy, on the Fife coast. And the meeting of Saturday 7 July 1951 was no exception. With an entry of some 100 competitors, riders that day were faced with the extremes of the British weather – from 'pouring rain to blinding sun' (*The Motor Cycle*).

The name R. McIntyre (number 27) was entered on the BSA Gold Star three-fifty referred to earlier, in both the 350 and 500cc classes. And light rain

Mercury Motorcycle Club badge.

was already 'polishing' the track when the 350cc heats were run. This resulted in speeds dropping and a number of crashes, none of which were serious. Most of the casualties occurred at the treacherous 'Snake', which concluded in a right-angle, downhill turn into the finishing straight.

The large entry of 47 riders for the 350cc heats did not include the previous year's winner, Denis Parkinson, but another well-known English rider, Bernard Hargreaves from Clitheroe, Lancashire, riding a Douglas Plus 90 flat twin machine, managed to take this title south once again. Bob McIntyre finished runner-up in both his heat and the final. Third was another BSA rider, M. Patey.

Then, after winning his 500cc heat, Bob suffered a retirement in the final, in both cases with his Gold Star three-fifty. In this latter event Jock Weddell (WDS) won (also setting the fastest lap of the day at 56.3mph) from W.G. Scott (BSA) and Bob's future great friend and eventual teammate in the Joe Potts squad Alastair King, on an overhead camshaft Norton.

Bob's rapid progress during 1951 was to be ultimately noticed by one of the very few trade concerns who were by then beginning to take a serious interest in motorcycle racing north of the border; Cooper Brothers of Troon. The next chapter in the Bob McIntyre story was just about to begin.

A ZB32 Gold Star BSA similar to the the one Bob made his road-racing debut on at Ballado Airfield Kincardine, 21 July 1950.

Chapter 2

Cooper Brothers

SAM and younger brother Leslie Cooper ran a successful motorcycle business during the early 1950s entitled, appropriately enough, Cooper Brothers, at 125–9 Templehill, Troon, Ayrshire, in the south-west of Scotland. At that time they were the main agents for several marques including Ariel, BSA, Corgi, Francis-Barnett, James, Royal Enfield, Triumph, Velocette, AJS and Matchless.

Bob McIntyre first sprang to the public's attention when he finished runner-up in the Junior Clubman's TT in June 1952; his first-ever visit to the Isle of Man. He also set the fastest lap on the Cooper Bros BSA Gold Star.

Bob after the race, being congratulated for his outstanding performance in setting a new class lap record on his first visit to the Isle of Man.

It was through the two latter marques, plus BSA, that the brothers were to sign Bob McIntyre for two years during 1952 and 1953.

As related in Chapter 1, Bob Mac had managed to beat Leslie Cooper in most of the races the two had competed in together during 1951 – Bob riding his friend Alan McKenzie's BSA Gold Star, Leslie Cooper aboard a new-that-year AJS 7R. As the latter machine was a much superior bike, older brother Sam Cooper was quick to realise that in Bob McIntyre there was a rider of considerable potential. And he was proved to be right!

So at the end of 1951 Sam Cooper – who was the senior partner in the business – asked Bob if he would like to ride for him in the Isle of Man Junior Clubman's TT of 1952 on a new BSA ZB32 Gold Star.

The history of this race series is outlined within a separate boxed section in this chapter, but suffice it to say that the Clubman's TT used the same 37.73-mile Mountain course as the legendary TT races. But the Clubman's event was for fully-equipped production roadsters only, out-and-out racers being barred. However, as Bob was to recall later 'it was not, however, in any way an amateur race.'

With the offer of the Gold Star for the Isle of Man came an offer of a job at Cooper Brothers, and so, in the winter of 1951, Bob switched employment. Bob said: 'Cooper Brothers lent me the Clubman's model that I would be racing in the TT to use for commuting between Glasgow and Troon, 30 miles away.' Bob was at that time still living at his parents' home in Harefield Drive, Scotstoun.

Prior to the Clubman's TT, Bob did only a couple of meetings in 1952. One was at Winfield in Berwickshire, where he won the 350cc race and came second (on the same 350cc BSA) in the 500cc event. Later the same month he finished second in a joint bike/car meeting at Beveridge Park, Kirkcaldy, in the 500cc final. Then, as Bob said, 'I rode the Gold Star down to Liverpool, and took it across on the boat to the Isle of Man.'

First Island impressions

Of his initial impressions of the Island, Bob was to admit that it didn't make 'any great impression on me.' This was because, in fact, he saw little of it except the circuit, Sam Cooper being impatient that the young McIntyre should use his time learning the course. Bob described it thus:

...he hustled me into a car with himself and an experienced TT rider of the time, Jack Slater. Sam had also raced in the island and the pair of them proceeded to drive me round the circuit, telling me how to ride it. They showed me braking points, told me which gear to use on each bend. I am sure it was all good advice, but by the time we got to Ramsey, I had to beg them to stop. Trying to absorb their ceaseless flow of information had given me a splitting headache.

Anyone who has ridden the Mountain circuit will no doubt be able to appreciate just why Bob McIntyre had ended up with a headache. Quite simply, it is the most difficult racing circuit in the world to learn. Learning it cannot be speeded up as Sam Cooper had attempted to do. Everyone is different. Some aspiring racers take years to learn it, whereas others can begin to learn it straight away. Even someone with the natural talent that Bob McIntyre was gifted with still had to learn this difficult course in their own time.

So Bob returned to the guesthouse in which he was staying, got out the Gold Star and set off by himself. He once admitted, 'I have never made a practice of walking round a circuit as some riders do, as one is not going to walk round in the race it seems to me pointless.'

So Bob rode round the course at touring speeds for some 20 laps before, as he said, 'I started using any speed.' And 'I found the length of the circuit overwhelming. There was so much to learn.'

A practice crash

Then came the start of practice – and a crash which was never reported by the press at the time. It came in the first practice session. This is how Bob described the incident:

I did one lap and was full of the joys of spring. I roared down from Brandish to Hillberry, with the intention of taking this fast right-hander flat out in top gear. I thought it could be done and it can be done. But I did not do it. I had forgotten to remove the centre stand from the Gold Star! It grounded, lifted out the back end of the bike and I came off. I was doing 100mph.

When Bob returned with the extensively damaged machine (mudguards, tanks and footrests needed replacement) he of course had to confess to Sam Cooper that he had crashed at high speed on the second lap of practice. Sam's reaction was that he wanted to pack the bike and Bob straight off back to

Scotland there and then. This was because he was convinced that his young and inexperienced protégé would 'kill himself if he continued.' But Bob told him that if 'he did not let me ride the bike he and I were finished.' The two men had a big scene. The result was that Sam Cooper agreed to let Bob carry on, providing he went cautiously '...which I did – until the penultimate practice anyway, when I put up quite a quick lap.' This incident showed up two things. First the McIntyre determination not to give in, second his ability to recover from a set-back. These were to be two pivotal traits which Bob McIntyre was to display for the remainder of his life.

By now, at the end of practice week, the 'crash' had largely been forgotten, with the rest of practice going smoothly. In fact, it has to be said, the incident was not generally known to have happened. With a race number of 76, Bob's entry was hidden in a 103-man field, of which there were to be 96 starters on race day. These comprised AJS (4), BSA (69), Douglas (4), Royal Enfield (2), Norton (14) and Matchless (3).

The notable riders were Bernard Hargreaves, Derek Ennett, Eric Housley, Ken James, Derek Powell, Owen Greenwood and Frank Sheene (father of Barry).

Following his sponsors' orders, Bob did not show his hand until the very last practice session, held on Friday morning, 6 June. The record lap of 29 minutes 35 seconds (76.55mph), established in 1951 by Ken James (Norton) in the 1951 Junior Clubman's, was broken by no fewer than four riders: R. Jones (BSA) 29m 27s (76.88mph), D. Ennett (Matchless) 29m 16s (77.36mph), K. James (Norton) 28m 27s (78.71mph) and finally R. McIntyre 28m 55s (78.30mph). So the Scottish newcomer had gone round quickest! This was a fantastic achievement considering he had never seen the circuit until little over a week previously. It was a full 40 seconds quicker than James's 1951 record. As Bob was later to recall: 'people sat up and looked; BSA's representatives in the Island became interested and vetted the machine for us. I had maintained it myself until then.'

In typical modest fashion Bob didn't mention that he had broken the lap record during practice in his 1962 book *Motor Cycling Today*.

The race
And so came Bob's first Isle of Man race, the 1952 Junior Clubman's TT. A scene-setting journalistic picture prior to the start of this event was contained in *The Motor Cycle* race report, dated 12 June 1952:

Clubs from all over the country were represented. Clubmates of competitors lined the course four deep to cheer their champions. For them the Clubman's race has a special significance. Many of them

1952 Junior Manx Grand Prix. Bob at the weigh-in on his Cooper Bros AJS 7R.

regard it as their private party. Every clubman worth his salt regards his club as the best there is, and, given a clear run, Tom or Dick or Harry, or whatever his name may be, is going to prove it today.

Although the history books show that Eric Housley of the Chesterfield Club won the four-lap race in 1 hour 54 minutes 25.2 seconds (78.92mph), it was the runner-up Bob McIntyre (riding for his local Glasgow Mercury Club) who really made his name that day. Bob's figures of 1 hour 55 minutes 17.4 seconds (78.52mph) don't really do justice to what he achieved. Not only was Bob a TT novice, whereas Housley was a 23-year-old motor mechanic who had already ridden in the 1950 and 1951 events, but also the young Scot didn't have a clear run. This is how he described the race:

...at the end of the first lap Eric Housley (BSA) led by twelve seconds. I was second, Ken James (Norton) was third, Derek Powell (BSA) was fourth and Derek Ennett (Matchless) fifth. All five of us had broken the previous year's record lap set by Ken James. However, my machine was not going as well as it should have done and on the second lap Ken James overtook me. By the third lap Housley was fifty seconds ahead of James and James was ten seconds ahead of me. My bike began to misfire. I do not know what made me do it but I shut the air

AJS 7R

At various times in his career Bob McIntyre rode the AJS 7R – the famous 'Boy Racer', stretching from the 1952 Manx Grand Prix through to the early 1960s.

The 7R was first announced in February 1948. And compared to the pre-war R7, the newcomer shared very little except the basic concept of certain design principles, including being an overhead single, with camshaft driven by chain, the latter with a Weller tensioner.

As for the 7R's frame, this was largely copied from the works E90 Porcupine twin, being a wide-spaced double cradle layout in welded steel tubing. The front forks were modified AMC Teledraulics (first used on the wartime G3/L model), while at the rear the fashionable swinging arm was controlled by a pair of oil-damped spring-controlled shock absorbers. In the braking department, conical hubs were employed.

However, the real centre of attention was the new 74x81mm 348cc single overhead cam engine. As with the pre-war AJS ohc singles, this was

the work of Yorkshire-born engineer Phillip Walker, then aged 47. He had worked with AMC for many years, except for a stint at the Handley-Page aircraft company for the duration of the war. To keep weight to an absolute minimum, wide use was made of magnesium castings and these were finished in a highly distinctive gold-coloured corrosion inhibiting paint.

The engine could not only trace its origins back to the original cammy AJS single of 1927, but it was to have a 15-year production run as the 7R, followed by an enlarged version, the 496cc (90x78mm) G50 Matchless which first arrived in 1958, but is still being built today, remaining a leading contender in classic racing events at club, national and international levels.

The aluminium alloy cylinder barrel featured a shrunk-in iron liner and was held in position by four long bolts which passed from the crank case right through to the cylinder head. A forged three-ring piston was employed together with a massive I-section steel connecting rod, the latter component featuring a bushed small-end and a Duralumin-caged single row big-end bearing. There were circumferential webs to the eyes of both the big and small-ends to provide additional strength. The solid steel crankshaft flywheels were drilled and recessed on their inner faces to accommodate the big-end bearing, thus keeping lateral width of the assembly to a minimum. The magnesium crankcases split vertically, while the timing cover encased a pair of oil pumps; the lubrication system was of the traditional British dry sump type with a separate oil tank.

A definite advantage of the 7R compared to its great rival the Manx Norton was the fully enclosed valve gear, although both engines used hairpin valve springs. Other features of the first 7R included an Amal TT carb, four-speed Burman close ratio gearbox and a dry multi-plate clutch.

Over its 15-year production life the 7R saw many changes aimed at keeping it competitive. The most important of these are as follows: new exhaust (1950); new frame (1953); new bore and stroke of 75.5x78mm

(originally 74x81mm) (1956); switch from Burman to AMC gearbox (1958).

From mid-1954 responsibility for the 7R development had switched to Jack Williams, following the death that year of H.J. (Ike) Hatch. Production of the 7R came to an end in 1962, although a few bikes were built from spares in 1963.

Several of Bob McIntyre's best moments came while riding one of the Plumstead factory's 7R models, such as the 1952 Manx GP Junior victory (and perhaps an even more notable runner-up spot on the same bike in the Senior a couple of days later); winning the prestigious Mellano Trophy at Silverstone in 1954 and 1958 and a magnificent third in the 1958 Junior TT behind the four-cylinder MV Agustas of John Surtees and John Hartle.

lever and that cured the trouble. A small splinter of wood had got in the jet and the bike had been running on a very weak mixture. Now I got my skates on. There was a lap and a half left of the four-lap race. In that distance I could not catch Eric Housley, although I cut his lead to thirty-two seconds at the finish.

In that final frantic high-speed last lap, Bob had not only overtaken Ken James to take runner-up spot, but also set a new class lap record of 28 minutes 16.4 seconds, a speed of 80.09mph.

Clubman's 350cc Junior TT – 4 laps – 150.92 miles

1st   E. Housley (BSA)
2nd   R. McIntyre (BSA)
3rd   K. James (Norton)
4th   C. Staley (BSA)
5th   D. Powell (BSA)
6th   H. Plews (Norton)

Getting underway at the start of the Junior Manx Grand Prix. Bob went on to score a sensational victory.

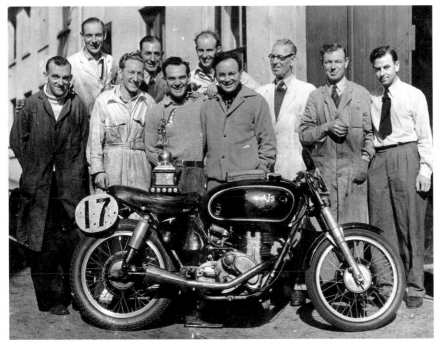

Bob and friends with the Junior Manx GP-winning machine and the winner's trophy.

Clubman's TT

The Clubman's TT ran for a decade from 1947 through to 1956. It was to prove a stepping stone for several future stars, including Geoff Duke and Bob McIntyre.

It was in January 1947 that the ACU (Auto Cycle Union) announced that it was to stage the first ever Clubman's TT in the Isle of Man programme. At the time some details had yet to be decided, but sufficient information was released so clubs and clubmen could be beginning to make their plans. The race was to be staged over four laps of the famous 37.73-mile Mountain course and would be open to nominated clubmen riding machines between 251 and 1000cc which were catalogued models, fully equipped. However, the exact definition of these last two words had yet to be fully clarified. For example, *The Motor Cycle* in their 16 January 1947 issue wondered if a racing machine such as a Manx Norton would be eligible.

Practising was to be undertaken at different times to that of the Junior, Senior and Lightweight international TTs. An interesting feature was that there would be compulsory refuelling during the race. A club entering a rider would be called upon to declare that the motorcycle concerned was according to the manufacturers' catalogue, which had to have been printed and published prior to the date on which entries closed. Some changes would be allowed, but only related to components such as spark plugs, tyres and chains.

As for the entry fee, this was to be two guineas (two pounds, two shillings), and the club entering the winning rider was to receive the Clubman's Tourist Trophy, and the rider a replica of this trophy.

The following month, February 1947, *The Motor Cycle* columnist 'Ixion' had this to say: 'The Clubman's TT is a bold experiment. The success or sudden death of the Wednesday race mainly pivots on (a) the enthusiasm with which clubs support it; and (b) the success of the officials in eliminating camouflaged trade machines (the terms 'amateur' and 'standard' are any organiser's nightmare).'

In total 65 entries were made for the inaugural Clubman's TT, held in June 1947. Several of these riders were to become well-known names in the sport during later years: Arthur Wheeler, Les Archer, Eric Cheney, Fron Purslow, Denis Parkinson, Allan Jefferies, Don Crossley, Phil Heath and Syd Lawton to name but a few. The three class winners were to be Eric Briggs (Senior), Denis Parkinson (Junior) and Basil Keys (Lightweight).

Twelve months later the Clubman's entry list had swollen to 101 – a full house as regards the number allowed in a TT at that time. The winner of the Senior event (riding a 998cc Vincent) was J.D. Daniels.

By 1949, there were simply too many entries for a single race to cope with. The Juniors (now referred to as the 350cc) ran concurrently with the 1000cc machines, whereas the 500cc bikes had their own race, as did the Lightweights, the latter being given their own two-lap race.

The 1949 Clubman's was notable on two counts: it provided future World Champion Geoff Duke with his first major road race victory (in the 500cc on an International Norton) and the BSA Gold Star scored its first TT win (Harold Clark, three-fifty).

In 1950 a ballot had to be held for the forthcoming Clubman's TT, so large were the entries. By now the 350cc class had become the most popular. In the race, six of the first 12 were Gold Stars, including first and second (B.A. Jackson and I. McGuffie).

By the time entries closed for the 1951 Clubman's races, there were virtually full houses for both the Junior and Senior events, but those for the 250 and 1000cc were so poor that these latter two classes were axed from the calendar.

Of the 41 finishers for the Junior race, over half were mounted on BSA Gold Stars, with the winner being Brian Purslow. His time for the four-lap, 150.92-mile race was 2 hours 10 seconds (75.36mph). The fastest lap was set by Norton-mounted K.R.V. James in 29 minutes 35 seconds (76.54mph). The Senior event was won by I.K. Archer (Norton), with Ivor Wickstead (Triumph) setting the fastest lap at 81.06mph.

When the 1952 Clubman's TT regulations were published in January that year, a new rule had been introduced. 'After Thursday 29 May any machine bearing racing number plates, whether observed or not, must not be used on any Isle of Man public highway except during practice hours and during the fifteen minutes before and after the official periods.' This directive also went on to say that any rider guilty of a breach of this regulation would be fined £5 and might be excluded from the races. Machines had to comply with local road fund licence and insurance requirements. This measure, it was said, had been forced on the organisers by what *The Motor Cycle* of 17 January 1952 described as 'Those thoughtless few who, in past years, have caused annoyance to the Isle of Man police and residents, by riding at high speed on open roads.'

When entries closed, there were a total of 105 riders for the Junior Clubman's, including three reserves. No fewer than 75 of them were BSA Gold Star mounted.

As this book reveals, a name destined for future greatness made his Isle of Man debut in the 1952 Clubman's Junior TT: Glasgow Mercury Club member R. McIntyre. But although Bob had the distinction of setting the fastest lap in 28 minutes 16.4 seconds (80.09mph), he didn't win the race. Instead, this honour went to Chesterfield's Eric Housley, who completed the four-lap event in 1 hour 54 minutes 28.2 seconds, averaging 78.92mph. Both Bob and Eric rode BSA Gold Star machines, as did the fourth, fifth, seventh, eighth, ninth and 12th men home.

The Clubman's TT was to continue for another four years – even then, it was the success of the BSA over other marques which finally sealed its fate. But it was responsible for producing two of the world's greatest racing stars during its 10-year history.

As Bob said later, 'that race made me. Finishing second and setting a new lap record on my first appearance in the Island drew a lot of attention to me. Sam and I had quite a night out.' And in truth Sam Cooper must have been mightily relieved that Bob had convinced him to stay on the Island!

Back in Scotland

Back in Troon the faithful BSA was stripped, rebuilt and sold. As Bob said, 'it had done its job.' It is believed to have been racing as late as the 1960s. Bob himself graduated to one of Sam Cooper's two AJS 7R models; the other being ridden by Leslie Cooper. As Bob had no machine of his own since selling the Ariel Red Hunter the previous year (as Bob said, he 'could not afford one'), Cooper Brothers always found a bike which he could ride to and from work (the 7R of course not being suitable for this purpose). Usually this daily transport was a BSA A10 Golden Flash, with a 646cc ohv twin-cylinder engine and plunger rear suspension.

Bob's next racing outing was a double victory on the 7R at the well-known Kirkcaldy races at the town's Beveridge Park on Saturday 5 July 1952. A contemporary race commentary described the setting thus: 'brilliant sunshine, tempered by a cool breeze off the Forth, made racing conditions ideal. Gaining in popularity each year, the meeting attracted 109 entries, which included such well-known riders as B.J. Hargreaves, R. McIntyre, J. McCredie, C. Bruce and J Weddell.'As was quite usual during the 1950s the 500cc final was broadcast live by the BBC from Beveridge Park – and thus had to be run dead on time. The course was by now ridden in an anti-clockwise direction, none other than Les Graham, the 1949 500cc World Champion, having voiced the opinion that it was faster.

The Motor Cycle, in its 10 July 1952 issue, had this to say:

> *Bob McIntyre, fresh from his success in the Clubman's Junior TT, brought further honours to the Glasgow Mercury MCC by winning both 350cc and 500cc classes. Riding a 7R AJS in both events, he was the star of the meeting; he established a new 350cc lap record at 60.07mph, and a new course record in the 500cc race of 60.37mph.*

In the 350cc race Bob beat Alastair King (Velocette KTT) and J.S. Blair (AJS), while in the 500cc final he won from Leslie Cooper (AJS) and W.J. Davie (Velocette).

Back to the Island

The next big event in Bob Mac's 1952 calendar was the Manx Grand Prix, held in September. By now the press had him in their sights as a leading contender – at least once practice week got under way. *The Motor Cycle* reported:

> R. McIntyre, who put up such a splendid performance on his first appearance in the Island last June when he gained second place and record lap in the Junior Clubman's TT has figured in the best three lap times each morning so far – twice in the Senior category and once in the Junior. Prior to June, McIntyre had competed only in local Scottish events. His mounts for the races are Sam Cooper's AJS and Norton on Tuesday and Thursday respectively. He says he is 'tickled pink' with the Featherbed Norton (on his first practice with this machine he returned second best lap time at a speed of over 86mph). His AJS appears to be in good fettle, too. It revs to over 7,200rpm on the Sulby Straight with a top-gear ratio of 5.14:1.

In the Junior event Bob was a member of the Kirkcaldy Club team, with J.S. Blair (also riding a Cooper 7R) and D.C. Birrell (Norton). But in the Senior, Bob was to abandon his Norton in favour of his three-fifty AJS. Why? Well, he was 'not completely happy with the Norton's front brake.' But what virtually no one realised was that Bob had suffered a broken collar bone a mere three weeks prior to the start of practice week and so almost missed being able to ride in the Manx GP at all!

The Junior race

The Motor Cycle race report headline dated 18 September 1952 shouted 'All Records Broken in Junior Manx.' The article went on to say:

> ...the 1952 Junior Manx Grand Prix, contested on Tuesday of last week over six laps of the IoM TT course, was won at the record speed of 85.73mph by 23-year-old Glasgow mechanic R.M. McIntyre riding an AJS. Bob's time of 2 hours 28 minutes 27 seconds for the race was nearly six minutes better than the previous record, set up by Robin Sherry the previous year.

This was a truly remarkable performance for someone who *The Motor Cycle* said was 'a comparative newcomer to road racing.' And it was during this race that the determined jutted jaw, which was to become such a McIntyre trademark, could be visually seen in his riding stance.

The second man home was the highly experienced Harold Clark, a consistent post-war Manx Grand Prix competitor, with Derek Farrant third. All three rode AJS 7R machines equipped with extra-large fuel tanks which enabled them to complete the six laps without refuelling.

The Motor Cycle report sets the scene for Bob's first Isle of Man victory:

> *…ten minutes before the start of the race, the clerk of the course announced that the meteorological report promised fair weather but the possibility of showers. The roads, wet in places from overnight rain, were drying rapidly, but were rather greasy under the trees on the approach to Ramsey. Promptly at 10.45am, to the crash of a maroon, the first man R.W. Porter (AJS) pushed off the grid and the race was on. Ninety-two others followed suit; the majority experienced no difficulty. There seemed to be the possibility of several scraps developing on the roads owing to the close starting of well-matched competitors. The most obvious example was No.17, McIntyre, and No.21, H. Clark, who thus started 40 seconds apart in that order.*
>
> *…by watching the rider's progress on the indicator clocks, it was apparent that McIntyre was thrusting his way through the earlier starters. He was the sixth man signalled at Ramsey, and he was followed at approximately starting time by Harold Clark. At Craig-ny-Baa, McIntyre had passed all earlier starters except No.2, D.J.P. Wilkins on a Norton.*

At the end of the first lap Bob led Harold Clark by eight seconds on adjusted time – thus leading the race. There was no doubt that even so early in the race these two riders were the most impressive. David Ley, commenting from the high-speed jump at the Highlander, described Bob's progress as 'sensationally fast.' Bob's first lap was 27 minutes 7 seconds, with Clark's 27 minutes 15 seconds.

At the end of lap 2, Bob's time showed that he had established a new Manx Grand Prix Junior record of 26 minutes 44 seconds (84.70mph). However, this was to be short-lived as Clark bettered this figure with 26 minutes 25 seconds (85.72mph) and so led the race by 11 seconds.

The announcer at the Highlander was again full of enthusiasm in describing Bob's riding, likening his style to that of World Champion Geoff Duke. Praise indeed! Even by the end of lap four Clark still led after again breaking the lap record. But on the fifth lap, as *The Motor Cycle* said, 'the fortunes of the leading pair fluctuated.' At the end Clark still led, but both had recorded identical lap times of 26 minutes 2 seconds.

Then, on the fifth and sixth laps, Bob succeeded in pulling back all the advantage Harold Clark had held. At the end of the race Bob led by well over half a minute. So what happened? This is how *The Motor Cycle* report described the end.

> *McIntyre's red light glowed and he hurtled over the line to receive the chequered flag. Immediately, Clark's light glowed. The seconds ticked by relentlessly – ten, twenty, thirty, forty – Clark could not win! He toured into second place with a smoking clutch; two of his five clutch springs had disappeared. What cruel luck after such a brilliant ride! Nevertheless, McIntyre's performance had stamped this unassuming lad as one who had a golden opportunity to reach the top flight.*

A star had been born that September day in 1952.

Junior 350cc Manx GP – 6 laps – 226.38 miles

1st	R. McIntyre	(AJS)
2nd	H. Clark	(AJS)
3rd	D.K. Farrant	(AJS)
4th	D. Ennett	(AJS)
5th	H.A. Pearce	(Velocette)
6th	K.R. Campbell	(Velocette)

An 'Amazing Senior'

If observers thought that was the end of the McIntyre magic that week, they were wrong. A mere two days later *The Motor Cycle* called the Senior Manx Grand Prix 'amazing.' And that's exactly what it was for one Robert Macgregor McIntyre.

Riding the same 348cc AJS on which he had won the Junior, Bob simply rode like a true master to claim second spot. Not only was he giving away 150cc to the 500cc machines, but he also improved on his winning Junior winning speed by almost 2mph. Harold Clark could do no better than finish fourth on a five-hundred Manx Norton! It was the stuff of legends; a performance which has hardly ever been matched in Manx Grand Prix history. As mentioned earlier, Bob had decided to ride his Junior AJS because of front brake problems during practice for the Senior Norton – even though he had recorded the fastest Senior practice lap in 26 minutes 13 seconds.

Obviously, Bob would have stood a better chance of victory on the larger-engined bike, but he was shrewd enough to realise that safety came first, even at this early stage in his career.

Coming out of Governor's Bridge dip on his way to second in the 1952 Senior Manx GP (still riding the 348cc AJS). It was a great result, but afterwards Bob wished he had ridden the Cooper Bros 500 Norton (which he had practised on).

'Like a midsummer day' was how one journalist described Thursday 11 September 1952. This was because the day dawned bright, clear, dry and with only a gentle breeze. Right from the start Bob showed his class and determination, by registering a standing start lap of 26 minutes 21 seconds. Even so, he trailed the leading rider Derek Farrant on a Matchless G45 twin by 25 seconds. At the end of lap two Bob was third, behind Farrant and Harold Clark (who was now riding a 499cc Norton).

By the end of lap four Bob was second to Farrant, a position he retained at the end of the sixth and final lap. *The Motor Cycle* commented: 'McIntyre received the chequered flag to complete his second brilliant ride in one week on the same 348cc AJS, having on this occasion outstripped every five-hundred except Farrant's Matchless twin.'

Senior 500cc Manx GP – 6 laps – 226.38 miles

1st   D. Farrant (Matchless)

2nd   R. McIntyre (348cc AJS)

3rd   P. Davey (Norton)

4th   H. Clark (Norton)
5th   D. Ennett (348cc AJS)
6th   D. Christian (Norton)

Of his Senior ride Bob said: 'Sam Cooper gave me a pretty free hand; his only instructions were to ride as hard as I could from the word go. I was learning from my growing experience on the Island and I managed to lap faster than I did in the Junior.'

The top three men in the 1952 Senior Manx Grand Prix. Left to right: Bob McIntyre, Derek Farrant (winner) and Peter Davey (third).

A debut at Silverstone

A couple of weeks after the Isle of Man came Bob's first taste of international road racing. As Bob himself said, 'It was the first time I had raced at the Northamptonshire airfield circuit.' The event was the Hutchinson 100 meeting organised by the BMCRC (British Motor Cycle Racing Club). It was staged on Saturday 27 September 1952.

This was the first time Bob McIntyre had come up against truly world-class stars – men like John Surtees, Ray Amm and Les Graham.

The youthful McIntyre was not fazed by this. In fact, he was sharing a front-row grid for the 350cc Championship race. As he recalled later, 'I went off like a rocket and after about the second corner I found myself in front. I was not expecting this. I thought wildly "what do I do now?" Then I remembered the words put in my ear by my sponsor a few minutes before: "Never mind them. Get on with it." So I tore on, leading everyone.'

At this stage it should be explained that the meeting was staged in truly appalling conditions of bitterly cold wind and heavy rain. In addition, things were made even more tricky by the amount of rubber and oil left on the track surface from car racing held on the circuit the week before.

The Motor Cycle race report published in the magazine's 2 October 1952 issue explains what happened next: 'Event 4, the BMCRC 350cc Championship Race, became interesting very early on. Last corner before the finishing straight is Woodcote, and it was wet and slippery. On lap 1, R. McIntyre (AJS) was the first man to appear; unfortunately, he was sliding along the wet tarmac at a high speed preceded by his machine.' Happily, the exit from this corner was very wide, and there was a large patch of grass which prevented Bob from getting anything more than a shaking. But as Bob recalled later, 'I was not alone in this indignity. I was picking myself up when George Brown landed at my feet. Soon there were five of us dismounted, all at the same spot and on the first lap. I was a very de-tuned young rider!

As Silverstone effectively brought the British racing season to a close, Bob then spent the winter months servicing and repairing touring bikes in the Cooper Brothers' Troon workshop.

The 1953 season

Then came the 1953 season, in which Bob again contested racing events in both Scotland and England with Cooper-supplied machinery. Bob's first visit to the Thruxton circuit in Hampshire occurred on Easter Monday 6 April 1953. After finishing third in his heat on the Cooper AJS, behind Michael O'Rourke (AJS) and Cecil Sandford (Velocette), Bob proved just how far he had come by coming home in the top six of a world-class field, with riders including O'Rourke, Sandford, Derek Farrant, Syd Lawton, Ken Kavanagh and John Surtees. A contemporary press report described the action:

> ...the 350cc final produced some very close racing. Kavanagh (Norton) led from start to finish, but was closely pressed by J. Storr (Norton) in the latter half of the race. J. Surtees (Norton) worked up to third place by lap 8 and, after recording the fastest lap so far, actually headed Storr by a few feet on lap 13. The latter, however, regained second place by no more than a wheel at the finish. Behind these leaders a terrific tussle was waged between C.C. Sandford (Velocette) and R. McIntyre, D. Farrant and M. O'Rourke, all on AJSs.

Silverstone again

Less than a couple of weeks later, on 18 April, Bob journeyed to Silverstone once again, for the popular *Motor Cycling* Saturday meeting. This time the conditions were bright, if a little breezy, and a vast crowd of almost 75,000 spectators witnessed some close and exciting racing. And it was at this meeting that Bob McIntyre did much to establish himself on the English short circuit scene.

The 20-lap 350cc race brought the Norton works team members to the line, but Geoff Duke, Ken Kavanagh and Ray Amm were equipped with production Manx models rather than their factory specials. It was also the last meeting at which Geoff was to be mounted on the British marque before signing for Gilera. AJS works riders were also out in this event, including Bill Doran. But the race was to result in a fantastic duel between John Storr and John Surtees (Norton). These two were never more than a few yards apart. Not far behind them, Bob McIntyre was unassailable in third place – a position he was to hold until the end of the 20-lap, 58-mile race.

Isle of Man TT

For many years, certainly during the Bob McIntyre era, the Isle of Man TT was the world's premier motorcycle racing event.

First employed in 1911 (though in slightly different guise), the legendary Mountain Course measured 37.73 miles in length and comprised roads which were the normal traffic arteries of the Isle of Man. To avoid too much interference with everyday trade on the Island, therefore, the pre-race practice periods took place largely in the early hours of the morning. Closure of the roads for both practice and racing required a separate Act of the Isle of Man Parliament every year.

The start, grandstand, scoreboard and pits were situated in Glencrutchery Road, high above the town of Douglas. Soon after leaving the slight rise of Brown's Hill, followed by the drop to Quarter Bridge, a slow right-hander necessitated hard braking, engagement of bottom gear and usually the use of the clutch.

Bradden Bridge was the next landmark, a spectacular S-bend over the railway and river, then on to Union Mills three miles from the start, winding and undulating, the course dropped down to the Highlander and through the bends at Greeba to Ballacraine (7.25 miles); a sharp right-hander.

The course was now very much out in the country, with the road twisting and turning through the leafy tunnel of the Neb Valley, past Laurel Bank and Glen Helen, then up the 1-in-10 rise of Creg Willey's Hill on to the heights of Cronk-y-Voddee. The descent of Baaregarroo before the 13th milestone section was generally held as being the fastest part of the course. It was followed by a tricky section ending with Westwood's Corner, a relatively fast left-hander.

Soon riders reached Kirkmichael (14.5 miles), with its second gear right-hander followed by a trip through the narrow village street, after which there was a winding but fast stretch to Ballaugh – with the famous humpback bridge where both wheels left the ground. Left, right, left – the trio of Quarry Bends were taken in the region of 100mph or more; the bends leading out on to the start of the famous mile-long Sulby Straight, with at its end an extremely sharp right-hand corner at Sulby Bridge (20 miles). Then came hard acceleration up to and around the long, sweeping left-hander at Ginger Hall. Through wooded Kerromoar and past the foot of Glen Auldyn, the circuit wound its way on to the town of Ramsey, where riders flicked right and left through Parliament Square in the very middle of the town. Then came the beginning of the long mountain climb, the road rising up May Hill to the testing Ramsey Hairpin (24.5 miles) and up again to Waterworks Corner and the Gooseneck.

Still climbing, riders passed Guthrie's Memorial and reached East Mountain Gate (28.5 miles) where the long gruelling ascent at last began to flatten out. A further mile on led to a quartet of gentle bends at the Verandah section, followed by the bumpy crossing of the mountain railway tracks at the Bungalow. The highest point on the course was at Brandywell, a left-hand sweep beyond the Bungalow, and from there the road began to fall gently, through the aptly named Windy Corner, a medium fast right-hander and the long 33rd milestone bend.

Kate's Cottage (300 yards past Keppel Gate) marked the beginning of

the flat out, exhilarating sweep down to Creg-ny-Baa (34.5 miles). Still dropping, the course swept towards the left-hander at Brandish Corner and down yet more to the fast right-hander at Hilberry.

With less than two miles to the finish there followed the short climb of Cronk-ny-Mona and the sharp right-hand turn at Signpost Corner. Bedstead Corner and The Nook followed in swift succession and within a quarter-of-a-mile it was a case of hard on the brakes for Governor's Bridge, an acute hairpin, which was the slowest corner on the course. The short detour through the hollow was a link to earlier days when it formed part of the main road. Once out of the hollow, riders accelerated into Glencrutchery Road less than half-a-mile from the grandstand and pit area.

In essence the course remains the same today, when at the beginning of the 21st century, the TT has long since lost its World Championship status. However, it still remains one of the most famous venues in motorcycle racing, attracting huge crowds every June; it was also the setting for some of Bob McIntyre's greatest-ever triumphs.

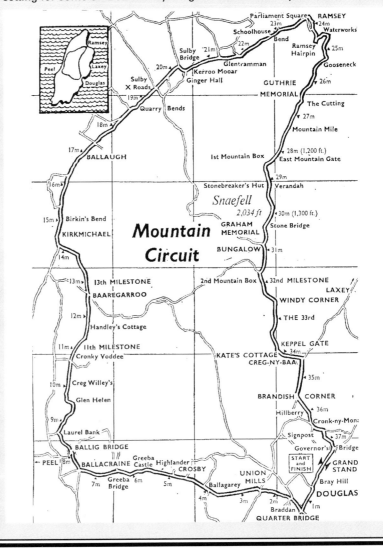

Back in Scotland a week later Bob was missing from the first race meeting of the season at Beveridge Park. Unfortunately, the event was marred by the first fatal accident at this circuit. In the first heat, J.S. Blair (who, riding a Cooper AJS, had been Bob's teammate in the Manx GP) hit a tree at Raith Bend and was killed instantly. Alastair King won the main race on another AJS 7R, with Leslie Cooper runner-up.

A day out with Vic Willoughby

Journalist and racer Vic Willoughby visited Bob, together with the Cooper brothers, at the Troon dealership – taking up a long-standing invitation. Vic had travelled north from the London offices of *The Motor Cycle* aboard a four-cylinder Ariel Square Four Mark 11, covering a distance of just over 400 miles in some seven hours.

The following day, Bob and Vic changed into leathers and, accompanied by Sam and Leslie Cooper, motored five or six miles to Heathfield Aerodrome with the firm's two racing Ajay models. As Vic Willoughby disclosed in a subsequent article published in May 1953, 'it is here that Bob pays periodical visits for riding practice on the perimeter and for engine testing on a grass-grown runway.' The Heathfield perimeter measured something in the region of three miles and featured 15 assorted bends and corners per lap, which Willoughby said 'give the rider no respite and demand intelligent line plotting, since frequently a seemingly unorthodox line on one bend is demanded by what follows. Moreover, Bob told me casually, the surface is bumpy. Just how diabolically bumpy was soon painfully obvious!'

Vic, in describing his experiences, provides a valuable insight into Bob's abilities to take things in his stride like few others – and his extreme fitness at this time. 'We warmed up the two engines, then set off in close company, with Bob in the lead to show me the way. A moderate pace on the early laps was gradually increased until soon we were circulating as fast as was consistent with safety. But oh, that surface! Suffice to say that the Boy Racers [the name by which the AJS 7R was commonly known], renowned for the excellence of their suspensions and steering, frequently shook their heads violently and jolted us six inches out of our seats. My wrists and lower ribs soon felt pulverised, but there is no opportunity to ease up at Heathfield. In spite of the strenuous conditions, Bob's style was immaculate and completely confident. His beautifully chosen line was consistent, lap after lap. Man and machine were as one.'

But perhaps the biggest contribution to the Bob McIntyre story which Willoughby revealed in the spring 1953 feature was the following observation: 'What manner of a man is this 24-year-old enthusiast who, on

his first three races in the Isle of Man has never finished lower than second?' He continued: 'Of medium height and powerfully built, he has a cheerful, yet serious, disposition. In my own associations with the racing game, I have always been deeply impressed by the genuine quality of the vast majority of its participants. McIntyre is no exception. Reserved in speech, a non-smoker and moderate drinker, his paramount interest is motorcycle racing.'

More of interest followed: 'Like his renowned countryman, the late Jimmy Guthrie, he believes that the best training for motorcycle racing is riding motorcycles.'

Willoughby concluded his appraisal: 'Successful road-racing men fall into two broad categories. Some – Geoff Duke is the outstanding modern example – rocket to the top in a seemingly impossible short space of time. Conversely, Guthrie, Scotland's greatest contribution to the racing game, took years to develop the perfections of style and technique which made him supreme in the middle-to-late thirties. It would be premature at this stage to class McIntyre with such peerless champions. But it is tolerably certain that no rising star ever displayed more native ability, sincerity and determination.'

North West 200

Then came Bob McIntyre's debut in Northern Ireland in no less an event than the annual international North West 200 meeting, which had first been staged in 1929. Once again he was lined up against the top stars – including the Norton factory team, featuring Ray Amm mounted on the revolutionary Kneeler machine. First Bob won the 350cc race. He made a flying start and held second place behind Norton star Jack Brett at the end of the first lap,

May 1953. Bob receives the 350cc winner's trophy at the North West 200. Other class winners were 500cc Syd Lawton (centre) and 250cc Arthur Wheeler.

with Amm fourth. Then Brett retired with engine problems and Bob assumed the lead, a position he was to hold until the end of some 150 miles. Amm had been challenging hard before he too retired after setting the fastest lap.

Bob also won the Handicap, which was open to all riders, to complete a very successful foray to Ulster.

A return to the Island

Next on the McIntyre schedule was a return to the Isle of Man for the TT. He was entered in both the Junior and Senior races on AJS machinery.

In the Junior, after putting in a best lap of 25 minutes 16 seconds in the Thursday evening 4 June session, Bob was lying fifth at the end of the first lap. Actually this was a magnificent showing, as all of the first eight riders bar himself were on works bikes. The full listing was as follows: 1st Rod Coleman (AJS), 2nd Ray Amm (Norton), 3rd Fergus Anderson (Moto Guzzi), 4th Ken Kavanagh (Norton), 5th Bob McIntyre (AJS), 6th Jack Brett (Norton), 7th Bill Doran (AJS), 8th Les Graham (MV Agusta).

This was a position which Bob was to hold until forced out on lap 3 with engine trouble. Because of this he was a non-starter in the Senior race. However, by holding fifth for two laps against the might of the factory teams, Bob had proved he was capable of mixing it with the best in the world; something which was not to go unnoticed.

After the disappointment of the TT came immediate success back home in Scotland when Bob won both his heats and finals on his Cooper AJS and a new Matchless G45 twin provided by the same source, at Beveridge Park, Kirkcaldy, on Saturday 9 July. There were four heats in the 350cc class, other winners being Leslie Cooper, J. Drysdale (BSM) and D.A. Richie (Velocette). In the final, Bob won from Alastair King (Velocette) and Leslie Cooper.

Rain, which had been threatening all afternoon, made its entry simultaneously with the first 500cc heat. Speeds immediately dropped sharply, and crashes were numerous. There were five heats, won by Bob, Richie, Alastair King, G. Olding (Velocette) and Leslie Cooper. In the final, the positions were Bob, Alastair King and D. Stewart (BSM).

A couple of weeks later Bob was at Charterhall on Saturday 23 July 1953. For the first time in their long history, the Scottish Speed Championships were held away from the West Sands at St Andrews. The new venue was the airfield circuit at Charterhall in Berwickshire. Measuring precisely two miles to a lap, the circuit featured not only a long main straight, but some interesting corners.

In contrast to Beveridge Park, the rain came early in the day, with improving weather later. In the Heavyweight (unlimited) Championship, Bob McIntyre, riding the Cooper Brothers Matchless G45 twin, was first away and led for the entire 10-lap race distance. Second and third positions were taken by Denis Parkinson and J. Bottomley respectively. There was also success for Bob in the three-lap 350cc race (from Leslie Cooper and Denis Parkinson, on AJS and Norton machinery), the 500cc (Mediumweight) Championship and a five-lap event for club teams.

Blandford Camp

The fourth International Blandford Camp Road Races were staged on Bank Holiday Monday 3 August 1953. Perfect weather conditions saw the lap record broken in all four classes.

In the first heat of the Junior race, for the *Daily Express* Trophy, G. Dunlop (AJS) won from H.R. Pearce (Velocette) and John Surtees (Norton). Then, fresh from victory in the French Grand Prix, World Champion Fergus Anderson won his heat from Bob and Derek Farrant (AJS). At the start of the Junior final, Anderson shot into the lead, but Bob's engine stalled on the line, meaning he was well down the field. However, this seemed to inspire him and in spite of his bad start, the Scot passed John Surtees on lap two and Farrant on the fifth circuit. At the end of the race, Bob was only 10 seconds adrift of the Moto Guzzi works star. The two of them shared the new lap record of 83.62mph. Considering this was Bob's first visit to the Dorset circuit it was an impressive performance, but although Bob finished third on his Matchless twin in heat two of the 500cc Avon Trophy race, he didn't feature in the first three of the final, which was won by Derek Farrant on another G45, with John Surtees (Norton) second.

A brilliant debut in the Ulster GP

Next came another visit to Northern Island, this time for the Ulster Grand Prix, held over the 7½-mile Dundrod circuit.

In the 350cc race run on Thursday 13 August 1953, Bob, on his privately entered Cooper 7R, was ranged against works teams from Norton, AJS and Moto Guzzi. And once again McIntyre showed that he was quite capable of holding his own against all comers, as *The Motor Cycle* race report in their 20 August 1953 issue reveals:

The three-fifties were despatched at 5.30pm – one minute before the smaller machines (the 350cc and 250cc races being run concurrently). D.K. Farrant, mounted for the first time on a three-valve factory AJS, made the most business-like start. But once the initial jostling for positions had settled, it was K.T. Kavanagh (Norton) who had outstripped the pack. Close on his heels was R. McIntyre on his standard, but extremely rapid, 7R AJS, Farrant was third.

During the middle of the race Bob dropped back to fourth – simply because the works bikes were so much quicker. However, as the later stages of the race were to prove, these highly tuned factory specials, in particular Nortons, seemed too highly stressed to maintain their searing pace. And at the end only two works bikes remained in circulation – Ken Mudford (Norton) and Rod Coleman (AJS), with Bob McIntyre sandwiched between the two. And this was how they finished, all three a lap ahead of the fourth placed man.

August 1953 at the start of the 350cc Ulster Grand Prix at Dundrod. Ranged against the factory Norton, AJS and Moto Guzzi teams, Bob (63) finished a brilliant second.

350cc Ulster GP – 28 laps – 207.45 miles

1st	K. Mudford (Norton)
2nd	R. McIntyre (AJS)
3rd	R. Coleman (AJS)
4th	H. Pearce (Velocette)
5th	M. Templeton (AJS)
6th	W. Campbell (Norton)

Although the factory MV Agusta and Moto Guzzi machines were non-starters, the 30-lap 500cc race promised exciting racing between the works AJS, Norton and Gilera teams, plus a certain Mr McIntyre, the latter now out on his Matchless twin. And as *The Motor Cycle* was able to report: 'R. McIntyre (Matchless) was repeating his tremendous performance of Thursday evening; lying fifth, he was heading factory riders of Norton, Gilera and AJS machines, and he continued to do so until a broken exhaust valve ended his scintillating display after eight laps.'

Aberdare Park and Snetterton

Next port of call was Aberdare Park in South Wales on Saturday 20 August, unfortunately a day marred by torrential rain. But even so the wily Scot simply adapted to the prevailing conditions, winning the 350cc final and finishing runner-up to John Surtees in the 500cc final. Again these results have to be put in the context of the fact that once again he was making his debut appearance at the circuit.

Seven days later, on 4 September, Bob and John Surtees again shared the honours at the race meeting organised by the Snetterton Combine at Snetterton in Norfolk. Although Bob's most striking success came in the 350cc class when he won both his heat and the final, the real controversy occurred in the bigger class.

His duel with John Surtees (Norton) in the 500cc heat (which Bob won) promised an exciting final as a climax to the afternoon's sport. But just prior to the final came news that Bob's Matchless G45 could not be persuaded to fire on more than one cylinder.

The Motor Cycle takes up the story:

> *However, after some discussion, McIntyre produced an immaculate 7R AJS and waited with other competitors, to move to the starting line; then after a few minutes he returned to the paddock. Obviously the organisers were determined to keep to the 351–500cc limit. It was rather puzzling, therefore, to observe the Scotsman, after a further*

interval, making his way once more from the paddock to occupy a vacant place on the starting grid. The crowd waited expectantly as a further rider-official discussion took place – and sighed in sympathy as McIntyre turned his machine round and started back to the enclosure.

Bob's exclusion robbed the race of any interest and allowed Surtees to win unchallenged. Unfortunately, this was one of those cases where officialdom spoilt everyone's enjoyment simply by being too rigid …

Oliver's Mount, Scarborough

With an entry which included the newly crowned 500cc World Champion (Geoff Duke, Gilera) and 350cc World Champion (Fergus Anderson, Moto Guzzi), the two-day international road race meeting at Oliver's Mount, Scarborough, on Friday and Saturday 18/19 September, promised some spectacular racing. Bob had entered both his Cooper machines, the 350 AJS 7R and 500 Matchless G45. But at Scarborough the Scot was not to recapture the form he had shown in recent events; his best finish being a fifth in the 350cc final, which was won by Anderson on his championship-winning Moto Guzzi. Later Bob admitted that Scarborough was not one of his favourite circuits.

Following the Scarborough meeting Bob then travelled overnight to Charterhall in Berwickshire, where he race tested the Joe Potts long-stroke five-hundred Manx Norton. In winning the 500cc race, he found his mount to be equal in speed to Denis Parkinson's prototype 1954 short-stroke Norton, on which the Yorkshireman had just won the Senior Manx Grand Prix.

On Saturday 26 September 1953, Bob was on top form at Silverstone, the scene of the international Hutchinson 100 meeting, finishing runner-up to Norton factory rider Ken Kavanagh in both the heat and final of the 350cc championship event.

But he found the going more difficult in the 500cc 20-lap Championship race, the last of the day. Not only was Kavanagh in this race, but also Dickie Dale on a works four-cylinder Gilera. And it was the latter who stormed into the lead at the fall of the flag. For over two laps he was slipstreamed by Bob on his Matchless twin. Then, on lap three, the Scot lost the tow. And from then on he was forced to concede places. Quite simply the pushrod twin was no match for the works bikes – or even for that matter the best of the privately-entered Nortons.

The curtain comes down

The curtain came down on the 1953 British road racing season at the recently opened Oulton Park circuit in Cheshire on 17 September. Situated in the grounds of Sir Phillip Grey-Egerton's estate near Tarporley, some 14 miles south-east of Chester, the circuit had been designed and laid down especially for racing. Measuring some 1.5 miles to the lap (it was later extended to 2.7 miles), the course was roughly rectangular in shape. It incorporated three sweeping right-handers, a right-hand hairpin, and a shallow S-bend.

In the 350cc final Eric Housley led (after victory in the 250cc race) but came to grief when he appeared to miss a gear and charged off the circuit at high speed, leaving Bob McIntyre (AJS) to win from Cecil Sandford (Velocette). In the 1000cc class, after winning his heat on the Matchless, Bob was unable to finish in the top three in the final, which was won by Norton-mounted Percy Tait.

After the season had ended, Sam Cooper told Bob that AJS were interested in signing him to ride in their works team for the 1954 season. Sam said that if Bob wanted to 'get anywhere' he had to join a factory team. So during the Earls Court Show in London during November 1953, Sam and Bob travelled south and had an interview with the AJS company representative, Jock West. The company was offering Bob a place in their team and a job in their factory. He accepted. And a new chapter was begun.

Chapter 3

AJS Works Team

EXCEPT for the very early days when he had ridden his friend Alan McKenzie's BSA 350cc Gold Star, all Bob McIntyre's road racing had been accomplished on machinery provided by Troon-based dealers Cooper Brothers, headed by the senior partner, Sam Cooper.

But as a professional racer at last, after accepting the offer of a works contract with AJS, Bob had to leave home. He found lodgings in the town of Sidcup in Kent, not far from the south-east London AMC works in Woolwich. As he recalled later, 'this was my first full year as a professional motorcyclist. Until now I had been an amateur in the sense that I had not earned my living by racing.'

Debut day at Silverstone

Bob McIntyre's riding debut for the AJS team came at Silverstone on 10 April 1954. *The Motor Cycle* dated 15 April sets the scene:

> *...an air of eager expectancy pervaded the precincts of Silverstone last Saturday morning. The first national road-race meeting of 1954 was about to begin. Factory and free-lance riders were eager to be off to a flying start in the new season. Likewise, factory technicians and private tuners shared a common anxiety to put to the test a winter's development work. Crowds of spectators thrilled to the sound of open exhausts and the sickly sweet smell of racing oil as they converged on their chosen vantage points.*

As an official member of the AJS squad, Bob's machinery for the 1954 season consisted of the three-valve single for the three-fifty class (sometimes a production 7R was also used), while his mount for the 500cc category was the 498cc Porcupine twin.

In the 350cc Championship Race, Norton team leader Ray Amm won quite comfortably and also established a new class lap record at 90.29mph.

Although he's smiling here, Bob McIntyre's 1954 season as a member of the factory AJS team was not a particularly succesful or happy time for the Scottish star. The bike is the 350 triple valve single.

In describing the action behind Amm, one commentator said, 'As the race wore on, the remainder of the field strung out into a procession.' McIntyre rode doggedly into second place on a notably slower machine and was followed by Surtees (Norton), Sandford (Velocette) and South African Rudi Alison (Norton).

The 500cc Championship Race saw Geoff Duke (Gilera) and Amm battle at the front of the field until the latter overrevved his engine and then dropped back, although he retained second place. Behind these two came a 'pulse-stirring struggle', as one newspaper described it, with Derek Farrant annexing third spot, while J.R. Clark (Matchless), R.D. Keeler (Norton), John Surtees (Norton) and Bob McIntyre fought their own private battle.

Next came a return for Bob to Blandford Camp in Dorset, where, as with Silverstone nine days earlier, the weather was fine and sunny. Held on Easter Monday 19 April 1954, Derek Farrant and Bob were to prove the most successful riders in the races the AJS teamsters contested.

In the 350cc heats, Farrant had won his, but Bob riding in the other had stepped off his machine at Anson Corner after establishing a new class record for the 3.2-mile circuit. However, he was able to remount and finish third. In the final, his teammate made a great start, whereas the Scot was less fortunate, his engine proving reluctant to fire, meaning he was last away. But riding with typical McIntyre grit and determination, he fought his way through the field to challenge for second spot after only two laps. At the end

AMC

The company registered as Associated Motor Cycles, popularly known as AMC, came about as a result of various takeovers. In 1931, at the height of the Great Depression, the Matchless concern (owned by the Collier family) had acquired AJS from the Wolverhampton-based Stevens Brothers; then following the takeover of Sunbeam by ICI (Imperial Chemical Industries) in August 1937 Matchless subsequently acquired the Sunbeam marque from ICI. This meant that the Colliers now owned three quite different marques – Sunbeam, Matchless and AJS – all famous brand names in their own right. The directors of the Matchless company decided that a more suitable name was needed to encompass all three. And so on 12 October 1937 the company was re-registered as Associated Motor Cycles Ltd.

In 1940, AMC sold the rights to the Sunbeam brand name to the BSA Group in Birmingham. During the war years only Matchless motorcycles were built by AMC; mostly the Teledraulic-equipped G3L 350cc ohv single. Events that crucially affected AMC during the war years were the deaths of Bert Collier in 1941, and Harry A. Collier in 1944. When the war ended in Europe on 8 May 1945, only Charlie Collier remained.

This was a much more serious blow than anybody outside the family could have envisaged, since young Bert Collier was just beginning to show he had all the hallmarks of being a brilliant designer, while the oldest brother, Harry A. Collier, was, at the time of his death, AMC chairman.

In June 1947 AMC took over the Coventry-based Francis-Barnett concern. This was followed up by James in November 1950. Finally, in February 1953, it was announced that the group had acquired the famous Norton company.

Although all this swallowing up of rivals might give the impression that when Bob McIntyre signed up to ride for AMC, via the AJS marque for the 1954 season, everything was rosy this was far from the truth, because that year was to be the last one that AJS or Norton would field works specials. And in addition by 1954 neither AJS or Norton was competitive at Grand Prix level, in the face of the overwhelming challenge from the likes of Gilera, MV Agusta and Moto Guzzi.

Not only this, but AMC dictated that AJS machines would be raced naked. This was in an era when comprehensive streamlining was being used extensively by rival teams. So not only were the single and twin-cylinder bikes no longer truly competitive, but the 'naked-only' policy also robbed the AJS riders of an additional 10mph when they could least afford to lose anything. The result was to be expected, with generally poor performances in the classic races in 1954.

As Bob McIntyre later recalled 'For the first time I was to race in the foreign Grand Prix, I went with the team to all the Classics, the big continental races, but I had little success.' To cap all this, Bob was 'not greatly impressed by the AJS organisation.'

This lack of success, combined with his love of his native land – and an intense loyalty to his sponsor Joe Potts – meant that Bob McIntyre was never really keen on being a full works rider after his AJS experience. And there is no doubt that this prevented even greater success than he actually achieved. In the author's opinion it also restricted his chances of becoming a world champion – an award which he richly deserved but never achieved.

he had closed right up to Farrant and also set the fastest lap at 82.88mph. Roles were reversed in the 500cc event, when Farrant and Bob, both riding production Matchless G45 machines, saw the former's bike prove difficult to start, whereas our hero was able to establish an early lead over the Australian Maurice Quincey (Norton). Bob maintained this lead to the end – also equalling the outright lap record with a speed of 85.91mph.

In the 16-lap Invitation race at the end of the meeting, Bob again established himself in the lead on his Matchless G45 twin, but was forced out on lap 12 with a sick engine.

Success in Ulster

On Saturday 15 May 1954, the famous North West 200 was held over the Portstewart-Coleraine-Portrush road circuit in Northern Ireland. This course, just over 11 miles to a lap, was triangular in shape. Two sides of the triangle were formed by a four-mile stretch from the start at Portstewart to Coleraine, and by the slightly longer, and much faster, section to Portrush. Running back to the start, along by the sea, was the base of the triangle, which *The Motor Cycle* reporter described as 'tortuous and deceiving' with many dips and rises. As in previous years, the three classes (250, 350 and 500cc) ran concurrently. Classes were set off at one-minute intervals, the 500cc men first.

In the Senior Bob was facing stiff opposition, which included the four-cylinder Gileras of Geoff Duke and Reg Armstrong. The Scot was aboard the G45 ohv twin he had ridden to victory at Blandford almost a month earlier.

From the drop of the flag, Armstrong's screaming Gilera four led the field from Dubliner Louis Carter (Norton) and Bob. But by the end of the first lap the two Gileras were at the front, followed by McIntyre. Duke was later to retire, leaving Bob to come home runner-up in the 18-lap, 198.90-mile race. Armstrong's winning time was 2 hours 8 minutes 44 seconds (92.81mph); McIntyre's 2 hours 10 minutes 47 seconds (91.35mph). The next man, J.J. Woods (Norton), was almost another seven minutes behind the Matchless rider.

Latest AJS models for the Isle of Man TT

Bob was entered for the TT on exclusively AJS machinery – a 3-valve single for the Junior (350cc) and one of the latest Porcupine twins for the Senior (500cc) – the latter having been considerably modified from the previous season and now sporting a deep, bulbous fuel tank, lower overall height and weir carburation. Notably, the steering head had been lowered by altering the angle of the top tube; the tube being slightly nearer to the horizontal than formerly, bringing the head 1½ inches lower than before. The weir principle of feeding fuel to the carburettor jet was not a new one. The object was to keep fuel in the jet chamber at a constant level and thus obviate fuel surge – arising from high-speed cornering and rapid acceleration and deceleration. A car-type diaphragm petrol pump was operated by a cam on the auxiliary shaft from the engine's timing case. This was needed because of the new fuel tank design. *The Motor Cycle* described the tank as 'reminiscent of a pack-mule with a low-slung load on each side.' The latest 3-valve single had also adopted a version of the new tank.

1954 TT practice got under way with an early morning session on Wednesday 2 June. The fastest lap was put in by Bob on the AJS 500 twin in 24 minutes 48 seconds (91.3mph). But for much of the rest of the practice week the Scot was not to feature on the leaderboard for either the 500 or 350cc classes. In fact, it was only on Friday and Saturday 11/12 June that Bob managed to get his Junior model on the leaderboard, being third and fifth fastest respectively. And he was not able to improve on his earlier speed on the five-hundred and did not feature at all. In fact, behind the scenes Bob was far from happy with his works AJS machines in the Island, finding them lacking both performance and handling over this most demanding of all circuits. He was also later to be extremely critical of the team's organisation.

All these problems were to show themselves in his results, or lack of them, in the 1954 TT series. First came the Junior race on Monday 14 June, which was contested before record crowds in superb weather. The AJS team of Rod Coleman, Derek Farrant and Bob McIntyre was ranged against factory machinery from MV Agusta, Moto Guzzi, Norton and DKW (although in fact the latter were to be non-starters).

At the end of lap one, Bob was lying seventh, having lapped in 25 minutes 30 seconds (88.80mph) compared to the race leader Fergus Anderson (Moto Guzzi) in 24 minutes 33 seconds (92.26mph). Of the AJS men, Coleman was the best – in fourth place.

But then came news that on lap two, Bob's bike had cried 'enough' and he was a retirement.

So now it was all down to how he would do in the Senior race four days later, on Friday 18 June. Unfortunately for everyone concerned, whether they were rider or spectator, the 1954 Senior TT was what *The Motor Cycle* editorial leader of the following week referred to as a 'debacle'. It continued:

Last Friday's International Senior TT came as a damping anticlimax to a period of magnificent racing. Eight days earlier, the Clubman's Trophy Races had been fought out in a speed and style normally expected from a field of international status; on the previous Monday the International Junior and Lightweight 250cc events had provided dramatic finishes, and, on the Wednesday, the Sidecar and Lightweight 125cc events had clearly done much in paving the way towards the Clypse course being used annually for small-capacity machines and sidecars. At the end of all this the Senior TT, renowned throughout the world as the blue riband of motorcycle racing, was as unsatisfactory as a badly managed firework display on a wet November 5. The result, based on three miss-bedevilled laps and one clearer lap, is obviously a disappointment, even to the victor.

As for the race itself, owing to the poor visibility, it was postponed twice. Then reports, subsequently proved incorrect, of a slight improvement in the weather, induced the stewards to permit a start at noon, one and a half hours after the scheduled starting time!

One race report simply said 'Catastrophic Four-Lap Senior TT.' Somehow 52 riders completed the shortened four-lap, 150.92-mile race, with Bob McIntyre finishing 14th, one place in front of Norton-mounted John Surtees. The 'race' was won by Ray Amm (Norton) with Geoff Duke (Gilera) runner-up.

The atrocious weather continues

Atrocious weather followed the Grand Prix circus to Northern Ireland, where the Ulster GP was staged on Thursday 24 June and Saturday 26 June 1954. As *The Motor Cycle* said, 'Atrocious weather marred the meeting, and spectator attendance was sparse.'

As the Gilera, Moto Guzzi and MV Agusta teams were absent, the results went to the German NSU marque in the 125 and 250cc classes, while in the 350 and 500cc races it was a straight battle between AJS and Norton at works level.

The 500cc race was held on the Thursday, but Bob McIntyre missed a gear and was forced to use the slip road at Deer's Leap. He lost so many places that to have attempted to catch the leaders on such treacherous roads would have 'constituted inexcusable folly' (*The Motor Cycle*), so he retired.

Two days later the weather was not much better, but things improved as far as results were concerned for the AJS man. The beginning of the 350cc race saw Rod Coleman retire due to illness, leaving Derek Farrant and Bob on the remaining AJS works models to do battle with the Norton factory trio of Ray Amm, Jack Brett and new signing Gordon Laing. From mid-distance the AJS pair speeded up – this coming after the Norton men had built up a commanding lead in the wet. But as the roads dried, the AJS duo began to whittle down the gap. Lapping faster than the leaders, they successfully challenged Laing, but, on the penultimate lap, Farrant locked his front wheel at the hairpin and slipped off. Bob's effort earned him a rostrum position, which was well-merited.

350cc Ulster GP – 25 laps – 185.39 miles
1st   R. Amm (Norton)
2nd   J. Brett (Norton)
3rd   R. McIntyre (AJS)
4th   G. Laing (Norton)
5th   L. Simpson (AJS)

A debut at Spa

Exactly eight days after his success in the 350 Ulster GP, Bob was making his debut at Spa Francorchamps in Belgium on Sunday 4 July, the scene of the next Grand Prix. Before this had come the practice sessions on Thursday, Friday and Saturday – again held in wet, cold conditions. However, by 1pm on Sunday the heavy rain had at least cleared to give cold and overcast conditions, but with dry roads.

The first race of the day was the 350cc event, represented by 10 nations and five marques, including works entries from AJS, DKW, Moto Guzzi and Norton. Fastest in practice had been Fergus Anderson (Moto Guzzi).

Unfortunately, Bob was on the back row of the grid. But after the first lap he was the leading AJS rider in ninth place. Then on lap four another downpour began, making conditions on the high-speed Spa Francorchamps circuit extremely difficult. But the Scot held on to the chequered flag, finishing sixth. The Moto Guzzi duo of Ken Kavanagh and Fergus Anderson finished an impressive 1-2, with the first DKW rider Siegfried Wünsche in third.

On paper, the 500cc race looked much more difficult, with a field of 28 representing eight makes of machine and the cream of riders from no fewer than 11 countries, including World Champion Geoff Duke, Pierre Monneret of France and Louis Simpson of Belgium on Gilera fours. Louis Simpson had replaced the injured Derek Farrant in the AJS squad.

At one-third distance Bob McIntyre lay sixth – an excellent showing when one considers the opposition. By then the retirements had begun and a couple of laps later he was the sole AJS still circulating. Coleman and Simpson had gone out within a few minutes of one another – Coleman with a broken gear selector spring, Simpson a suspected fuel pump failure. Monneret was to fall from his Gilera twice – the second time sustaining an injury that forced his retirement from the race. Then Bob forced his Porcupine twin ahead of

Geoff Duke (right) with fellow works Norton rider Ken Kavanagh, after finishing first and second respectively in the 350cc Italian GP at Monza, 9 September 1951.

Geoff Duke

In the book *Motor Cycling Today*, published in 1962, Bob McIntyre said he considered the two greatest riders of his era to have been John Surtees and Geoff Duke.

Geoff was born in St Helens, Lancashire, in 1923, the son of a baker. He first caught the motorcycle bug as a small boy, watching sand racing on the beaches of Southport and Wallasey – and riding pillion behind his brother Eric, some nine years his senior. Later Geoff and a school friend clubbed together to purchase their first motorcycle when Geoff was only 13. They could not ride it on the public highway but learned to ride on farmland.

After beginning work as a mechanic at a telephone exchange at the age of 16, Geoff purchased a Dot two-stroke. Then at 18 he volunteered to be

Duke winning the 500cc race on his Gilera four, Silverstone, 10 April 1954.

an Army dispatch rider, but found he would only be accepted as an instrument mechanic. However, this got him into the Royal Signals, so Geoff joined and subsequently made such a nuisance of himself that he was transferred to DR (Dispatch Rider) duties. This led to the chance of riding for the army's display team and meeting a certain Hugh Viney (the legendary AJS trials ace and four-times winner of the Scottish Six Days Trial).

When Geoff was demobbed in 1947 he used his gratuity to purchase a BSA single and got a job at the same factory preparing trials bikes and riding them. His trials results were noticed by Norton teamster Artie Bell, who, after seeing him ride in Yorkshire, introduced Geoff to the Norton management. This resulted in the offer of a job, which was enthusiastically accepted. After riding a 500T ohv single in trials for his new employer, Geoff transferred to road racing.

During the 1948 Manx Grand Prix (his first-ever road race) Geoff Duke was leading when forced to retire with a split oil tank. The following June he returned for the Senior Clubman's TT and won at a record speed of 82.97mph. Three months later he won the Senior Manx and took runner-up spot in the Junior event. Geoff was promoted to the full Norton works team, managed by Joe Craig, for the 1950 season.

A series of tyre problems meant that Norton did not have a very good 1950, even though they debuted the new Featherbed chassis. But from then on, until he quit the Birmingham factory in the spring of 1953, Geoff and Norton could do no wrong; winning the 350/500cc world titles (the first time this had been achieved) in 1951, followed by the 350cc championship in 1952.

But by now the four-cylinder Italian models were at last outpacing the Norton singles, so Geoff signed for Gilera, winning the 500cc title for the next three years in 1953, 1954 and 1955.

Politics and accidents did much to restrict his efforts in 1956 and 1957 and then Gilera quit. But it was during this time that he was largely responsible for recruiting Bob McIntyre into the Arcore squad.

During 1958, Geoff rode a works BMW Rennsport in the 500cc class and his own private Norton in the 350cc category. Then, in 1959, in what was destined to be his final racing year, Geoff rode works Benellis in the 250cc and Nortons in the larger classes.

Unlike John Surtees, Geoff Duke's attempts to make the transition from two to four wheels, with Aston Martin in 1952, proved something of a failure; he soon switched back to motorcycles. But there is no doubt that Geoff Duke was one of the very greatest of all motorcycle racing stars, and one of the very smoothest top-liners ever.

Martin with four laps to the finish. Unfortunately, the roles were reversed a lap later, meaning that Bob McIntyre was fourth when the flag finally fell – but it was still an excellent result. His time was 1 hour 14 minutes 28.1 seconds, an average speed of 105.97 mph.

500cc Belgian GP – 15 laps – 131.5 miles

1st   G. Duke (Gilera)

2nd   K. Kavanagh (Moto Guzzi)

3rd   L. Martin (Gilera)

4th   R. McIntyre (AJS)

5th   K. Campbell (Norton)

6th   G. Murphy (Matchless)

Dutch TT

After the Belgian GP, competitors moved on to Assen in Holland for the next round, which was staged six days later on Saturday 11 July 1954. Here Bob repeated his fourth and sixth places gained in Belgium – but in reverse, coming sixth in the 500cc race behind Duke (Gilera), Anderson (Moto Guzzi), Carlo Bandirola (MV Agusta), Coleman (AJS) and Dickie Dale (MV Agusta). Considering there were two four-cylinder bikes behind him – Nello Pagani (MV) and Hans Vear (Gilera) – this was a good result.

But it was the 350cc race where the Scot did best in Holland with a fourth place.

350cc Dutch TT – 12 laps – 122.88 miles

1st   F. Anderson (Moto Guzzi)

2nd   E. Lorenzetti (Moto Guzzi)

3rd   R. Coleman (AJS)

4th   R. McIntyre (AJS)

5th   K. Hoffmann (DKW)

6th   A. Montanari (Moto Guzzi)

Compared to earlier results, those gained by Bob in the German GP at the 7.1-mile Solitude circuit were disappointing – although there were reasons for them. Some half a million spectators attended the meeting beneath a sweltering sun, held at a venue which twisted and turned uphill and downhill among beautifully wooded hills overlooking Stuttgart.

It had all looked so promising when Bob had gained an instant lead as the flag dropped at the start of the 14-lap, 99.57-mile 350cc race. And it was an exciting one. By the end of lap one, Bob held third, behind Anderson (Moto Guzzi) and Amm (Norton). He was followed by Brett (Norton), Kavanagh and Lorenzetti (Moto Guzzi) and his teammates Coleman and Farrant; the latter making his first appearance since his accident in Ulster.

The two top Guzzi riders (Ferguson and Kavanagh) and Amm pulled out something of a lead over the others. The AJS riders 'fought like tigers' with Lorenzetti. McIntyre and Coleman, in turn, passed the Italian, only to be repassed within a few miles. Brett lay seventh, but the pace was too hot for Farrant and he dropped back to eighth.

By half distance Bob pulled into the pits for attention to his twistgrip and lost several places before being able to restart. But many riders were suffering from either engine failure or the effects of melting tar on the road surface around the circuit. Eventually, Bob had climbed back to eighth, a position he held to the end, behind teammate Farrant who was seventh. The race was won by Ray Amm, from AJS team leader Rod Coleman.

In the 500cc race Bob was the first AJS rider home in seventh position, one place better than Coleman. Geoff Duke won on the Gilera from Ray Amm (Norton) and Gilera teammate Reg Armstrong.

Thruxton and Silverstone

Bob McIntyre's position as a works rider for AJS in 1954 meant that his British appearances were generally restricted that year. However, he did take in the international meeting at Thruxton on Bank Holiday Monday 1 August. But, as with earlier British short circuit meetings that year, he rode production 7R and Matchless G45 models rather than the three-valve single and Porcupine twin works bikes.

Thruxton resulted in a pair of third places in the 350 and 500cc finals. Bob finished behind Fergus Anderson (Moto Guzzi) and John Surtees (Norton) in the smaller class, whereas on the Matchless twin he was still bested by the

April 1954, the Silverstone Saturday international meeting. In the 500cc race Bob (50, AJS Porcupine) leads teammate Derek Farrant (49), John Surtees and Ray Amm (Nortons).

same riders, but with Surtees now the victor. Six days later the highlight of Bob's year came at Silverstone, when he won the coveted Mellano Trophy at the Hutchinson 100 meeting at the Northamptonshire circuit on Saturday 7 August. The famous award was the BMCRC (British Motor Cycle Racing Club) oldest challenge cup, which was first put up in 1925. This trophy had been awarded for different performances on different occasions. In 1953 it was reserved for the rider whose average speed exceeded the previous lap record for the class by the greatest margin. But because of heavy rain and a partially flooded track, it was fortunate that a clause in the regulations concerning the award also read 'to the rider whose average speed most nearly approached the existing lap record.'

In the non-championship races, Bob won the 350cc event from Surtees – and also set the fastest lap of 88.61mph. In the 500cc race he beat Surtees again, but finished runner-up to Geoff Duke (Gilera). In the 20-lap 350cc Championship, Bob was third, behind race winner Surtees and Cecil Sandford (Velocette).

Because of the extreme weather conditions, the stewards reduced the length of the last race – the 500cc Championship – from 20 laps to 10. Ironically, the race was run in bright sunshine, though the track was still awash. Derek Farrant and Bob McIntyre declined to take part, since they were not happy with the handling of their AJS Porcupine twins on the slippery road surface.

Swiss Grand Prix

The Swiss Grand Prix at Berne was yet another to feature wet roads for the majority of the meeting. The Bremgarten circuit, situated in woods to the west of Berne, measured 4.5 miles to a lap and remained much as it had been in pre-war days. There was a mixture of all types of riding, with both fast and slow corners. Many considered it to be the perfect riders' course, demanding machine speed, handling and rider skill in equal measure.

Rod Coleman

New Zealander Rod Coleman was a teammate of Bob McIntyre's during the latter's time as an AJS works rider in 1954.

Rod had made his own AJS debut in the 1951 Ulster Grand Prix. However, back home he had grown up as part of a motorcycling family, his father, having earned fame in the US as 'Cannonball Coleman', had also ridden in the 1930 TT (on a Royal Enfield in the Junior and a Rudge in the Senior – retiring in both).

As for Rod himself, although he had learned to ride a bike before he was 10 years old, he intended becoming a doctor. He pursued medical studies and passed his intermediate examination at Otago University in 1944. It was during these student days that he took up grass track racing as a hobby and, from that time on, his medical ambitions began to be less of a priority.

When Rod decided to abandon his studies in favour of the family business, his father gave him every encouragement – and here developed the urge to take up racing. He made his debut in this branch of the sport in 1947, on a pre-war Velocette in the New Zealand Grand Prix at Christchurch. Although gearbox trouble put him out of the race, his enthusiasm had been kindled.

In 1949 he decided that a racing visit to the Isle of Man was essential, so he saved the money to make the trip to Europe as a privateer. This began his association with AJS, as on arrival in England he collected a 7R from the Plumstead factory. But 1949 was not to be capped with success – just the reverse in fact as he crashed in practice, breaking his jaw in the process.

He gave Europe a miss in 1950 and instead raced the 7R together with an ex-Les Archer five-hundred overhead camshaft Velocette back home in New Zealand.

Official recognition by his country came in 1951 when, together with Len Parry and Ken Mudford, he was sent to the Isle of Man by the New Zealand Auto Cycle Union. His TT race debut proved a brilliant success. In the Junior event, Rod finished eighth on his 7R at 85.26mph – the second non-factory rider home. Then, when lying fifth in the Senior race (on a Manx Norton) a broken chain put an end to a couple of superb rides.

After the TT, Rod joined his two fellow countrymen on a tour with the Continental Circus. He soon proved his Isle of Man performances were no flash in the pan. Not only did he win a couple of minor international meetings, but more importantly his displays in the Dutch TT and Belgian and French Grand Prix were even more impressive. In these he was usually first privateer in his races and in Holland finished a brilliant fourth in the 350cc race, headed only by two works AJSs and a factory Norton.

This resulted in the chance to ride a works AJS Porcupine in the 500cc Ulster Grand Prix. And what a baptism! In appalling conditions on the old Clady circuit, Coleman held third spot behind the Nortons of Geoff Duke and Ken Kavanagh, before being forced to retire with a bout of misfiring caused by waterlogged electrics.

His only other works rides that year came at Monza in September 1951, when, after a sixth in the 350cc race, he challenged the leading Gilera until magneto trouble sidelined his efforts.

Then came three seasons as a full-blown member of the AJS factory team, during which time he tasted real successes (including victory in the 1954 Junior TT) and frustrating experiences with the Porcupine, particularly in the TTs of 1952 and 1953.

His best world championship placings were fourth in both the 350 and 500cc series of 1954. He also continued to campaign his own 'private' 7R and 500 Manx Norton machines back home in New Zealand between the European series.

Rod was married in Birmingham at the end of 1954, the couple sailing for New Zealand shortly afterwards. With AJS quitting Grand Prix racing at the end of that year, Rod Coleman announced his retirement from European competition.

New Zealander Rod Coleman, a teammate of Bob's in the 1954 factory squad.

The 250cc race was the only one held on Saturday 21 August, with the 350cc race the first on Sunday. The 21-lap race covered 95 miles and it was very much a case of Moto Guzzi, then Norton, then AJS. With Anderson and Kavanagh dominating the proceedings, Amm and Brett on their dohc Nortons were third and fourth, with Coleman and McIntyre fifth and sixth respectively. Other works models from Moto Guzzi and AJS were placed in the top 10.

But in the 500cc Grand Prix, Bob was forced to retire on the second circuit with waterlogged electrics.

Then it was back to Britain to bring down the curtain on another season – and, as it was to transpire, Bob McIntyre's career as an official AJS rider.

Bob putting the works three-valve AJS through its paces.

The annual International Gold Cup meeting at Oliver's Mount, Scarborough, was staged over Friday and Saturday 17/18 September 1954. And, for once that year, there was an abundance of fine weather throughout the entire meeting.

The first 350cc heat was dominated by Bob, who led from start to finish; heat two went to John Surtees (Norton) and the third to P.H. Carter (Norton). In the final, Surtees got away to a flying start and the AJS works pair of McIntyre and Farrant could not make up this lost ground, finishing in that order.

The 350cc competition had been run on the Saturday, and the 500cc heats and final took place the following day. There was the added threat of Geoff Duke and Reg Armstrong on four-cylinder Gileras, and Dickie Dale on an MV four. But it was Bob who led the final into Mere Hairpin on the first lap, followed by P.D. Davey (Norton) and Geoff Duke (Gilera). As *The Motor Cycle* reported:

> *The young Scot held his first place until the third lap, when Duke took charge and established a record lap for the East Yorkshire venue. Surtees eventually got past the Scot, due to the much more easy-to-ride Norton single. Behind these three came Dickie Dale, John Hartle and Fox, with Armstrong seventh.*

Next came the first-ever road race meeting at the Aintree course, Liverpool. The three main events were won by Geoff Duke (499cc Gilera), Pip Harris (499cc Norton sidecar) and Bob McIntyre (348cc AJS).

Ray Amm, Norton's number one works rider in 1954.

Amm, with wife Jill and his mother.

Measuring three miles to a lap, the Aintree circuit ran alongside the famous Grand National horse racing course.

The 15-lap 350cc race saw a talented sextet of riders leading the field, comprising Brett, Amm and Surtees (Norton) and Coleman, Farrant and McIntyre (AJS). But it was the young Scot who was to emerge victorious by dint of some excellent riding.

In the 1000cc race, John Surtees rode brilliantly to split the Gileras of Geoff Duke and Reg Armstrong. Then came Rod Coleman (AJS), P.H. Carter (Norton) and Bob McIntyre sixth. There is no doubt that Bob found the smaller AJS a more competitive package, certainly on the short circuits.

And so came to an end the McIntyre-AMC alliance. As he was later to recall:

> For the first time I was to race in the foreign Grand Prix. I went with the team to all the Classics [not strictly correct], the big continental races, but I had little success. I got places, plenty of seconds and thirds, but I did not win anything of note. My teammates, Rod Coleman and Derek Farrant, did not do well either, apart from first and second places in the Junior TT. It was a year of Norton successes.

There were a number of 'political' reasons why the AJS team did not do well in 1954, which are explained in a boxed section covering the AMC (Associated Motor Cycles) group. His lack of success would also hamper Bob's willingness to sign for other factories in the future, which was to be a vital reason for his ultimate failure to win a World Championship title – something he so richly deserved.

Bob during the Junior TT in June 1954. At the end of lap one Bob lay seventh, but he retired on the following circuit.

Chapter 4

Joe Potts

IN BOB McIntyre's own words:

The year 1954 was not a happy year for me. Inevitably I felt rather a new boy, this being my first season in the Grand Prix class. I did not even enjoy the foreign travel. On my first trip I probably ate the wrong things; at any rate I was sick and left with a lingering mistrust of the continental food. On top of all this I was not greatly impressed by the AJS racing organisation.

So when the racing season ended, in late September 1954, Bob left AJS and London and went back to his native Scotland and began a partnership with Joe Potts which was to continue for the rest of his life. As Bob said, 'A mutual friend had introduced us some time before. Joe had raced 500cc cars and later built his own – 'JP' cars.'

As described in a separate boxed section within this chapter, Joe Potts had a number of business ventures and so, because of these ongoing commitments,

At the end of 1954, Bob left AJS and London and went back to his native Scotland and began a partnership with Joe Potts, which was to continue for the rest of his life. He is pictured at Brough, on 3 April 1955, on a Potts Norton.

Another Brough shot of
Bob with the Potts Norton.

he decided to retire from active participation. But he found he had to indulge
his desire for speed in some way. He did so by purchasing a Manx Norton and
tuning it. George Brown rode it for the Potts équipe in 1953 and Vic
Willoughby in 1954. For 1955 this sponsorship went to Bob McIntyre.

The deal was that Bob should also look after the motorcycle side of Joe
Potts's business. But as Bob was to recall, 'Unfortunately we had only one
showroom and cars and motorcycles do not mix happily, and we soon

Bob's great friend and travelling companion, fellow racer Alastair King, seen here during the 1961 Senior TT in which he finished fourth, averaging 97.52mph. Bob came home runner-up at 99.20mph.

Alastair King

As Les Weir said in the May 1959 issue of *The Scottish Clubman* magazine: 'There is only one thing between Alastair King and Scotland's motorcycle crowns – and that's Bob McIntyre'. Some might have considered themselves unlucky to be separated from greater glory by one such dominant figure, but not Alastair. As he said himself, 'It's a greater glory to be second to Bob, than to win without him'.

Alastair King's first race was on a Norton International at Errol Aerodrome in spring 1951. Contrary to regulations, Alastair managed to reach the starting line without a lap of practice and astonished himself by not only reaching the final, but finishing in sixth position.

For the 1952 season a more serious approach was made, with the purchase of a Velocette KTT Mark VIII. But against the latest AJS 7R and Featherbed Manx Nortons, which were beginning to appear north of the border, he had to ride extremely hard to get the many local successes he achieved that year.

1953 was the year of the first new bike, and that was purchased principally for the Senior Clubman's TT. The choice was the newly released Featherbed-framed International and, entered by the Mercury Club, Alastair finished fifth at an average speed of 81.77mph. Following his Isle of Man showing he was offered the loan of an AJS 7R from the Cooper Brothers équipe for the Manx GP in September 1953. However, the result was not what everyone had wished for; far from it. Not content with dropping the machine within a mile of the start on the first lap at Quarter Bridge, some helpful spectator removed the plug lead in an effort to prevent the engine over-revving. With surplus fuel all over the place, it would be an understatement to say that King's hopes went up in smoke. The resultant pyre was, as one commentator put it 'second only to Hiroshima', and was of such note that it was photographically recorded on

Alastair with his 499cc
Norton at Oulton Park
c.1960.

no less a front page than the following day's *Daily Express* newspaper! In
1954 Bob McIntyre joined the AJS works team and Sam Cooper offered
Alastair one of his immaculately prepared 7Rs. On this he swept the
boards locally and made some credible forays south of the border.

The Senior Clubman's TT was tried again, this time on one of the new
DB34 Gold Star models. He not only won at a record average speed of
85.76mph, but also set a new class lap record of 87.02mph.

Ill luck again dogged Alastair in the Manx Grand Prix, when he was
robbed of almost certain victory in the Junior event when his 7R's engine
seized on the last lap at Kirkmichael; but he did have the satisfaction of
setting a new Junior lap record at 87.77mph.

But worse was to come, because as Alastair was to recall 'the year is
better forgotten as one stroke of ill-luck befell another.' First Sam Cooper
pulled out of the racing game, and although Eric Bowers generously put a
couple of machines at Alastair's disposal, injuries and mechanical failures
won the day.

Then, in 1956, business returned to normal and success followed
success all over Scotland. That was until the ill-fated Manx Grand Prix came
around in September. With a headline 'Terrific Struggles' *The Motor Cycle*
was able to report that although Alastair King had 'broken the lap record
twice' the Scot had also been forced out with only a few miles to run: 'the
big-end had gone.' Riding a Manx Norton he did, however, manage to raise
the lap record to 91.07mph; this was to stand for several years.

For 1957, Alastair joined Joe Potts, which of course made him a
teammate of Bob McIntyre, although the two men had been close friends
for a number of years and members of the same Glasgow-based Mercury
Club. With Potts machinery Alastair recorded many victories in Scotland,
plus the likes of Brough, Silverstone and Oulton Park. This too was the year
of his first TT. After valve trouble in the Junior, in the Senior TT (the eight-
lap Jubilee event won by Bob on a Gilera in which the latter set the first
100mph lap) Alastair brought his Potts Norton home in seventh and was
rewarded with his first Replica.

Potts machinery was again used in 1958, with early success at places such as Oulton Park, where Geoff Duke was vanquished. There was also a terrific duel between Alastair and Bob at Charterhall, in which Alastair finally managed to cross the line first. June once again brought the TT and with it the cruellest luck of all. After finishing sixth in the Junior, in the Senior race things were virtually in the bag with ample time in hand when disaster struck at Kirkmichael and Alastair crashed heavily, causing damage to his elbow which resulted in three months of enforced rest.

Back in the saddle in September 1958, Alastair's successes were once again immediate. At Oulton Park, for example, only John Surtees on his works four-cylinder MV could stay in front of the speedy Scot.

Easter Monday 1959 at Oulton Park saw Alastair chalk up victories in the 250, 350 and 500cc classes, a feat enjoyed by only the really talanted riders.

Then came the TT with truly brilliant performances: a third in the Junior behind the MVs of Surtees and Hartle and one better in the Senior class when Alastair came home runner-up to John Surtees's MV four, followed by a sixth in the 500cc Ulster Grand Prix a couple of months later.

But it was not until 1961 that he was to repeat this sort of form. This time it was in the Ulster and Italian rounds of the World Championships that his best results were forthcoming. After a fourth in the Senior TT, Alastair took third in the 500cc Ulster (behind Hocking's MV and Hailwood's Norton) and second in the 350cc race riding a works Bianchi twin (again behind Hocking's MV). Then came Alastair's finest Continental Grand Prix result – a second behind Mike Hailwood in the 500cc Italian GP at Monza in September 1961.

Besides riding the AJS and Norton bikes in the bigger classes – plus a works Bianchi in the 350cc division – King also raced a Ducati 125 and a Benelli 250; the latter for Shrewsbury rider/dealer Fron Purslow.

Then came Bob McIntyre's fatal accident at Oulton Park on August Bank Holiday Monday 1962. Following Bob's death a few days later, Alastair announced his retirement from the sport which the two great friends had loved so much. Alastair rode (in a demonstration) Bob's McIntyre Matchless G50 special at the Remembrance meeting run at Oulton Park in October 1962 – then hung up his leathers for good.

Sadly, Alastair was to suffer a fatal car accident in his native Scotland during the early 1970s.

Alastair and Bob in fine form. Note those bar prices!

Brough Airfield, East Yorkshire in April 1955. John Surtees (23) leads Bob; both are mounted on Manx Nortons.

Bob receives the victor's laurels after winning the main race of the day on 3 April 1955, the Brough 25. Bob won from John Surtees and Dave Chadwick; all rode Nortons.

realised that we could bring in more money by racing motorcycles than by selling them.' And so the McIntyre/Potts alliance decided to stop selling them and 'have a real go at racing them'. From that time onwards, all Bob McIntyre did was to prepare and race machines.

This meant hard but enjoyable work. As a works rider Bob had only to get himself to the race meetings and ride. But now he had to maintain the bikes. Bikes for the 1955 season meant 350 and 500cc Manx Nortons – the former being added to the squad in time for the forthcoming season. As Bob said later:

I had to transport them to meetings – in a small Bedford van I had acquired – and attend to everything. As a works rider I had been guaranteed a minimum salary which the firm would make up if the prize money failed to reach that figure. Now I had to win if Joe and I were to continue. Races abroad were out of the question.

Bob got his 1955 season under way at Brough Airfield in East Yorkshire on Sunday 3 April. Following a week of superb spring weather, there was low cloud and rain to greet spectators and riders alike in time for practice. But fortunately the clouds rolled by and the crowd of some 14,000 spectators witnessed some exciting racing over a dry track. In the 350cc final Bob finished third, behind the Norton-mounted John Surtees and K.H. Patrick (BSA). But in the main event of the day, the Brough '25', Bob won from Surtees, with Dave Chadwick third on another Norton.

Then came two meetings over the Easter weekend: Snetterton on Sunday 10 April and Oulton Park on Monday 11 April.

At the Norfolk venue thousands of enthusiasts braved the persistent drizzle to attend the event, which was organised by the Snetterton Combine of Norfolk and Suffolk motorcycle clubs. And they were rewarded with a high standard of racing. In the Junior and Senior races it was very much a case of who would emerge victorious between John Surtees (now riding works development Nortons) and Bob McIntyre on his Potts-entered production Manx Norton models.

Unfortunately Bob was to be a non-starter on his smaller model, but in the main race of the day on his 499cc bike he finished runner-up to Surtees.

The following day at Oulton Park there were big crowds (a record attendance of over 30,000). Organised by the Wirral 100 Club and sponsored by the *Daily Herald* newspaper, there were factory-supported riders among the 206-entry list. These included AMC (John Clark, Derek Ennett and Bill Lomas) and Norton Motors (John Hartle).

Bob put up a tremendous performance to finish runner-up on his streamlined Potts Norton in the 1955 Junior TT. When one considers that he was beaten only by Bill Lomas on a works Guzzi, it proved his mastery of the 37.73-mile Mountain circuit.

The main race of the day was the 19-lap, 52.5-mile Silver Jubilee Cup for machines up to 1000cc. After winning his heat Bob was among the 27 starters for the final. Terry Shepherd (Norton) made a lightning start and for three laps held a seven second lead over P.H. Carter (Norton). But next time around Bob McIntyre, who had been sixth on lap one but had been gobbling up places

rapidly, flew past Carter and was quickly catching up the leader. Shepherd's lead dwindled until, on lap 12, the pair hurtled down the finishing straight side by side. Bob was forced to give way at Old Hall Corner and for a further lap was content to ride in Shepherd's slipstream. This move paid off, as next time through Old Hall Corner, Shepherd overdid things and crashed out. Although he was not badly hurt, he was unable to continue. This left Bob in a commanding position, nearly half a minute ahead of the next man, Bill Lomas (Matchless). Bob then wisely eased his pace, but even so he lapped R.H. King (Norton), who was in seventh position. Bob went on to win and also set the fastest lap at 82.1mph.

Oulton Park 1000cc Silver Jubilee Cup – 19 laps – 52.5 miles

1st   R. McIntyre (Norton)
2nd   P.H. Carter (Norton)
3rd   W.A. Lomas (Matchless)
4th   E.B. Jones (Norton)
5th   G.E. Read (Norton)
6th   G.E. Leigh (Norton)

Record-breaking Silverstone

Just under two weeks later Bob was racing at the annual *Motor Cycle* supported Silverstone Saturday meeting on 23 April 1955. The main events of the 13-race programme were the international BMCRC Championship encounters. But Bob's three-fifty was not yet back in action, so he was only present in the 500cc class. Even so he made an impressive showing, finishing third behind World Champion Geoff Duke (Gilera) and John Surtees. There is no doubt that both the Gilera four and Surtees's works development Norton were considerably quicker than the Scot's Potts Norton. As *The Motor Cycle* commented:

> *For the length of the race, third place was disputed by no fewer than five riders in one of the closest struggles ever seen. The stalwarts were R McIntyre, Brett, RD Keeler, riding Nortons, and Clark and Perris on Matchlesses. Deservedly, success went to McIntyre, who had been riding in particularly determined style.*

At Aintree on Saturday 30 April, Bob McIntyre had a particularly successful day, not only winning two races, but also finishing runner-up in a third. The other star of the meeting was Cecil Sandford, who had works Moto Guzzi singles for the 250 and 350cc events.

In the 350cc race Sandford's Moto Guzzi was simply too fast for all the opposition, including Bob's Norton. But of the others, who included the likes of Dave Chadwick and Mike O'Rourke, Bob came out on top.

Next came the 1000cc race, which Bob won from E. Pantlin and P.H. Carter (Norton); the Scot also set the fastest lap at 77.81mph. Finally came the Solo Handicap race, which saw another victory for Bob – and another fastest lap, this time circling at 78.26mph. All-in-all it was a highly successful 'trip down south' for the McIntyre effort. *The Motor Cycle* described the Solo Handicap thus:

The meeting ended with a solo handicap event over 20 laps. The field comprised the 10 fastest riders in the 250cc race and the first 15 finishers in each of the Junior and Senior events. The two-fifties were dispatched 3m 40s ahead of the 350cc machines, which in turn had a 35s initial advantage over the five-hundreds. Cann (248 Moto Guzzi) immediately took the lead and, at half distance, the order behind him was T.E. Fenwick (248 Moto Guzzi) and BT Rood (249 Velocette). R. McIntyre (499 Norton), who had been tearing through the field, was in sixth place and gaining about 10s a lap on the leader. Chadwick (348 Norton) was riding with great dash and lay seventh, ahead of Sandford on the three-fifty Moto Guzzi. McIntyre took the lead on lap 17.

After Aintree came another visit to the picturesque Oulton Park circuit, now extended to 2.76 miles, on Saturday 7 April. After taking part in what was described as a 'stirring battle' in the first heat of the 350cc Championship Race with Bill Lomas (AJS) and Cecil Sandford (Moto Guzzi), Bob was a non-finisher in the final after the plug on his smaller Norton oiled-up and he was subsequently flagged off for receiving outside assistance.

In the 1000cc Championship event, after winning his heat, Bob was to finish runner-up to a record-breaking John Surtees (Norton) in the 19-lap final. It should also be pointed out that the likes of John Surtees had machines for not just the 350 and 1000cc, but also the 250cc. Bob was definitely at a disadvantage during this period of his career, when he needed the maximum amount of track time.

Overnight Bob travelled north of the border, to add to his recent successes by winning both the main races at Errol airfield (halfway between Perth and Dundee) on Sunday 8 May 1955. The meeting, organised by the Perth Club, was run over the well-known figure-of-eight two-mile course, and though the corners had been artificially tightened, both lap and race speeds were faster than before – due to the high quality of riding displayed by Bob.

Aberdare Park, south Wales, was the setting for this lovely period shot of Bob and a young admirer, 18 June 1955.

This was followed six days later by a visit to Aberdare Park, in South Wales, on Saturday 14 May. Once again John Surtees was the man who dominated, with Bob McIntyre the closest opposition, finishing runner-up in the 350, 500 and unlimited events. The Scot also won all three of his heats that day. The course at Aberdare Park measured 1,320 yards to the lap and wound through beautiful, tree-lined glades.

John Surtees also did the winning at Brands Hatch the following day, on Sunday 15 May. But in fairness, John was already a Brands specialist, whereas it was Bob's first visit to the Kentish circuit.

One report of the Brands action said:

> *M.P. O'Rourke (AJS and Norton) got the nearest to Surtees in the 350 and 500cc finals. R. McIntyre rode as stylishly as Surtees but his Norton seemed to lack speed; for example, though he started well in the three-fifty final, leaving Surtees still on his feet, by the end of the third lap McIntyre lay third behind Surtees and O'Rourke. He was also third in the Handicap (on his five-hundred Norton) and fourth in the 500cc final.*

On Sunday 22 May Bob was back in action at Errol when the Dundee & Angus Club staged a road race meeting over the popular circuit. And again it was McIntyre who took both the 350cc and 1000cc races, and set up the fastest laps.

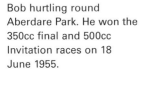

Bob hurtling round Aberdare Park. He won the 350cc final and 500cc Invitation races on 18 June 1955.

Best wishes
~~Lambert~~

Joe Potts

Joe Potts's motto was 'have the right man handling the twist grip'. And in Bob McIntyre and Alastair King it is easy to see just how true this saying really was.

Like many other leading entrants and tuners, Potts had been a keen motorcycle racer himself, from 1930 to 1934. He competed in grass and sand races in his native Scotland on Sunbeam machinery. Then, after a lay-off of some 13 years, which of course included the war period, Joe Potts decided on a comeback. But this time, in 1949, it was on four wheels, starting with a Cooper car. At this time he was already manufacturing small batches of his own JP racing car. In a strange irony he did not race his own cars, at least not at first, initially preferring to stick with the Cooper. Although Joe Potts was an excellent engineer, he got his friend and chief mechanic, Willie Rogerson, to design the lightweight chassis (formed by two parallel steel tubes on each side) for the rear-engined JP car. It may surprise readers to know that in the early 1950s Joe Potts had an engineering staff of some 120 employees. In total, some 30 examples of the JP racer were produced, powered by a variety of engines, notably JAP and Vincent HRD. His dealings with the latter concern, which was based in Stevenage, Hertfordshire, brought Potts into contact with the legendary George Brown, and the common interests and mutual enthusiasm of the pair led to Joe Potts purchasing a Manx Norton. Tuned and modified in typical Potts fashion, this machine carried George Brown to a highly acclaimed seventh place in the 1952 Senior TT. George continued riding for Potts in 1953, then in 1954 his place was taken by motorcycling journalist Vic Willoughby.

But it was with Bob McIntyre that the Potts reputation was truly cemented. The first time that Bob rode for Joe was at a Charterhall meeting towards the end of the 1954 season. McIntyre won the 500cc event, putting one across several better-known riders on the very latest short-stroke models. In 1954 Bob had signed up to ride works AJS models (advised to do so by his then sponsor Sam Cooper), but after a season which Bob was later to say he had 'not enjoyed', he was back as a privateer with the Potts équipe for 1955 and 1956. Even with a Gilera contract for 1957, Bob McIntyre still continued to ride Potts machinery when he was able. Then, when Gilera retired from Grand Prix racing towards the end of 1957, Bob was back to ride Potts machinery, which by now usually consisted of an AJS 7R for the 350cc class and a Manx Norton for the 500cc category.

Even when Bob rode for Bianchi (1961) and Honda (1961 and 1962), he stipulated that he must be free to ride for Potts in non-championship events; both factories agreed to this request.

In many ways the career of Alastair King was overshadowed by his more famous travelling partner, but in truth he was a brilliant rider in his own right. Jimmy Buchan was another who benefited from Potts's support. But although he was one of the most well-known figures in British racing during the 1950s and 1960s, motorcycle racing for Joe Potts was little more than a hobby, for the rest of the time he spent carrying on the family business in the Glasgow suburb of Bellshill. This business was quite extensive, comprising a garage with sales, servicing facilities, car hire, a 24-hour breakdown service – Joe Potts was even a funeral director, this latter business venture coming prior to his engineering and motor trade connections (in fact it still survives in Bellshill).

Joe Potts always protested that he was no technician. Even so, he displayed a shrewd appreciation of mechanical fundamentals. His approach to a task was logical and his methods meticulous, and this combination meant that his riders achieved considerable successes at all levels.

My research has revealed that Joe Potts was a generally well liked, decent man, keen to help others. However, my good friend David Tonge, who acquired much of the late Reg Dearden's Norton spares inventory, was to receive something of an ear-bending session when he asked Joe how he got on with the Norton factory: 'They (Norton) have been most unhelpful, simply because we have been beating them.'

Bob McIntyre's mentor, Joe Potts, 'Scotland's High Priest of Tune'. This photograph was taken in May 1956.

Back to the TT

Probably the major part of Bob McIntyre's 1955 season was his planning and preparation for the TT. Just how much can be seen from the fact that in the early morning practice session for the 500cc Senior he took his Norton around second fastest (behind Geoff Duke's Gilera four) and in front of Ken Kavanagh (Moto Guzzi), Fergus Anderson (Moto Guzzi), John Surtees (Norton) and Jack Brett (Norton). And remember, all these other riders were aboard full works or works development models.

For the Island Bob's 499cc Norton had been equipped with a home-made system of oil cooling for the exhaust-valve guide. The Scot recorded the fastest lap for a private rider during the entire practice period – and also achieved the same distinction with his Junior mount. The latter had been fitted with a fully streamlined aluminium 'dustbin' fairing.

In the races that followed the name Bob McIntyre was to be a talking point all around the famous Mountain circuit, with some outstanding riding.

The 1955 Junior TT was contested over dry roads and was to be one of Bob's finest performances up to that time. Besides the factory development AJS and Norton models, Bob's biggest challenge came from the Italian Moto Guzzi factory. But one of their riders, Dickie Dale, had been involved in a motor accident, suffering a cracked shoulder bone. This meant that Guzzi signed Bill Lomas as a replacement to partner Ken Kavanagh, Cecil Sandford and Duilio Agostini (no relation to 15-times World Champion Giacomo). Factory policy meant that both Norton and AJS factory-entered models were in unstreamlined form, whereas the Moto Guzzis had full streamlining, which pundits said was worth up to 10mph on the faster sections of the course. This feature was copied by the Potts Norton ridden by Bob McIntyre in this race. The pre-race favourites were one of the Guzzi riders or John Surtees. Nobody seemed to be considering Bob or his Potts Norton, which after all were private entries.

At the end of the first lap it was revealed that Surtees had gone round in 24 minutes 47 seconds, with all the Guzzi riders slower. Then came an explosive surprise – Bob McIntyre on the Potts-tuned Norton was dead-heating with Surtees. Incredible, but true! But even better was to come, with Bob leading the race by the end of lap two. This is how one commentator saw things:

> *McIntyre, that brilliant Scot who in the saddle looks so much like Duke, pulled out all the stops. Through Union Mills and Glen Helen his torso was welded to the tank top. Up Snaefell climb he was brilliance personified. His fantastic challenge paid off and at the end of the lap he headed Surtees by 18 seconds.*

Bob Mac continued to lead the race until lap five. This is where the Scot probably made the mistake which was to cost him the race. As *The Motor Cycle* said:

McIntyre's halt (for his pit stop) was leisurely, perhaps too leisurely, for he took 27s – and calmly reported a slight loss of compression! Sandford's stop took 25s and Surtees 22s. It was then that realisation dawned – the chief leader board shuffle need not be temporary. Lomas went straight through. He was not going to stop for fuel at all, for the Guzzi's 7½-gallon tankage was enough for the full race distance.

This was to be a bitter lesson for Bob and the Potts équipe – and something they would copy from Guzzi in the future – pannier tanks contained in the fairing sides! *The Motor Cycle* continued:

The gallant Scot's Herculean effort seemed doomed to failure after all for, at the end of the fifth lap, he was signalled as second, 4s behind Lomas and 12s ahead of Sandford. One against two in such close scrapping makes difficult odds.

At the end of the seven-lap, 264.11-mile race Lomas emerged victorious from Bob, with Sandford third and John Surtees fourth. And John, Bob and Cecil Sandford were to win the Club Team Award (for BMCRC). Lomas's winning time was 2 hours 51 minutes 38.2 seconds (92.31mph), Bob's 2 hours 52 minutes 38.2 seconds (91.79mph).

Junior TT – 7 laps – 264.11 miles
1st   W. Lomas (Moto Guzzi)
2nd   R. McIntyre (Norton)
3rd   C. Sandford (Moto Guzzi)
4th   J. Surtees (Norton)
5th   M. Quincey (Norton)
6th   J. Hartle (Norton)

Interviewed after the finish, Bob cheerfully announced that he 'could have tackled another lap', but his Norton would not have been so willing. The engine had begun to lose power shortly before his pit stop and, though the deterioration was not serious for a while, it became more pronounced during the final circuit. Later, it was discovered the lost power was due to valve-seat distortion.

The Senior race

As *The Motor Cycle* reported: 'For nearly three-quarters of an hour last Friday, the world thought that the Isle of Man Mountain course had been lapped for the first time at 100mph.' But then it was announced that Geoff Duke and his Gilera had missed this feat by half a second with a speed of 99.97mph.

In the race the lowest position which Bob held was eighth (on lap five), but he completed the first lap in fifth – an identical position to that which he was to hold at the finish of the seven-lap race (the same distance as the Junior race of four days earlier). But this time he beat Bill Lomas, who was seventh, again riding a works Moto Guzzi. Bob again held the distinction of being the first non works-supported entry to finish and also a member of the winning club team (BMCRC – G.E. Duke, J. Surtees, R. McIntyre).

Senior TT – 7 laps – 264.11 miles

1st	G.E. Duke (Gilera)
2nd	H.R. Armstrong (Gilera)
3rd	K. Kavanagh (Moto Guzzi)
4th	J. Brett (Norton)
5th	R. McIntyre (Norton)
6th	D. Ennett (Matchless)

Bob also won *The Motor Cycle* Cup, awarded to the entrant who was a signatory of the dealer's agreement (Manufacturers' Union) whose rider improved by the greatest margin on the average time of the first 20 riders in the International Senior, Junior or Lightweight 250cc races. This was for runner-up in the Junior race: 'Joseph Potts'. It is also interesting to note that Bob decided not to use streamlining on his Senior Norton. Though he considered it had 'consistently' improved the top speed of his Junior machine, he was 'not entirely happy with the handling at high speed.' He was also forced to use his reserve five-hundred for the race. It was virtually brand new and had received 'less attention and tuning.'

Someone who was notably impressed by Bob's 1955 TT performances was the then current 350cc World Champion and Moto Guzzi team manager Fergus Anderson. He pointed out that 'Bob McIntyre had a normal four-speed box' (against the five-speed assemblies on the works Guzzis). Fergus also revealed, 'There is only one rider I would have taken on had it been possible… and his name was Bob McIntyre!'

Back to the short circuits

Following the TT, it was back to the British short circuits. Bob's first outing was at the televised meeting at Aberdare Park on Saturday 18 June. The TV presentation went out live and, as one race report of the meeting said: 'Perfect weather, which had almost certainly been conjured up by the Welsh gods, meant that spectators at the venue and before their TV screens enjoyed an afternoon's good racing.' The invitation race for the Welsh TV Trophy comprised two heats and a final, all shown on television. During the first few miles of the final Peter Ferbrache's 499cc (Hartley-Ariel) led, but Bob, who had drawn a back-row grid position, was soon very close behind and moved ahead to take the lead, which he held to the end, also setting the fastest lap.

It was unanimously agreed that the 12-lap 350cc event, which followed the presentation of the Welsh TV Trophy to Bob, was the best of the day. The winner, once again, was McIntyre (Norton). He set the seal on a most successful day with a class-record lap of 49.6 seconds. Again he had to come through to victory from a poor grid position.

For the second time the Scottish Speed Championships were staged at the well-known Beveridge Park venue in Kirkcaldy. The date was Saturday 2 July 1955 and Bob was simply in a class of his own. During the meeting he broke his own 350 and 500cc lap records no fewer than four times!

The 350cc Championship was run off in three five-lap heats and a 10-lap final. In the final McIntyre led from start to finish and was never seriously challenged. On the fourth lap he broke his 1953 record of 60.88mph with a lap in 1 minute 20.8 seconds, equal to a speed of just over 61mph.

Four five-lap heats, two five-lap semi-finals and a 10-lap final were required to decide the 500cc Championship. Bob, who in his heat had twice hoisted the 500cc lap record with times of 1 minute 19.8 seconds (62mph) and 1 minute 19.6 seconds (62.2mph) won the second semi-final with ease and in doing so again broke the record with a sizzling circuit in 1 minute 18.4 seconds (63.1mph), the fastest of the day. As a contemporary race report said: 'The final was more or less a repetition of the 350cc event, McIntyre way out in front, riding a beautifully judged, unhurried race just fast enough to keep well out of challenge distance.'

On Saturday 30 July Bob scored three out of three wins at the Cheshire Centre's Oulton Park meeting on his Potts Norton machines. *The Motor Cycle* dated 4 August 1955 said spectators 'saw first-class riding, not least among which was the polished display of the brilliant R. McIntyre, who began his August Bank Holiday weekend activities well by winning every event in which he entered – three in all.'

As at the earlier visit to Oulton that year, Terry Shepherd and Dave

Chadwick provided the main opposition. Mike O'Rourke and Frank Perris were also in the frame, but none could touch McIntyre that day.

The opposition was much tougher two days later, on Monday 2 August, at the ACU sixth International Road Races, held at the Thruxton circuit near Andover, Hampshire. This meeting, like Oulton on the Saturday, was favoured with fine, dry weather. The meeting had attracted an unusually large number of acknowledged star riders, including the new 350cc World Champion Bill Lomas and his teammate Dickie Dale on works Moto Guzzis, plus the Norton and AJS teams. Riding unfaired bikes Bob gained fourth and fifth places in the 350 and 500cc finals respectively.

Ulster Grand Prix

When the Ulster Grand Prix took place in mid-August, Bob's main opposition again came from the AJS, Norton and Moto Guzzi works teams. For the 350cc event, as he had in the TT, Bob's Norton sported the fully streamlined aluminium shell.

Bob signing autographs at the 1955 Ulster GP. He is seated here on his 348cc Potts Norton, the same bike as he used in the TT. He finished fifth, averaging 87.10mph.

The meeting was held with unbroken blue skies and vast crowds. On Saturday 13 August the attendance was estimated at 100,000. The 1955 Ulster consisted of only three races (250, 350 and 500cc). The Dundrod circuit was some 7.5 miles long and considered a true rider's course. It had many bends and its corners were varied in nature from very slow to ultra-fast.

There were also severe gradients at times; the 500ft climb from Cochranstown to Hole in the Wall was a real test of machine stamina. But there were also some long, full-bore stretches where the works bikes were at a distinct advantage.

The 350cc race was run on Thursday 11 August. Ranged against the solitary Potts Norton were the Moto Guzzi team (Lomas, Sandford, Dale and Agostini), Norton (Surtees, Brett and Hartle) and AJS (Perris, John Clark and Derek Powell) – nine machines in all. With a race distance of 20 laps (148.18 miles) it was a test of endurance for both rider and bike. The final finishing order was Lomas, Hartle, Surtees, Sandford, McIntyre, Murphy, Brett, Powell, Clark and Perris.

In the 500cc race, held on the Saturday, Bob managed to go one better, with fourth place (behind Lomas, Hartle and Dale), the race distance having been increased to 25 laps (185.23 miles).

On Sunday 21 August at Errol airfield Bob suffered his first defeat in his native Scotland for some considerable time. In the 350cc open event he had to concede second best to Alastair King (AJS) for the entire 10-lap race. A period race report described it thus:

> McIntyre lay in King's slipstream and made many unavailing attempts to pass. On the ninth lap he did manage to get ahead but held the lead for only a few yards until King took him again on the Pits Bend and stayed in front for the remaining lap.

However, in the 1000cc race Bob, obviously out to avenge his previous defeat, took the lead from the very start and his progress was such that he was lapping the slower men before half-distance.

Bob's next outing came at Snetterton, Norfolk, on Saturday 10 September. This meeting had attracted an excellent entry, with John Surtees and Bob sharing the honours in which these two riders came up against each other, McIntyre winning the 350cc event, Surtees the 500cc. In both cases their main challenger was Mike O'Rourke (AJS).

The International Scarborough Gold Cup meeting was staged over Friday and Saturday 16/17 September. The entry included Geoff Duke (Gilera), the Norton team of Surtees, Hartle and Brett and the German Karl Lottes on a works DKW. In the 350cc final on the first day Bob brought his Potts Norton home third, behind the factory Nortons of Surtees and Hartle. But Bob was unplaced the following day in the 500cc event, which was won by Geoff Duke and his screaming Gilera four from Surtees and Hartle.

Scarborough was followed by another meeting enjoying international

Bob (1) leading John Hartle, Olivers Mount, Scarborough, September 1955. The Scot finished third, Hartle second in the 350cc Junior final at this international Gold Cup meeting.

status, at Aintree on Saturday 24 September. Unlike earlier motorcycle events at the Liverpool circuit, this time there was a large number of spectators, estimated to be some 30,000.

But as *The Motor Cycle* commented in their issue of 29 September 1955: 'For once R. McIntyre's best efforts in tuning and riding his Nortons were not enough to keep him up with the factory riders.' And so he finished sixth in the 350cc race and fifth in the 500cc. The Aintree course was very much about speed and little else. For the record Surtees (Norton) won the 350cc, Duke (Gilera) the 500cc.

The following day, Sunday, Bob was at Brough, East Yorkshire. Here he once again did battle with John Surtees. After both winning their 350cc heats, Surtees managed to keep in front of Bob to the flag. Then Bob retired in the third heat of the 500cc event and thus did not take part in the final.

The annual Hutchinson 100 meeting at Silverstone on Saturday 1 October 1955 saw Bob reclaim his crown as the man fully capable of giving the works bikes a run for their money. He was to end the day with three second places and a fourth – a truly magnificent performance considering the array of international talent lined up against him. In fact only John Surtees could best

Bob, except in the 500cc Championship race when Surtees won from Duke (Gilera) and John Hartle (Norton), with Bob next.

The Motor Cycle described Bob's performance in the 350cc Championship event:

> *For the first half of the race the struggle for second place was so close and so fierce that it was difficult to separate the six riders involved – McIntyre, Hartle and Brett on Nortons, Sandford (Moto Guzzi), J.R. Clark and R.N. Brown (AJS). McIntyre's doggedness prevailed and he drew away from the bunch to finish little more than 20s behind the winner.*

Sunday 2 October saw many of those who had raced at Silverstone the day before fight it out over the 1.24-mile Brands Hatch short circuit. Watching them was a record crowd of over 60,000 spectators – with many more unable to get into the famous Kentish venue. In the 15-lap 350cc race local star John Surtees beat Bob into second, with Bob Brown (Norton) third.

Bob was without his 500cc Norton, so rode a BSA in the 1000cc Invitation race, finishing third behind Surtees and Alan Trow (Norton), these two riders having beaten World Champion Geoff Duke (Gilera) in the 500cc event. And so another season came to an end, with Bob having made a successful transition from works entry back to privateer.

Far from a quiet winter

If readers imagine that Bob then had several months with nothing much to do, they would be completely wrong. In fact there were three new bikes to prepare, as Bob would be riding 246, 349 and 499cc Joe Potts Nortons during the 1956 season.

The powerplant of the two-fifty had begun life as a 349cc Manx Norton assembly. But with the Potts équipe's efforts, the cylinder barrel was shortened and sleeved to a bore dimension of 70mm. In order to reduce the stroke to 64mm, the original flywheel assembly was axed in favour of a one-piece crankshaft carrying an outside flywheel. The light-alloy connecting rod was split across the big-end eye, which was equipped with a white metal Vandervell-type shell bearing. Machined from a solid billet of high-duty steel and subsequently heat-treated, the crankshaft had standard-size main bearing journals, 1in diameter on the timing side and 1½in on the drive side. The ball and roller timing side main bearings were one-offs. The diameter of the big-end bearing was 1½in. To ensure adequate lubrication for the plain bearing big-end, oil pressure had been upped to 60lb/sq in, this having necessitated the

The Potts 248 Norton Special as it appeared when it debuted in spring 1956. The specification included 8000rpm, 100mph (161kph) in unstreamlined form, Earles-type front forks and 2LS front brake.

use of a synthetic rubber oil seal where the big-end feed jet entered the crankshaft at the offside (right) end.

The cylinder head had been machined from a stock three-fifty Manx Norton casting and the inlet valve was of a slightly smaller diameter than the standard 40M three-fifty Manx. Camshaft profile had been determined by the Potts machine shop, while the carburettor was a 1½in Amal GP instrument.

Of conventional duplex-loop pattern, the frame was constructed in 1½in diameter Reynolds 531 tubing; the swinging arm fork was manufactured from 16-gauge Accles and Pollock tubing. Both swinging arm fork and front fork assemblies (the latter of the Earles pattern) featured tapered stanchions. The 2LS front brake was of the latest Manx Norton design, with a floating shoe plate and a torque linkage designed to isolate fork action from braking torque.

In naked form the machine was capable of reaching a genuine 100mph, with peak power being produced at 8000rpm.

A triple victory in East Yorkshire

The first road race meeting of the 1956 season to be held at the Brough circuit in East Yorkshire was staged on Good Friday, 30 March. This saw Bob victorious in all three solo finals – the 250, 350 and Unlimited Brough '25' – and the Scot also set the fastest lap in each. The first victory came on the smallest Norton, when Bob won some half a lap in front of runner-up Ted Fenwick (Moto Guzzi) and fellow Scot Charlie Bruce (Velocette). In the 350cc final, it was Bob from George Catlin and Alastair King (all Norton mounted). Then, in the main race of the day, the Brough '25', it was McIntyre, Alastair King and B.J. Thompson (Matchless).

A similar state of affairs was repeated on Easter Monday, 2 April, at Oulton Park, with the flying Scot winning the 250, 350 and 500cc classes. Riding at his very best at both Brough and Oulton, no other rider was able to mount a successful challenge to Bob.

As *The Motor Cycle* dated 12 April 1956 was able to report:

Bob (81) lapping a slower competitor on his way to three wins (250cc, 350cc and Brough '25') at Brough on 30 March 1956. He set the fastest lap in each of the races.

Highlights of last Sunday's road-race meeting at Snetterton, organised under a regional-restricted permit by the Snetterton Combine, were undoubtedly clashes in the 250cc and 500cc events between MV Agusta-mounted John Surtees and Bob McIntyre (Nortons). Both riders delighted the large crowd with dashing displays of riding skill but the superior acceleration and speed of the MV Agustas enabled Surtees to win more or less as he liked, though for McIntyre it can be said that he was never very far behind.

The Motor Cycle's race report referred to Bob's effort to stay with the much faster MV-mounted Surtees as 'gallant.' But in both cases, the Scot was forced to concede victory.

The two heats for the 350cc event were won by Ernie Washer (AJS) and Bob. In the final, our hero was pursued by Mike O'Rourke (AJS) for three laps. Thereafter Bob drew away to win by some distance. Although badly boxed in at the start, Alan Trow (Norton) rode a great race to pip O'Rourke for the runner-up berth by less than four lengths. Bob McIntyre set a new class lap record of 82.69mph.

Waterlogged Silverstone

There was all-day rain for the BMCRC Championships at Silverstone on Saturday 14 April 1956. And except for a win in the 1000cc championship race (after winning his heat), Bob had a miserable day – as his hopes of a potential victory in the 350cc class had been shattered when he was forced to retire in the opening heat when his Norton stopped with waterlogged ignition.

He had elected not to bring his smaller Norton to the Northamptonshire circuit.

The following weekend, on Sunday 22 April, Bob was back on home soil in Scotland. The venue was Errol Airfield between Perth and Dundee. He won all three classes he contested: 250cc from Charlie Bruce (Velocette), 350cc from Jimmy Buchan (Norton) and the 500cc from Alastair King (Norton); also setting the fastest lap in each race.

And it would have been a repeat performance on 28 April at Charterhall had not mechanical trouble forced Bob's retirement in the 350cc class.

Certain victory slipped from Bob Mac's grasp in the international North West 200 on Saturday 12 May 1956, when after setting the fastest lap of the meeting in 6 minutes 58 seconds (95.25mph), he struck problems at the three-quarters race distance with a split fuel tank. And as *The Motor Cycle* reported: 'To add to his difficulties there was a misunderstanding over signalling at a time when, had he continued his effort, he would probably have gained second place; as it was he dropped out.'

He then travelled overnight to the Perth club's Errol meeting where he won the 250 and 1000cc races and finished runner-up to his pal Alastair King in the 350cc event. However, it should be pointed out that he was forced to use his 250cc Norton in this latter event. Losing 100cc, he just couldn't make up the power loss, but tried everything possible including slipstreaming the larger engined bike – and on occasions even leading it! Not for the first time he displayed that McIntyre fighting spirit, not conceding victory until the flag fell at the very end of the final lap.

For the second year running Bob won the Brough '25' on his Potts Norton, 30 March 1956.

Typical scene at Errol Airfield, *c.*1956.

Challenging Duke at Oulton

The Whitsun Monday meeting at Oulton Park on 21 May 1956 featured Bob McIntyre and Geoff Duke, the two main stars of the day. After Bob had chalked up victories (and fastest laps) in the 250 and 350cc classes, the vast crowd got ready for the main race, the 351 to 1000cc final. *The Motor Cycle* sets the scene:

> *Thirty-two riders massed on the grid for the start of the 19-lap Senior Championship (up to 1000cc) final for the Britannia Vase. When the starting signal was given Duke's Gilera, placed on the second row, could be heard bursting into song at least two bars ahead of the main crescendo. In fact, before the starter had rolled up his flag the red Italian machine had gained more than 30 yards on every other machine and was streaking away into the first corner. At the end of a lap Duke held a 6 second advantage over second man G.T. Salt, while McIntyre (Norton), probably the only rider present capable of putting up a serious challenge, lay fourth.*

By the end of the second lap Bob had established himself in second place, a position he was to hold until the end of the race.

So already that year he had proved himself capable of being the best single-cylinder rider when faced with the two main contenders for the 1956 500cc World Championship – John Surtees (MV Agusta) and Geoff Duke (Gilera). As events were to prove, his efforts had not gone unnoticed.

Back to the Island

Next it was back to the Isle of Man for the TT. In 1956 Bob was entered in three events: 250, 350 and 500cc. The Scot was now being seen as a major contender for honours. In the 'Who Will Win?' in *The Motor Cycle* dated 31 May 1956, Michael Kirk viewed Bob McIntyre in the following terms:

> *He is a private owner who had chosen to ride Joe Potts' Nortons in spite of at least two invitations to go foreign. Last year he finished second to Lomas and led for the first four laps. Lomas went the full distance without refuelling and McIntyre not only stopped but later lost compression through a faulty valve seat. This year, too, Lomas will almost certainly go through non-stop and the fact that McIntyre's Norton was fitted with pannier tanks in the North West '200' is significant. Barring trouble McIntyre could win, and is more likely to cause Lomas to call for aspirin than anyone other than Lomas'*

teammates and Sandford (DKW). As a rider he is in the Duke-Surtees-Lomas bracket. If he once again beats the factory Nortons no one would be surprised.

Bob had two fairings of identical shape on the Island, one in aluminium and the other in glass-fibre. They were lower and of a more rounded cross-section than his previous streamlining. They also featured a higher nose to avoid the need for cooling ducts for brake and engine. The four-point attachment to the machine was noted by one journalist to be 'remarkably simple, neat and robust.' A length of 1½in diameter steel tubing was clamped to the front down-tubes of the frame and there were two stub tubes, one on each side of the forward engine plates. Coupling all four to similar-size stubs within the fairing were lengths of large-bore rubber hose clamped by jubilee clips. At some 10lb bare, the fibreglass shell was approximately half the weight of the aluminium assembly; these fairings were interchangeable on all three engine sizes of the McIntyre Nortons. Interestingly, Bob's three-fifty featured oil cooling of the exhaust valve, in the same fashion as the earlier factory Nortons.

Later in the practice week Bob was reported to be considering abandoning his streamlining for the races. This was not so much to do with the machine's

Bob pushing his three-fifty streamlined Potts Norton into action during practice at the 1956 TT. After such a successful 1955 TT, 1956 was dogged by retirements.

behaviour in high winds, but because of his inability to corner as fast as when the bikes were naked. And he openly admitted that the latest streamlining 'gives less improvement in performance than last year's pattern.' In the end, Bob chose to race his Senior and Junior Nortons without streamlining, but with pannier tanks giving a total capacity of nine gallons.

Retirements all round

Unfortunately, the actual races of the 1956 TT series were to prove a big disappointment for the McIntyre camp. Firstly, after constantly putting his Norton on the 250cc leaderboard (usually third or fourth) and thus splitting the works teams, Bob was unable to use the bike in the race due to mechanical problems. Then in the Junior (350cc) race his Norton developed an oil leak and he was forced to retire at the end of the second lap. Finally, in the Senior (500cc) race event he was forced out on the second lap with a sheared pannier tank bolt.

This run of misfortune then continued at Thruxton on Saturday 23 June, when Bob and Alastair King, riding a 499cc BSA Gold Star, were again to strike trouble. This time the retirement was caused by a crash, which Bob sustained while duelling for the lead in the opening laps of the nine-hour race for production bikes at the Hampshire circuit. One report said:

At noon the flag went up. The surging mass of machines, exhaust blending with exhaust, swept off into Club Corner. R.E. Jerrard (BSA) led from Bob McIntyre (BSA) and at such a knottage to suggest a sprint rather than a marathon. The Jerrard-McIntyre duel was short-lived for, at Windy Corner, with only 2½ laps completed, Jerrard spun and McIntyre ran into his machine. Both men came off and Jerrard was taken to hospital though his injuries were not severe.

Bob's only injury was to a hand – but this was to sideline him for some three weeks.

Bob being congratulated after winning the 500cc British Championship title, Thruxton, 6 August 1956.

His return to racing came at the second annual Southern 100 meeting over the Billown 4½-mile road circuit in the Isle of Man near Castletown, in the south of the Island on 12 July 1956.

The 350cc race opened proceedings. From the drop of the flag Bob went into the lead – a position he was to hold for the entire 50-mile race distance, followed by Dave Chadwick (Norton) and Terry Shepherd (Norton). Alastair King (Norton) was fifth. For 15 laps of the 500cc event the pattern of the 350cc race was repeated – McIntyre well out in the lead. But then the effects of the hand injury which he had sustained at Thruxton came to the fore; this resulted in the Scot dropping back to fourth. But at least he did have the satisfaction of setting the fastest lap in the big race with a speed of 82.7mph.

A triple at Beveridge Park

Even though his right hand was still so tender from his Thruxton spill that he could hardly operate the front brake, Bob, riding the Joe Potts Nortons, simply 'ran away' with the 250, 350 and 500cc classes at Beveridge Park, Kirkcaldy, on Saturday 14 July. As *The Motor Cycle* said: 'His success came as a fitting compensation for missing the 'double' in the Isle of Man.' On his five-hundred Norton, Bob equalled his own circuit lap record of 63.1mph.

Another triple looked on the cards exactly two weeks later at Aintree, on Saturday 28 July 1956, when he won both the 350 and 500cc events at the national Red Rose meeting, and was leading the 250cc event when his chain came off on the first lap. The opposition included the likes of Bob Anderson, J.R. Clark, G.A. Murphy, Derek Minter and Terry Shepherd.

Over the August Bank Holiday, Bob raced at Oulton Park on Saturday 4 August where he finished runner-up in the 350cc race to World Champion Bill Lomas (Moto Guzzi), won the 250cc from Bob Brown (NSU) and set

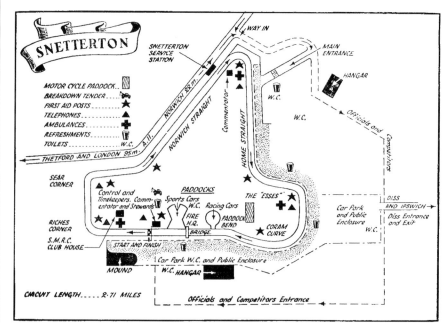

Making his debut at Cadwell Park Bob finished third in the 350cc and...

...runner-up in the 500cc races on his Potts Norton machines; in both cases his riding number was 21 and the date was 16 September 1956.

the fastest lap at 76.58mph, but retired in the 1000cc race with a broken footrest.

The following day, on Sunday 5 August, Bob won all his three classes at Snetterton in Norfolk. It remained fine all day, while admission (for spectators) was free for the first time since the circuit was opened (due to the Sunday Observance Act, which was in place at the time). Besides setting the fastest lap in each of his races, the Scot also established a new lap record in the 350cc class; in the Junior final he lapped at 83.37mph to better the existing record he held jointly with Alan Trow.

British champion – twice

On 6 August 1956, Bob McIntyre became British Champion on his 248cc Potts Norton. The venue was Thruxton Airfield, the scene of the ACU

International British Championships meeting. The eight-lap Lightweight (250cc) Championship saw the names of Bob McIntyre, Geoff Monty (GMS) and Percy Tait (Beasley-Velocette) as the main contenders. And sure enough at the end of the first lap this trio was well ahead of the field, the Scottish star in the lead. It soon became evident that Tait and Monty could not hope to hold McIntyre's streamlined Norton and by half-distance Bob had a lead of more than a quarter of a mile. Near the end Tait's carburettor main jet became blocked, resulting in the loss of several places, and Basil Keys (Norton) came through to take third. Bob not only won the prestigious title of 250cc British Champion, but also set the fastest lap of 77.55mph.

Next came the Junior (350cc) championship race. After winning his heat, Bob led Bill Lomas (Moto Guzzi) at the end of the first lap of the final. But a lap later the positions were reversed, with the pair already well in front of the remainder of the field. Even at the end of the 18 laps the Scot was only four seconds adrift of the 1956 350cc World Champion. This was an impressive result because the next man – Terry Shepherd (Norton) – was a full one minute in arrears.

Finally, after yet another heat win, came the 500cc British Senior Championship (again over 18 laps). True to form, Bob jumped ahead at the start. But his right hand (injured during the Thruxton nine-hour race a few weeks earlier) was tiring and he was having difficulty maintaining his lead over Terry Shepherd and John Clark (Matchless). With three laps to go it appeared as if Shepherd might chalk up a surprise win. But Bob, sensing his rival's bid, gritted his teeth and pulled out enough speed to win by some 250 yards. The famous McIntyre determination had seen him through again.

Bob was double British Champion!

More bad luck

Next came another visit to Errol Airfield. But as *The Motor Cycle* dated 16 August 1956 reported: 'Bob McIntyre does not seem to have reached the end of the streak of bad luck which has dogged him so persistently this season.' Yes, he did win the 250cc event, but in the 350cc race he retired with engine gremlins, while in the 500cc class gearbox trouble caused his retirement. His friend Alastair King thus took two victories.

Then came a month's break from racing until a rash of meetings at the end of September and into the first week of October 1956.

The first of these came at Scarborough's Oliver's Mount circuit international Gold Cup. The heats were held on Friday 21 September, the finals the following day. Bob won both his 350 and 500cc heats – and the 350cc final (from Peter Murphy and Dave Chadwick). In the 500cc Gold Cup

race Bob led Geoff Duke (Gilera) for the first three laps, but Duke took the lead from then on, with the Scot in close company. At the finish, Geoff Duke and Bob swapped machines to do a lap of honour. At the time everyone thought this act simply 'a pleasant end to two days of really keen racing' as one journal recorded. But few could have guessed another reason for Bob McIntyre's Gilera ride – he was about to become a works rider again!

Next day Bob made his debut at Cadwell Park, Lincolnshire. After winning the 250cc race (from Percy Tait and George Catlin) the Potts Norton rider went on to finish third (to Peter Murphy and Bernard Codd) in the 350cc and runner-up (behind John Hartle) in the 500cc event. Considering he had never seen the tight and difficult circuit before, Bob's performance was excellent. *The Motor Cycle* reported the 500cc race thus: 'The 20-lap Senior championship brought out the best from both Hartle and McIntyre. Hartle led at the end of lap 1 and he was still leading at the finish, but it was far from being a walk-over. McIntyre rode with grim determination and once, at the foot of the Mountain, got within an ace of overtaking his rival.'

Bob racing at Snetterton on 5 August 1956. Besides setting the fastest lap in each of his races, the Scot established a new lap record in the Junior (350cc) final at 83.37mph.

Total War at Silverstone

The headline read 'Total War at Silverstone.' And that was precisely what race fans witnessed at the BMCRC's international Hutchinson '100' meeting at Silverstone on Saturday 22 September. Although Bob only scored one victory in five races, he nonetheless was a serious contender in all of them with his forceful riding. His victory came in the second 500cc race, where he also put in the fastest lap (92.38mph), but it was the final race of the day, the 20-lap, 350cc Championship race, which really caught the imagination. *The Motor Cycle* of 27 September 1956 described the action:

McIntyre, Brett, Perris, Brown, King, Hartle, Codd and Shepherd drew front-row positions. The flag fell and Brett streaked away into the lead. But as the field rocketed down the straight to begin the second lap McIntyre led with Hartle second and Brett third. A lap later Hartle was in front. At the end of lap 4 Hartle still led, with McIntyre second and Brett tucked in behind. Less than two machine lengths separated all three and they were fast pulling away from King in fourth place. By the end of the following lap McIntyre had somehow forced his machine to the front, next time round Hartle was back in the lead with Brett still third. The excitement was heart-stopping! At the end of the eighth lap it was Brett who was in front and Hartle dropped behind McIntyre. Again and again the lead changed hands and the three were never more than feet apart. It was fantastic!

And so it was to continue, with Brett eventually winning from Bob with Hartle third. What a race! As for the rest of the pack, they were a long way to the rear, having their own private battles all the way down the field. But again Bob McIntyre had shown that in 1956 no other privateer could match his performances – Brett and Hartle were Norton works riders, but as had been the case so many times that year Bob had kept his bike up at the front where usually only factories flew.

The following day, Sunday 23 September, Bob was in action at Brands Hatch. After finishing runner-up to Mike O'Rourke (203cc MV) in the 250cc event, Bob continued in the same vein, recording runner-up spots in three more races (350, 1000cc and Slazenger Trophy). Essentially one man was responsible for preventing a McIntyre victory: Norton works rider Alan Trow, Trow being on home territory, living just a few miles from the Kent circuit.

The next McIntyre visit was to Aberdare Park in South Wales on Saturday 29 September, where he scored three wins in three rides – a feat he was to repeat at the south London Crystal Palace circuit on 6 October. And although this was Bob's final race meeting of the 1956 season, things were far from a normal end-of-season feel. Behind the scenes several parties had been jostling for the Scot's signature, notably Gilera and MV Agusta.

In the 11 October 1956 issue of *The Motor Cycle* Bob's plans were revealed. He had signed to race 350 and 500cc Gilera fours in the following season's Grand Prix races. But as the report outlined:

> *One of the most pro-British of the present generation of racing men, McIntyre had joined the Gilera team not so much with the idea of cashing in on his riding ability as much as from a desire to contest the classics on equal terms with other top-ranking riders while he is still at the height of his form.*

But until only a few days before, just who would gain Bob's signature was far from certain. This is what John Surtees told the author: 'Towards the end of 1956 I had been asked by MV Agusta to recommend someone who could be signed up for the 350/500cc classes.' At first John recommended his great friend and teammate at Norton, John Hartle. But this was not possible because Hartle was the doing his National Service in the British Army. The other choice was Bob McIntyre. So John Surtees, together with Count Domenico Agusta's friend Bill Webster, travelled to Aberdare Park, where Bob was competing on Saturday 29 September 1956. He told the author that an arrangement between McIntyre and MV was 'virtually settled.' But then he read *The Motor Cycle* news story a few days later that said that Bob had signed for Gilera. John continued: 'I rated Bob highly enough, particularly in the Isle of Man, to think it better to have him on an MV alongside me, rather than on a Gilera.'

And so Bob McIntyre's immediate future had been decided. And as history shows, the 1957 season was to provide some of Bob's greatest moments in the sport.

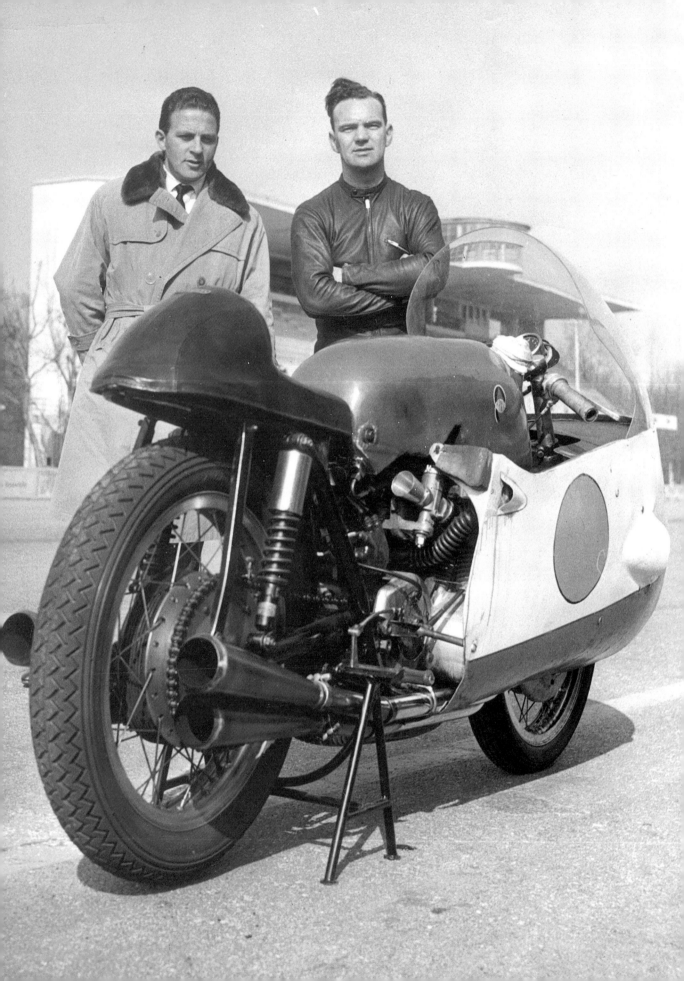

Chapter 5

Gilera

FOLLOWING Bob McIntyre's brilliant ride in the 1955 Junior TT, when he almost won the race from a host of factory entries including the likes of Moto Guzzi, Norton and AJS, the Scot was considered as one of the world's top motorcycle racing prospects.

At the end of that year, he was invited to join the Italian Gilera team, led by World Champion Geoff Duke. However, by the time of the offer, Joe Potts and Bob had already concluded their plans for the 1956 season, and so the offer was declined.

The Gilera offer is repeated

As Bob was later to explain:

> *At the end of 1956 the offer was repeated. Gilera contacted me while I was at Scarborough (via Geoff Duke). I had already discussed the question with Joe Potts. He knew that to win Classic races I needed better mounts than he could provide for me. It was just not possible to match the multi-cylindered Italian fliers, the Gileras and MVs, on a private single-cylinder British machine.*

There was, as explained at the end of the previous chapter, a serious bid for Bob's services from Gilera's big rivals, MV Agusta. And earlier there had also been interest from Moto Guzzi.

So Bob flew to Italy – and had a meeting with Giuseppe Gilera, boss of the factory which bore his name.

The factory was based in Arcore, on the outskirts of Milan. Bob recalled:

> *I was introduced to Mr Gilera – a thorough gentleman. I explained to him my position. I knew Gilera were interested only in the Classic races and the TTs. I would ride for Gilera in these events – but when Gilera did not require my services, I must be free to ride in races at*

Bob at Monza in March 1957, with his new teammate, the Italian Libero Liberati.

The four-cylinder Gilera
engine.

home on Joe Potts' machines. Gilera were not over-keen on the idea, but when they saw that I was not going to sign under any other conditions, they agreed. I was signed up without even a try out on a four.

Even so, at the beginning of October 1956 Bob had at last track-tested the four-cylinder Gilera in Italy – after already signing on the dotted line. The venue was Monza, almost on Gilera's doorstep. As one report of the time explained: 'Rain, wind and a slippery surface prevailed when McIntyre tried out the fours at Monza recently. Nevertheless, he put in some hard riding and reports that he was extremely impressed by the power and superb handling of the models.'

Although Geoff Duke took his Gilera to South Africa over the winter months, his new teammate stayed at home in Scotland. Another issue was the Suez Crisis, which seriously affected all forms of motorsport during much of 1957 – many events being cancelled, although this did not happen to the Grand Prix or Isle of Man TT. Elsewhere in the UK petrol rationing was a serious problem.

In mid-March 1957, Bob was back in Italy. He had once again been to Monza to put in some testing with the four-cylinder Gilera. He was able to report that he was 'most impressed' and that ridden 'practice-fashion' as distinct from 'racewise', the 'surging power had not proved difficult to control.' It was also the first time the Scot had ridden the Gilera on dry roads. His first race, he said, would be at Imola on 22 April.

Bob's debut was at the international Shell Gold Cup meeting staged over the 3.1-mile Imola track just east of Bologna in northern Italy and saw a vast crowd gathered in brilliant sunshine. But for many of the star riders present it was not a happy day. Both Geoff Duke and Bill Lomas sustained injuries, which were to prevent either taking much more interest in the 1957 season, while Bob was forced to halt at his pit in the 350cc race, the stop robbing him of a possible victory. The result was eventually: 1st L. Liberati (Gilera), 2nd A. Montonari (Moto Guzzi) and 3rd R. McIntyre (Gilera). Both the race and lap speeds were new records – set by Liberati. In the 500cc, both Liberati and Bob retired their Gilera fours with mechanical troubles. This race saw victory go to Dickie Dale riding the revolutionary Moto Guzzi V8.

In the 8 May 1957 issue of *Motor Cycle News* it was reported that:

Bob McIntyre will again be riding the Joe Potts outside flywheel 250 Norton in the Lightweight TT. Last year after putting in some really

Gilera four-cylinder

The Gilera four-cylinder first hit the headlines in April 1937, when Piero Taruffi broke the one-hour speed record previously held by Norton rider Jimmy Guthrie at 114mph. Taruffi raised this to 121.33mph over a 28-mile course comprising a section of the Bergamo-Brescia *autostrada*. The motorcycle the Italian was piloting was a fully enclosed, liquid-cooled four-cylinder model developed from the earlier Rondine design, itself conceived from the even older GRB (Gianni, Remor, Bonmartini) air-cooled four of the mid-1920s. As for Gilera itself, the marque had been founded by Giuseppe Gilera in 1911 (see separate boxed section within this chapter).

Signor Gilera had been shrewd enough to realise the Rondine's potential, with the basic design being steadily improved through an intensive racing and records programme until 1939. Gilera was on course to achieve supremacy in the all-important 500cc Grand Prix class. Twice during that year rider Dorino Serafini achieved magnificent victories – beating BMW on its home ground in the German Grand Prix and winning the Ulster Grand Prix at record speed.

When racing resumed again after World War Two, the use of supercharging had been banned, so Gilera returned with new air-cooled fours designed by Ing. Piero Remor. Then, in late 1949, Remor quit to join rivals MV Agusta. However, Remor's exit left his former assistants at Gilera, Franco Passoni and Sandro Columbo, to carry out a redesign, which meant that in effect Gilera stayed ahead of MV, thanks to a lighter, more powerful engine during much of the 1950s.

Gilera's first world title came in 1950 (the second year of the FIM official championship series), when Umberto Masetti took the crown. From then on success followed success, particularly after Englishman Geoff Duke

The Italian Carlo Bandirola with one of the 1949 four-cylinder Gileras that year.

joined the Arcore factory in the spring of 1953. Duke brought with him the ideas of a new chassis which greatly improved the handling.

In eight seasons from 1950, Gilera riders Masetti, Duke and finally Libero Liberati won the 500cc championship no less than six times, winning 31 races in the process. It was on a Gilera too, that the subject of this book, Bob McIntyre, scored a historic Junior and Senior TT double in 1957 and became the first man to lap the legendary 37.73-mile Mountain course at over 100mph. In addition, there were also the performances of the sidecar ace Ercole Frigero, who was consistently successful, but is today almost totally unknown. For several years Frigero was second only to the great Eric Oliver (Norton) in the World Sidecar Championship.

The four-cylinder 500 Gilera, which ran from 1948 and displaced 496.7cc (52x58mm), was joined by a smaller 350 version in 1956. This latter engine displaced 349.7cc (46x52.6mm). As ridden by Bob McIntyre both sported five-speed gearboxes, telescopic front forks, duplex, steel cradle frames and twin shock, swinging arm rear suspension.

When Gilera retired from the sport it did so on a crest of a wave, with a series of record-breaking achievements at Monza in November 1957, crowned by Bob McIntyre's incredible 141.37 miles in a single hour on one of the 350cc four-cylinder models; the Monza surface for the speed bowl was in such poor condition at this time that riding the 500cc version was considered too dangerous.

Although Gilera made a number of much-publicised comebacks during

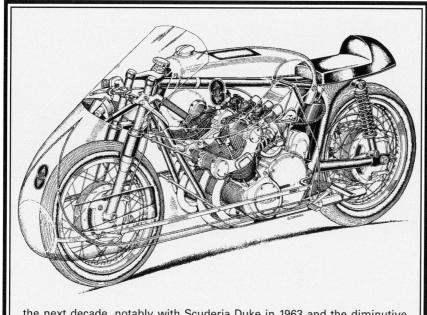

the next decade, notably with Scuderia Duke in 1963 and the diminutive Argentinean Benedito Caldarella a year later, the Arcore company was never to recapture its former glory.

Leading Liberati at Imola on the 500cc Gilera, 22 April 1957. Bob was later to retire with mechanical problems.

quick practice laps he had serious engine trouble during the final training session which could not be repaired in time for the race.

The Australian Bob Brown was chosen in mid-May to replace the injured Geoff Duke in the Gilera team for the Isle of Man TT. This was because Libero Liberati, the best of the Italian contracted riders, did not have any Isle of Man experience and so could not take part.

At the same time it was revealed that Brown and Bob McIntyre would be testing their bikes in the Isle of Man to determine whether they would be using the full streamlining.

Errol Aerodrome on Sunday 12 May saw Alastair King beat Bob in the 350cc final, after the former had made an overnight dash north from Aintree (where he had scored a double victory on his Nortons). And Alastair was only yards behind Bob in the Unlimited final and the Handicap. In the 350 race Alastair and Bob were just feet apart throughout the race. Unfortunately, Bob didn't get to the line with his streamlined two-fifty Norton, and the race was won by Dan Whelan (Velocette).

The German Grand Prix
Exactly seven days after racing at Errol, Bob McIntyre was at Hockenheim for the German Grand Prix – the first round of the 1957 World Championships.

Mounted on four-cylinder Gileras, he finished a close second to teammate Libero Liberati in the 500cc race – continually shattering the lap record for this fastest of all circuits, until he raised it to over 129mph! Earlier he led the 350cc race by a huge margin until he fell off on the last lap.

This is what Alan Bruce (the *Motor Cycle News* German correspondent) had to say:

Bob McIntyre was the star of the day and in my humble opinion would just about have taken the pants off the 'Duke' [Geoff Duke] today on this particular circuit. He should have won both the main races by miles, for in the '350' he stepped off on the last part of the last lap when about 1 minute in the lead. In the 500 he took the lead on the second lap, ran out of road on the next, dropped back to eighth, got back to fifth for a long time, then third and – with several lap records, including one at over 129mph – missed the top money by just half a second!

Another report said: 'Few of the German spectators appeared to have heard of Bob McIntyre when he came to the line with a Gilera four for the

The first round of the 1957
World Championships was
at Hockenheim. Bob is
seen here, nearest the
camera, prior to the start;
he finished second, but set
the fastest lap.

20-lap 350 race, for which there were 30 starters. And after he had been leading for several laps many were convinced he must be Geoff Duke!'

In the early practice periods for the following week's Golden Jubilee TT races, it was Bob McIntyre who set the pace. On Monday morning, 27 May 1957, out on the three-fifty Gilera four, the Scot lapped at 94.19 mph – only a fraction behind the record class speed of 94.61 mph – set up by Ray Amm (Norton) in 1954.

Then, on the Monday evening, Bob recorded the fastest Senior lap at 97.37mph. This was a pattern which was to remain for the rest of practice week. He rounded things off in the final session for the Senior and Junior races with a speed of 98.04mph in the bigger class (compared to John Surtees at 95.51mph on the MV four). The Junior (350cc) class seemed much more open, with close competition from Surtees and Moto Guzzi teamsters Dickie Dale and Keith Campbell, plus Gilera teammate Bob Brown.

McIntyre wins fastest Junior
The *Motor Cycle News* dated 5 June 1957 simply said: 'Bob McIntyre, Scottish rider of an Italian Gilera, won the Golden Jubilee Junior TT in the

Isle of Man on Monday at the record speed of 94.99mph. He also put in a record lap – his first, from a standing start, at 97.42mph.' These then were the bare facts. But what was Bob's race really like?

Another race report sets the scene:

> *After a week of practicing in weather of almost unparalleled perfection, the Jubilee TT programme is about to start in a blaze of June sunshine. So far as the starting area is concerned, that is, for there has been a blanket of sea mist just off-shore and occasionally drifting towards Snaefell Mountain, at the moment completely obscured from sight by the fog. Officials are confident, however, the cloud will have disappeared from the Isle of Man by 11am, when today's race is due to start – good argument in its favour for having put the time back an hour this year.*

About to start the 1957 Junior TT. Bob won and set the fastest lap.

The Junior race opened the TT programme and was run over seven laps of the 37.73-mile Mountain circuit, a total distance of 264.11 miles. There was

a 10-second interval between numbers, whether there was an actual starter or not. The original entry list totalled 89, but this was reduced to 77. As for the works entries, starters were two Gileras (Bob McIntyre and Bob Brown), one MV four (John Surtees), three AJSs (Peter Murphy, Keith Bryen and Derek Powell), three Nortons (Jack Brett, Alan Trow and John Hartle) and the Moto Guzzi team of Keith Campbell, Dickie Dale and John Clark, plus Arthur Wheeler on an ex-factory Guzzi.

With five minutes to go, it was reported that the last of the swirling mist had disappeared from the top of Snaefell road and visibility was perfect all around the course, with a very slight breeze.

Flat on the tank of the Junior Gilera. The full 'dustbin' streamlining was worth up to 10mph, but could be dangerous in high cross winds.

As Bob McIntyre was race number 79, he had the added problem of overtaking riders on his way up the leaderboard. Even so, it was announced that number 79 had broken the class lap record from a standing start, getting round in 23 minutes 14.2 seconds, an average speed of 97.42mph. Bob was the first lap leader – with an initial advantage of over 3mph over second man John Hartle.

But if he or anyone thought this race was a certainty they were rudely awakened when, after setting up a new lap record on the first circuit, Bob was delayed on the next lap. And when he did, eventually, arrive at the start/finish line to complete his second lap, he halted at his pit. As the *Motor Cycle News* race report said: 'He is there a long time and again as with Surtees, it is plug trouble. So Mac looks like slipping down the leaderboard before he re-starts.' What happened was this, in his own words:

I took the lead on the first lap and set up a new record of 97.42mph. A good start. But coming round Quarter Bridge I had thought the 350 went off song a bit. At Governor's Bridge I knew something was wrong but before I could diagnose the trouble with confidence – it was an oiled plug – I was past the pits at Bray Hill. And the Gilera was on three cylinders.

At the end of the third lap, Bob was third behind race leader Dickie Dale (Moto Guzzi) and John Hartle (Norton). And he visited the pits again (for 40 seconds) to refuel.

Crossing the finish line to win the 1957 Junior TT.

By the fourth lap the wind had got up and heavy clouds were closing in round the circuit, but Bob, now lapping at over 97mph again, was once again the leader, followed by Campbell, Brown and Surtees.

This state of affairs was to continue until the end of the race. As an example of his progress, by the beginning of the seventh and final lap, he had fewer than a dozen men ahead of him, although his riding number was 79.

One report of the day described the finish: 'McIntyre, on his red and white Gilera, comes home to applause of the packed grandstand. There is no doubt about the fact that this very game Scot is a popular winner.' Bob completed the seven laps in 2 hours 46 minutes 50.2 seconds, an average speed of 94.99mph. Fifty-three riders finished the race and Bob was also a member of the winning BMCRC team (McIntyre, Surtees and Wheeler).

Junior TT – 7 laps – 264.11 miles
1st   R. McIntyre (Gilera)
2nd   K.R. Campbell (Moto Guzzi)
3rd   R.N. Brown (Gilera)
4th   J. Surtees (MV Agusta)
5th   E. Hinton (Norton)
6th   G. Murphy (AJS)

Giuseppe Gilera

Born in a small village near Milan on 21 December 1887, Giuseppe Gilera, and his younger brother Luigi, did more than most to transform the face of motorcycle racing. For it was Gilera, rather than any other factory, who introduced the across-the-frame four-cylinder to Grand Prix racing. Others such as MV Agusta, Benelli and Honda took up the layout, but it was Gilera who got in first.

Others may have noticed the possibilities of the machine raced by the Rome-based Rondine squad during the mid-1930s, but Giuseppe Gilera was the one who took the opportunity by purchasing the design rights.

The Gilera works at Arcore, just outside Milan.

Piero Taruffi (in white overalls) with the record-breaking streamlined Gilera on which he clocked over 170mph in October 1937. Also in the picture are Giuseppe Gilera (centre) and Ing. Piero Remor (in light coloured suit).

The Rondine became the Gilera in 1936. And after almost three years of development it became the Champion of Europe in 1939. Quite simply, provided it kept going, the 500 liquid-cooled supercharged Gilera had a turn of speed which nothing else on two wheels could catch in the months leading up to the outbreak of World War Two.

Giuseppe Gilera was also a talent scout and gifted engineer. For starters, he not only coped when Ing. Remor left for MV Agusta at the end of 1949, but also helped to develop Remor's air-cooled, normally aspirated four into World Championship material. In this he was greatly helped by the procurement of the services of Geoff Duke, whom he finally signed early in 1953 (after making his original advances as early as 1950).

Duke was later to recall: 'he was a fabulous man – a real gentleman, and most generous, not just a boardroom figurehead. You couldn't fault him on a single thing'.

Duke quit Norton to sign for Gilera. In his first year, 1953, he won the 500cc world title – the first of his three consecutive individual world crowns for the Arcore factory.

It was Geoff Duke who was largely responsible for Gilera signing Bob McIntyre, who was to give Giuseppe Gilera not only the marque's crowning glory of the first official 100mph lap of the legendary 37.73-mile Isle of Man circuit and the Junior-Senior TT double in the 1957 Golden Jubilee Tourist Trophy, but also in the One-Hour world speed record (achieved at Monza in November 1957).

Then Gilera quit the sporting scene (except for trials), but their influence was felt in the years that followed, first by MV Agusta and later by the Japanese Honda team.

Sadly, for Giuseppe Gilera himself, his later years were to be filled with great disappointment. First, his beloved and only son, Ferruccio (then only 26 years old) died of a heart attack while on a business trip to the Argentinean Gilera subsidiary in October 1956. Then, during the 1960s, he was forced to fight an uphill battle, in a declining motorcycle market, to keep the company he had created afloat. It proved to be a feat that, ultimately, even he was unable to achieve, with Gilera being taken over in 1969 by the Piaggio organisation.

Only a few short months later, on 21 November 1971, Giuseppe Gilera passed away. He was 83 years old.

Protar model of Bob's 1957 Senior TT Gilera, made by Ian Welsh.

A 'cert'

A 'cert' is what Cyril Quantrill said in his 'Who Will Win The Senior?' feature in *Motor Cycle News* dated 5 June 1957. He said: 'On practice form Bob McIntyre is the nearest thing to a "cert" that we have had in the Island since Geoff Duke walked away with his Norton 'double' in 1951.'

And it so it proved, with the following week's *MCN* of 12 June 1957 reporting:

For the second time in a week, Scotsman Bob McIntyre demonstrated last Friday that he is more than a brilliant rider – he is one of the greatest tacticians the sport has ever seen... In winning the Golden Jubilee Senior Tourist Trophy Race for Moto Gilera, he became the first man ever to lap the Isle of Man 37.73-mile 'Mountain' circuit at over 100mph, yet after the fourth lap, by which time he had put the lap record up to 101.12mph, he progressively eased the pace while still keeping a sufficient margin over John Surtees (MV), who was second throughout.

Of course, on paper it all sounded so easy. But it most certainly was not. For example, after refuelling Bob ran straight into trouble. As he explained later:

I accelerated away. A stone hit me, thrown up by the wheels of another rider I was about to lap. It was probably no bigger than a pea, but at 100mph it felt like a brick. It caught me between my goggles and my crash helmet and cut my left temple. I felt dazed and sick, it brought tears to my eyes and I felt blood running. But fortunately, the rush of cold air coagulated the blood above my goggles.

Bob passed John Surtees (number 4) on the road during the fifth lap – and from then on knew he had just to keep going with John in his sights to win.

Thirty-eight riders finished the race. And Bob became not only the first rider to lap at 100mph, but also the sixth in TT history to record a double victory, the previous men being Tim Hunt (1931), Stanley Woods (1932 and 1933), Jimmy Guthrie (1934), Geoff Duke (1951) and Ray Amm (1953). All except McIntyre rode Nortons.

Senior TT – 8 laps – 301.84 miles

1st	R. McIntyre (Gilera)
2nd	J. Surtees (MV Agusta)
3rd	R.N. Brown (Gilera)
4th	R.H. Dale (Moto Guzzi V8)
5th	K.R. Campbell (Moto Guzzi single)
6th	A. Trow (Norton)

Since his lead was nearly 2½ minutes on corrected time, Bob McIntyre had slowed considerably on the last lap and Surtees had overtaken him on the drop to Craig-ny-Baa. Bob thought that the addition of the eighth lap constituted an unnecessary strain on the riders of factory multis.

Interestingly, the Scot's victorious machine featured a smaller top tank and two pannier tanks, whereas Bob Brown's Gilera had carried his seven-gallon fuel load in one conventional tank.

Post-race activities

Considering that they had just covered nearly 302 miles on the world's most gruelling road race course at average speeds approaching 100mph, the first three machines finished in 'remarkably good condition' (*The Motor Cycle*) and looked capable of 'covering several more laps at similar speed without further attention.'

All three machines had combustion chambers in near perfect condition, 'a smooth, thin film of carbon and no sign of undue heat.' The 3.50-section rear tyre on Bob's Senior-winning Gilera was little more than half worn, while front tyre wear was even less. Both tyres were worn more on the right than the left – not surprising considering that the course ran clockwise.

Team manager Roberto Persi doing his best to hide Bob and chief mechanic Fumigala after the 1957 TT victory.

Bob with Gilera team manager Roberto Persi at the 1957 TT.

A serious-looking Bob pushing his Junior Gilera.

There was virtually no oil on the walls of the rear tyre, though a small amount was trapped in the welled-section alloy wheel rim. The power unit was oil-free externally, while brake, clutch and chain settings were not in need of even minor adjustments.

The following is a list of equipment used on Bob's 1957 Senior TT Gilera machine:

Hepolite piston rings
Dell'Orto carburettors
KLG sparking plugs
Lucas magneto
Avon tyres and tubes
Ferodo brake and clutch linings
Bowdenex control cables
Smiths rev counter
BP Super Plus fuel
Castrol oil
Woodhead rear suspension units

There was great cheering when Bob McIntyre went up to receive his array

This photograph, taken during the eight-lap Senior TT, is inscribed 'Best wishes, Bob McIntyre'.

of trophies at the traditional post-race prize-giving ceremony. His double victories were extremely popular.

Back to the short circuits

Then it was back to the mainland and a return to the short circuits on Joe Potts's Norton machinery.

Bob with the 500 Gilera at the bottom of Bray Hill during the 1957 Senior TT.

A magnificent photograph of Bob McIntyre setting the first-ever 100mph TT lap record, during the 1957 Senior – 101.12mph (162.7kph) on lap four.

Winning the 1957 Senior TT, 12 June 1957.

A proud moment. Bob with his mother Elizabeth after the 1957 Senior race. It's possible to see the cut above Bob's left eye that came from a stone thrown up by another rider.

Gilera's renowned mechanic Fumagali during the 1957 TT period.

Bob receiving the Senior TT trophy after completing the Senior/Junior double in 1957. There was never a more popular winner.

Only three days after his record-breaking Senior TT victory, Bob was making the news again, with *The Motor Cycle* dated 13 June 1957 headlining: 'That Thistle Again' continuing: 'Bob McIntyre (Norton) in Scintillating Form at Oulton Park on Whit Monday Repeats His Junior and Senior TT Successes in the Les Graham Trophy Race.'

Held over 19 laps of the 2.7-mile Cheshire parkland circuit, the main race of the day was the Les Graham Trophy event. This was expected to produce a battle royal between Bob and John Surtees (both Norton mounted), respective winners of the qualifying heats. *The Motor Cycle* described the action which took place:

Expectation was realized in the early stages. Under the bridge and past the pits at the end of the opening lap came a seemingly never-ending stream of riders with, at their head, McIntyre and Surtees almost side by side. By lap 2 the pair had already drawn clear of the

John Surtees

Born in the pretty village of Tatsfield on the Kent-Surrey border, a couple of miles south of Biggin Hill airfield, on 11 February 1934, John Surtees was one of two riders Bob McIntyre considered the greatest of his generation (the other was Geoff Duke).

John's first motorcycle race came as a 14-year old when his father, Jack, recruited his services as a sidecar passenger. The pairing actually won the event but was subsequently disqualified because of John's age.

His first solo victory came at 17, at the tree-lined Aberdare Park circuit in South Wales. He was riding a 499cc Vincent Grey Flash single which he had constructed while serving his apprenticeship at the company's Stevenage works.

Except for a 1953 TT practice accident while riding an EMC 125, John would have been a Norton teamster that year. As it was, Norton retired from fielding full Grand Prix 'specials' at the end of 1954. However, John

This special greeting was presented to Bob by the Manx Motor Cycle Club to 'record our congratulations on your tremendous performance in winning the Junior and Senior Tourist Trophy Races in this their Jubilee Year.'

(together with John Hartle and Jack Brett) was signed to race works development Manx models for the 1955 season; he responded by having an excellent season, the highlight of which was winning the British Championship title.

Then he signed for the Italian MV Agusta concern to race its four-cylinder models during the 1956 season. In doing this, John was following in the footsteps of Geoff Duke (although Duke had gone from Norton to Gilera). John made his MV debut at Crystal Palace near his south London home in April 1956 in winning style. Then he went on to win the 500cc World Championship title – even though he suffered a fall in Germany at the Solitude circuit. Although he had broken his right arm, which effectively kept him out of racing until the following year, John had already amassed enough points to carry off the title.

Although he could only finish third behind the Gilera pairing of Libero Liberati and Bob McIntyre in the 1957 500cc title race, he had the honour of giving MV its first-ever victory with the smaller 350 four at the Belgian Grand Prix in July 1956.

Then came the golden trio of double 350cc and 500cc World Championship title years, when John won just about everything in 1958, 1959 and 1960. Having nothing else to prove in the two-wheel world, Surtees moved to four wheels, first as a driver for Ken Tyrrell, then as a member of the Lotus F1 team. In 1962 came a switch to a Lola, plus drives in a Ferrari 250 GTO in sports car events.

Next came a move into the full Ferrari team, competing in the 1963 and 1964 Formula 1 series. In the latter year he won the world title and thus became the only man ever to achieve the feat of taking the premier championship crowns on both two and four wheels.

After Ferrari came a spell with Honda, whom he joined for the 1967 season, and finally BRM in 1969.

Then he founded his own team, Mike Hailwood being among his drivers. Team Surtees was disbanded towards the end of the 1970s, its F1 'position' being acquired by Frank Williams.

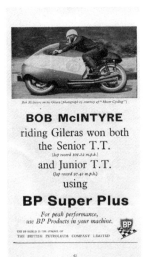

BOB McINTYRE
riding Gileras won both
the Senior T.T.
(lap record 101.12 m.p.h.)
and Junior T.T.
(lap record 97.42 m.p.h.)
using
BP Super Plus
For peak performance,
use BP Products in your machine.
THE BP SHIELD IS THE SYMBOL OF
THE BRITISH PETROLEUM COMPANY LIMITED

field, as had Alastair King, third place man, all alone of the howling pack. Excitement mounted around the course as Surtees took a momentary lead – which the Scot snatched away from him almost as quickly as he had gained it. But with seven laps gone, McIntyre had eased comfortably ahead of Surtees. As the race drew to its close, so McIntyre's determination became further underlined. His lead over Surtees increased by 10s, 12s then to 15s.

What this race proved without doubt was that Bob McIntyre was at the very peak of his form. Surtees was the reigning 500cc World Champion, and Bob had beaten him both in the Isle of Man and when they were more equally matched on single-cylinder Nortons.

Another McIntyre double

Another McIntyre double, but on Nortons this time and over the 2.5-mile Oliver's Mount, Scarborough, circuit, was the highlight of the two-day Cock o' the North meeting on Friday and Saturday 14/15 June 1957. But there was stiff competition from the likes of John Surtees, Jack Brett, Dave Chadwick and Alastair King.

The following weekend came the Scottish Speed championship at Errol Airfield, near Perth. One newspaper report said: 'Recipe for a successful meeting: take one road-race circuit, add Bob McIntyre, Alastair King and the Joe Potts' stable of Nortons, drop the starting flag and stand clear!'

Bob and Alastair duelled in no fewer than four main races that day (250, 350, 500cc and Unlimited). And what a treat Scottish fans had from their two favourite heroes.

Typical was the 500cc final. Quickly into the lead went Perth's own Jimmy Buchan (Norton), with Alastair King hot on his heels. But where was Bob McIntyre? Most untypically he had been dead last away; the fans heaved a sigh of disappointment, but it was premature – the race had only just begun. Soon King edged Buchan aside and meanwhile Bob was storming past the pack. As *The Motor Cycle* described:

Riding with tremendous zest he weaved through the straw-bale chicanes to gobble up the field one by one and strenuous though the efforts of King and Buchan may have seemed, they paled into insignificance as Bob swept past them with a sizzling record lap at 71.2mph.

In the 250cc race tuner Joe Potts was heard to comment that he was 'not feeling too happy with the wee bike.' But he was worrying unduly, for Bob

The race which probably cost Bob McIntyre the honour of becoming a world champion – the 1957 500cc Dutch TT at Assen. Here he leads John Surtees (MV). Bob crashed when trying to win after losing time due to plug trouble. The subsequent injury was to dog him for throughout the remainder of the season.

seemed to make easy work of his victory. Bob also took the 350cc final – from Alastair King – but Alastair had a victory at last in the Unlimited race, with McIntyre closely following his friend home.

A decisive setback

Then came the next round of the World Championships at Assen in Holland, the scene of the Dutch TT on Saturday 29 June, and with it a decisive setback for Bob McIntyre.

The Motor Cycle dated 4 July 1957 tells the story:

The lights blink to green. A heaving, sweating mass of riders shove their machines into action. The scream of fours and the shriek of a lone eight rise high above the crackle of twins and the bellow of singles. Two machines streak ahead, their riders masters among supermen, and lap after lap they hurtle round a 4.79-mile circuit lined by thousands upon thousands of spectators stewing in the harsh, unrelenting glare of the sun shining from a steel-blue sky. Each of the pair knows that one slip may cost him the race and each is determined to win. Then, with seven laps completed, the rider in second place suddenly detaches himself from his rival's slipstream and pulls into his pit. His machine does not feel as it should. Mechanics put their fingers on the exhaust pipes to locate a faulty plug. Plug leads are checked and at the same time the rider pulls his machine back on compression in readiness to rejoin the race. Meantime five of the men behind him have gone through, and when he eventually pushes off he is over a minute behind the leader. Slowly but surely he whittles down the gap, hurling his aluminium-clad projectile through the never-ending succession of twists and curves at a speed which would make lesser men dizzy. Soon spectators with stopwatches are saying that he may win – if he can keep up his white-hot pace. If he manages to bring off the near-impossible it will be a victory by one or two seconds. He is gaining 5s a lap, there are seven to go and he is 30s behind. Then, two laps later, a hard Dutch voice booms through the loudspeakers: 'Bob McIntyre is gevallen!'

And so, in an instant, Bob not only crashed out, but with the advantage of hindsight, also put his chances of becoming 500cc World Champion virtually out of reach. So what really happened? Here is how Bob saw things in his own words: 'I was catching him (Surtees) and should have passed him a couple of laps from the end but I was trying too hard ... I left the road and went into a ditch. When John took the chequered flag I was on my way to hospital with concussion.' Also – unknown to him, or anyone else at the time – he had broken a bone in his neck. And it was this injury which was to effectively prevent him being crowned champion.

Besides the tremendous effort described above, Bob had finished runner-up (behind Keith Campbell's Guzzi) in the earlier 350cc race. But it had been a close-fought thing, with the lead changing hands between Campbell and McIntyre on several occasions. And it was slower riders who eventually determined who got victory. One report said: 'McIntyre got the neck of the chicken when it came to passing slower competitors. He was baulked time and time again.'

Finally, before leaving the 1957 Dutch TT, it should be mentioned that Bob was the fastest man that day when he set a new lap record in the 500cc race at 85.53mph.

Bob's injuries in Holland meant that he was a definite non-starter for the fourth round of the World Championships, the Belgian Grand Prix at Spa Francorchamps.

It was not until Saturday 27 June – some five weeks – that Bob McIntyre was fit enough to race again. This event occurred at Crimond Airfield in northern Scotland. As usual north of the border, Bob's main opposition came from Alastair King. After Bob had easily won the 250cc race, the pair got down to 'a tooth and nail' (*The Motor Cycle*) scrap in the 350cc race, which culminated in a grandstand finish. The two riders rocketed out of the final corner side by side and streaked towards the line – Alastair scratching the win by a mere half a wheel. But Bob got his revenge with victory on his 500cc Norton in the Unlimited Championship race.

The following weekend came the British Championships at Thruxton. However, Bob was an absentee since his return to racing in Scotland had revived the headaches which had resulted from his crash at Assen in late June. This also ruled him out of the BMCRC programme at Oulton Park the same weekend.

A Grand Prix comeback in Ulster
Bob made his return to the World Championship trail at the Ulster GP on Saturday 10 August 1957. Because of petrol rationing being in force when the

Romolo Ferri during his attempt at the 100-kilometre class record at speed on the Monza banking. Ferri's machine was a 125cc Gilera twin.

Record Breaking

In the first half of the 20th century, record breaking was at least as important as any Grand Prix victory. Because of this, most manufacturers strove to take records from one another. This included the likes of Harley-Davidson, Indian, Brough Superior, BMW, Norton, Moto Guzzi and many more.

Besides the outright land speed record, the other really prestigious goal was the One Hour figure. When Gilera announced their intention to quit the Grand Prix scene, the Italian marque decided to go out on a high by bagging as many records as possible at Monza in autumn 1957. For most of these record attempts they used home-grown talent such as Alfredo Milani and Romolo Ferri. In mid-November 1957, as a final gesture before putting their machines into mothballs, the Gilera company sent for Bob McIntyre to make an attempt on the coveted One Hour figure, at that time held by the British Norton concern. This had been captured by Ram Amm, using a specially streamlined 500cc works racer, when at Montlhéry in 1953 he had put 133 miles under the wheels of the bike in 60 minutes.

Here, in Bob McIntyre's own words, is how Gilera's attempt proceeded:

We were to use a 350cc machine. It was virtually a standard four-cylinder model of the type I had been racing in Junior events, except that I had put sidecar springing on the rear end to stop the machine bottoming on the bumpy Monza circuit. I had jacked up the front end springing with little aluminium distance pieces and I had a special streamlining shell which covered my forearms and part of my legs. We were using the high-speed banked circuit. I had been on a banked circuit only once in my life; that was at the Motor Industry Research Association test track in England with a Porcupine AJS in 1954 and that was nothing like so fast. My practice laps were a bit hair-raising and I felt sure that the bike would not last out an hour at the speed expected. I feared bits would fly off. But we went ahead. The official chronometers were started and I went tearing off to see how much ground I could cover in an hour. I had screwed up the friction damper of the twist-grip throttle to the hardest position so that the throttle would stay open. It was a bit difficult going up through the gears but once I was in top gear the throttle was opened fully and I left it like that. I was soon hitting the banking at 155mph. Because of the bumps I had to stand up on the footrests, holding on to the handlebars grimly as though I was riding in a scramble. But with the banking, it was more like riding a fairground wall of death.

Monza, 13 November 1957. Alfredo Milani sets a new world one-kilometre sidecar speed record.

Then, after fifteen minutes, the bike stopped. It was a magneto fault. As I had not thought any machine could last out at such sustained speeds on such a surface I was not over-surprised. My immediate reaction was one of relief. It looked as though the attempt was over for the time being. I was booked to return home next day and it is a complicated matter to organise the timekeepers and official observers for a world record attempt. It is also an expensive matter and that was the factor that decided the issue. After a conference, the Gilera chiefs pleaded, 'Don't go away'. They put the machine into a lorry and roared off to the factory, which is about five miles from Monza. Inside a couple of hours they were back. A new magneto had been fitted. Now I had to start all over again. Fifteen minutes flat out riding had been *wasted. Up through the gears I went again. Round and round I tore, the throttle wide open, just concentrating on staying on. My legs ached, my arms throbbed from the constant vibration. At the end of the hour they put out the flag for me and I came in. They had very nearly to lift me from the machine. My wrists were swelling up and my feet were sore. The instep of one of my boots had been broken by the jarring of the footrest beneath it. The machine finished in almost better condition than I did. It was in perfect order except that one small bracket holding the streamlining had fractured. I had covered 141 miles in the hour and set a new world record. I had also gained the record for the standing start 100 kilometres with a time of twenty-six minutes twenty-eight seconds – a speed of 137mph.*

What Bob did not mention fully was just how bad a state the Monza speed bowl section was in at the time. It was truly awful, with an uneven surface – but that surface was in a bad state of disrepair, breaking up and crumbling in many places. Why wasn't a 500cc machine used? Well, this would have been suicide!

As Mike Hailwood was to say in 1964, after finally breaking the record: 'There has never been a more magnificent ride than that made by Bob McIntyre when taking the record at 141.27mph on a 350 Gilera four on the Monza track in 1957. Only riders who have attempted that circuit can truly appreciate the sheer guts and brilliant riding which made Bob's effort possible. I should hate my effort at Daytona, when I set a new hour record of 144.82mph on my 500 MV Agusta to be even compared with Bob's. There is just no comparison. I don't think I'm chicken and, believe me, both myself and Count Agusta would have preferred to have made the record attempt at Monza, but after circulating there during practice for the Italian car grand prix in September, I knew it was just impossible.'

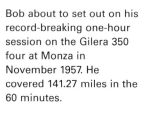

Bob about to set out on his record-breaking one-hour session on the Gilera 350 four at Monza in November 1957. He covered 141.27 miles in the 60 minutes.

plans were made, the Ulster that year was confined to one day and not spread over two days as was customary. Compressing the programme into a single day necessitated shortening each of the races so, in order to keep the distances for the solo races, it was decided to axe the sidecar classes.

As *The Motor Cycle* race report of 15 August 1957 reveals: 'The last-minute excitement whetted the crowd's appetite for the 350cc event. McIntyre had ridden in practice and elected to start with the proviso that if his head troubled him, he would retire.' Besides his Gilera teammates (Libero Liberati and Geoff Duke), Bob was ranged against Keith Bryen and Keith Campbell (Moto Guzzi), John Surtees (MV Agusta) and all the leading single-cylinder riders including John Hartle, Jack Brett and Dave Chadwick (Nortons) and Peter Murphy (AJS).

At the start, Bob's machine coughed and began to misfire. He was forced to stop and change a plug before getting away – in last position. As a newspaper report said: 'Many places back, McIntyre was in brilliant form and sweeping through the field like a tornado.' Soon he was up to 10th place – a fantastic achievement. With six laps of the 7.23-mile Dundrod circuit completed he was ninth; seven laps, eighth; eight laps, fifth. As *The Motor Cycle* described: 'It was fantastic. With nine laps gone he had Liberati in his sights.' But unfortunately then the gremlins struck and that was as far as he got. His engine went off song at the Hairpin on lap 10 and he retired. And with Keith Campbell winning, all hope of the 350cc world title had gone.

The final race of the day (and the only one run on dry roads) was the 500cc event. Included in the line-up were Duke, Liberati and McIntyre on Gileras, Campbell and Bryen on Moto Guzzis and a pair of MV Agustas ridden by John Surtees and Terry Shepherd. Bob's bike was unstreamlined for this race.

At the end of the first lap the order was Surtees, Liberati, Brett (Norton) and McIntyre. A lap later Bob had moved up to second. Then he dropped back to seventh. But then he started moving up the field again, helped by Surtees's retirement with a faulty magneto. At the end it was Liberati, McIntyre and Duke to give Gilera a 1, 2, 3.

500cc Ulster Grand Prix – 20 laps – 144.6 miles

1st   L. Liberati (Gilera)
2nd   R. McIntyre (Gilera)
3rd   G. Duke (Gilera)
4th   G. Tanner (Norton)
5th   K. Bryen (Moto Guzzi)
6th   T.S. Shepherd (MV Agusta)

Bob on his way to victory in the 350cc Italian GP at Monza, 1 September 1957.

This meant that the 500cc class in the title race was still wide open. Previously John Surtees, Libero Liberati and Bob Mac were tying with 14 points each. Liberati, by winning the 500cc race at Dundrod, now had 22 points and Bob, who finished second, 20. So should the Scot win at Monza and Liberati finish no higher than third, our hero would secure the title. With Surtees retiring in Ulster his chances of retaining his world crown were now slim indeed.

Racing takes its toll

There is no doubt that even competing in the Ulster GP had taken a massive toll on Bob. He was a non-starter at Errol the following weekend, and two weeks later at Crystal Palace on Saturday 17 August Bob was pronounced 'unfit to ride'. He had previously been expected to provide the main opposition to local hero John Surtees. However, since the Ulster, he had been troubled by a recurrence of headaches and, though he was present at the south London circuit, his role was one of spectator and moral support for his friend Alastair King. The latter finished third in both the 350 and 500cc finals.

The sixth and final event in the 1957 World Championship calendar was the Grand Prix des Nations on Sunday 1 September on the ultra-fast Monza circuit near Milan. The circuit measured just over 3.5 miles (3.57 miles to be exact). The question was, would Bob McIntyre be fit enough to take part?

When the day dawned the weather was cool and without a breath of wind; just about ideal for racing. The circuit was packed with thousands of vociferous Italians – all ready to give their undying support to their hero, Libero Liberati. Keith Campbell had already secured the 350cc title following his win in Ulster, but this was fortunate, as during training at Monza he had crashed one of the Moto Guzzi V8 models, breaking his collarbone and thus putting himself out of the running at Monza.

As *The Motor Cycle* reported:

Undoubtedly the most exciting race of the day was the 350cc event – contrary to expectations. Campbell's absence seemed to make a win for Liberati a virtual certainty, for McIntyre was known to be off-colour physically and Geoff Duke's form had not quite regained its fine edge. Surtees was riding brilliantly but his three-fifty MV lacked the speed of the Gileras.

A mechanic pushes away the 350 Gilera after the Monza victory.

The 500 Gilera which Bob was due to race, but never did, in the paddock at Monza.

But it was to be Bob McIntyre and Moto Guzzi's 50-year-old veteran Alano Montanari who were to be the surprise packages.

In a tightly packed bunch at the end of the first lap, Liberati led Surtees, McIntyre, Giuseppe Colnago (Moto Guzzi) and Alfredo Milani (Gilera). Just astern were Geoff Duke, Keith Bryen (Moto Guzzi) and Montanari.

McIntyre 'whipped' past Surtees on the next lap and Colnago followed suit a lap later, while Montanari displaced Bryen. As *The Motor Cycle* described:

> *The hysterical cheers which greeted the leader's passage through the start on the first three laps gave way to an uncanny hush on the fourth lap; McIntyre had tired of shadowing Liberati; and led him by 60 yards. During the same lap Montanari moved up from seventh position to fifth by calmly out-braking Duke and Milani.*

From this point on Bob slowly but surely drew away from Liberati. And then Montanari continued his progress up the field to displace Liberati. But in trying to peg back McIntyre, Montanari simply tried to achieve too much, resulting in a spot of grass tracking at Vedano – which caused his retirement. Bob went on to win by 32 seconds from Colnago, who had got the better of Liberati two laps from the finish.

But it was to be a bitter-sweet win for the Scottish star as he was violently sick after the finish – and his headaches had returned. Factory boss Giuseppe Gilera then promptly packed him off to hospital for attention. It was there that the medical staff discovered that Bob had broken a bone in his neck, which was responsible for all the problems he had suffered since the Dutch TT. The Scot was to stay in a Milan hospital for some time.

350cc Italian GP – 27 laps – 96.47 miles

1st	R. McIntyre (Gilera)
2nd	G. Colnago (Moto Guzzi)
3rd	L. Liberati (Gilera)
4th	A. Milani (Gilera)
5th	A. Mandolini (Moto Guzzi)
6th	J. Hartle (Norton)

So Bob was prevented from battling with Liberati for the 500cc crown. In the event the Italian won the race and thus became the 1957 500cc World Champion. Bob was runner-up (and third in the 350cc class).

Bob's Gilera teammate and the 1957 500cc World Champion, Libero Liberati.

The 500cc race gets underway at Monza – without Bob – he was already on his way to hospital.

Gilera quit

A few days after Monza came the bombshell that Gilera (to be joined later by Moto Guzzi and FB Mondial) were to quit GP racing. This of course meant that Bob, together with the other Gilera-contracted riders, including the new 500cc World Champion Libero Liberati and Geoff Duke, would be without machinery for 1958. At the same time came news that Joe Potts had acquired one of the later type AJS Porcupine twins at his workshop 'for development purposes.'

The main reasons Gilera put forward for their decision were:

Constantly increasing costs of development and maintenance

High cost of competing at the various meetings

'Uncertainty' about the much-debated streamlining

Differences of opinion about the use of foreign riders

Likelihood of the introduction of new racing formulas within a short time

Actually, the above were in reality a cover for the *real* reason, which was falling sales of series production roadsters. Quite simply the small, affordable family car had arrived and motorcycle sales across Europe were suffering. This was a trend which would only accelerate during the 1960s.

In the 2 October 1957 issue of *Motor Cycle News* there was a story in the 'Paddock Gossip' column by Mick Woollett. It read:

> *News of Bob McIntyre is that he has been ordered complete rest for two months. The cause of his trouble has been found, one of the vertebrae in his neck had a piece broken off when he crashed in the Dutch TT. This break was missed until after Monza when he was so badly affected following his victorious ride in the 350 class that he could not turn out in the 500cc race. Now that the cause has been pinpointed the doctors are certain that he will be one hundred percent fit for next season. There seems little doubt that he will be mounted on the Joe Potts 'Porcupine' and I hear that good progress is being made with the first of these machines. As reported earlier the capacity is being reduced from 500 to 350cc.*

Actually, in different ways, both the main sections of the *MCN* news story were to be proved wrong. Firstly, as covered in a separate boxed section in this chapter entitled 'Record Breaking', Bob was to be back in the saddle of one of the works Gileras, lightly modified for a successful attempt on the World One Hour speed record in a little over a month from when the story was written. And as for the Potts Porcupine, the project was never to be raced.

In the author's opinion the entire motorcycle was simply too heavy to make the transition from a five-hundred to a three-fifty; something Joe Potts no doubt realised himself in due course.

The idea behind the transformation of the Porcupine engine from 500 to 350cc was as follows: the engine, said to be one of the last works units built in 1954, was having both its bore and stroke altered to reduce the capacity – this, said Joe Potts, 'would result in a slightly oversquare engine.' Already (November 1957) the special crankshaft, cylinder heads and connecting rods were being made. The engine would be mounted in the frame at an angle of 45 degrees – as with the last Porcupine models – and not almost horizontally as with the original version. For a start 'the normal four-speed gearbox will be retained but if the model goes well it is hoped to get a five-speeder.' After tests with the completed engine, the building of a new frame was planned.

On Wednesday 27 November 1957 Bob McIntyre entered the history books when he broke the world 350cc-class 100km and One Hour records at Monza. Before letting the Scot get involved the Gilera factory put him through a medical examination to ascertain that everything was absolutely in order after his Dutch TT crash. It was, and so history was made for both the company and Bob himself. The One-Hour record (for all engine sizes) was to stand until broken by Mike Hailwood on a works MV Agusta four-cylinder *five-hundred* at Daytona in early 1964.

Then, in the middle of December 1957, came news that among the machinery in Joe Potts's workshop for the following season was an AJS 7R. The machine was at that point being rebuilt and would join several of the famous Potts stable of Norton machinery. It was also stated that 'good progress' was being made with the AJS Porcupine that was being modified to 350cc. But even then Joe Potts appeared to be hedging his bets on the latter project.

So, as 1957 came to an end, it was very much a case of preparing for the new season – which would be back as a privateer for McIntyre, rather than a full-blown works-supported entry. However, there was the prospect of riding in a lot more races and sharing the companionship of men like Joe Potts and Alastair King.

As for Gilera, Bob was always to hold them in the highest regard. He later recalled: 'The Gilera race organisation was the finest I have encountered. The mechanics were excellent. They were all Italian but there was always one or two who spoke some English.' This was in stark contrast to the critical views he had of his time as an AJS works rider in 1954.

Of course, his time with Gilera had also provided one of the true highlights of his racing career: the Junior/Senior TT double victories.

A 1958 photograph of Bob, a hero both sides of the border.

Chapter 6

Back as a Privateer

AFTER the highs and lows of his season as a factory Gilera rider, for 1958 Bob McIntyre returned to his roots in Glasgow and resumed a full-time association with the Joe Potts équipe. This also meant that he often travelled with his close friend and Potts teammate Alastair King, with whom he was able to resume the comradeship the two men enjoyed. In many ways this lifestyle suited Bob better than being a member of a works team. Not only was he at home in Scotland more, but he also worked on the machine he raced himself. He also had three years left of his four-year rolling contract with Gilera (which expired at the end of 1960), so his options for

Bob with his racing buddy Alastair King in the Potts Belshill garage in spring 1958. Bob had resumed his role as a privateer after the year with Gilera. The number plates each record successes gained by Alastair, Bob and Jimmy Buchan.

One of the 1958 McIntyre lightweight-framed machines (seen here with Denis Gallagher, 250 Velocette engine *c*.1960). With the larger Norton engines the handling was not up to scratch, so Bob reverted to the standard Norton Featherbed for the rest of the 1958 season.

joining another works team were limited. To maintain this he simply had to resign each year.

In the 19 February 1958 issue of *Motor Cycle News* something of a progress report appeared:

> *I had a word with Bob McIntyre the other day. He said that although the conversion of the Porcupine engine to 350cc was going well it was now almost certain he would be riding Nortons in both classes for the first part of the season at least. These will definitely be Joe Potts' machines and the '500' will be a '90-bore' and that the 350 has been modified on similar lines to the '500' and will have a bore of 78mm as against the standard 76mm.*

There was also the issue of streamlining. The full 'dustbin' type that Bob had used on his TT-winning Gilera fours was now banned by the FIM from international events. However, strangely, the British Auto Cycle Union decided to allow such fairings for its national and club events as the 1958 season began. Also, it was reported that for the first time in years the Scottish ACU was to enter a team in the TT. This squad would comprise Alastair King, Jimmy Buchan and Bob McIntyre. The last time the SACU had a team in the Isle of Man was in 1954 when they won both team awards in the Junior and Senior Clubman's events.

Bob had a quiet debut to the new season, when at Oulton Park on Easter Monday 7 April 1958 he was forced out of the 19-lap 500cc final, when lying second to Terry Shepherd (Norton), before retiring with front fork trouble. In the 350cc race he was unplaced. The day belonged instead to Alastair King, who took both the 350 and 500cc races from a star-studded entry, which included the likes of Geoff Duke and Bob Anderson (Nortons). Three days earlier at Brands Hatch on Good Friday, 4 April, Bob had been unplaced and troubled with 'suspension problems.' Why? Well, his machinery was newly-built Norton Specials. Unfortunately, as *Motor Cycle News* reported in their 16 April 1958 issue: 'Preparation had to be rushed and suspension troubles put paid to any hopes of victory.' Details of the special bikes included a purpose-built lightweight frame with a single tapered down tube at the front. The gearbox was mounted further forward and at an angle, allowing a short direct gear lever to be used. The engine lubrication oil was carried on the front right of the fuel tank. The weight (of the five-hundred) had been cut down to 274 pounds without petrol and oil – a saving of nearly 50 pounds against a standard production Manx model. As for the engine, this incorporated a 90mm cylinder bore, a special two-piece crankshaft (similar to the old works

Factory photograph of the
1956 Manx Norton.

Featherbed Manx Norton

Ulsterman Rex McCandless was responsible for the design of the
Featherbed frame, and powered by a works dohc Norton single-cylinder
engine this made its debut in the spring of 1950. Initially ridden only by the
works riders, such as Geoff Duke and Artie Bell, the first over-the-counter
'customer' examples arrived the following year. In both cases this
signalled the end of the old plunger-framed 'Garden Gate' models (which
in works guise had debuted during the 1936 TT and in production form had
been sold from 1946).

The Featherbed (thus named thanks to rider Harold Daniell saying it felt
like a 'feather bed' during a test session) created a sensation when it made
its winning entrance at the Blandford Camp circuit in April 1950. Geoff
Duke was in the saddle that day, as he was when, wearing his innovative
one-piece skin tight leathers, he won the Senior TT a couple of months
later. Although Geoff didn't win the 1950 World Championship (due to a
succession of tyre problems), the same rider-machine combination took
the 350/500cc World Championship double in 1951, retaining the 350cc
crown for Norton in 1952.

For 1951, the production Manx models were given the Featherbed
chassis for the first time, together with several other improvements
pioneered on the 1950 works models. It is also worth pointing out that the
production machines were constructed in a different area of the
Bracebridge Street, Birmingham, factory and were the responsibility of
Edgar Franks (later design chief at the Ambassador works) rather than Joe
Craig.

The pukka works specials were raced until the end of 1954. Then, with
Joe Craig in charge, works development versions of the standard
production version were entered in selected meetings by the trio of
Surtees, Hartle and Brett. The over-the-counter customer Manx 40M
(350cc) and 30M (500cc) continued with yearly updates until production
finally came to an end in 1962. During the 1950s 'customer' meant
someone who was approved by the company. This approval meant the

Lovely period shot of Northampton dealer/racer Joe Glazebrook (seated on bike), 348cc Manx 40M; 1961 Isle of Man TT.

Early version of the Featherbed-framed production Manx Norton, with Denis Parkinson aboard, Brough, 1954.

rider had to use his new machine in an international event, such as the TT, Ulster Grand Prix or a Continental European Grand Prix.

The first (1951) production Manx models displaced 499cc (79.62x100mm) and 348cc (71x88mm). Then, for the 1954 season, there was a major engine redesign, with shorter-stroke dimensions: 86x85.62mm for the larger unit and 76x76.85mm for the three-fifty.

There were also detail changes in most years, including: Amal GP carburettors (1952); rotating-magnet magneto (1956); coarser-pitch bevel gears (1957); AMC gearbox (1958); redesigned vertical drive-shaft (1959); Amal GP2 carb (1961); dual 7in front brakes (1962).

During much of the 1950s, Norton engines were widely used in Formula 3 (500cc) racing cars. But Norton would not supply separate engine and transmission, instead customers had to purchase a complete bike and dispose of the cycle components themselves. This meant that redundant Norton Featherbed frame assemblies were used to house a variety of other engines; notably 500 and 650cc Triumph twins. And thus the now-famous Triton special was born.

There is no doubt that top entrants, such as Joe Potts, were able to enjoy a liaison with the Norton works, which was useful to their riders – in Potts's case Bob McIntyre and Alastair King. During the late 1950s, development engineer Doug Hele carried out an extensive programme of improvements to the Manx, which benefited the marque and those who rode the double cammy Manx racers.

type) with crankpin integral with the driveside flywheel. A special big-end, with 14 rollers (instead of the usual 12), was employed in conjunction with a special connecting-rod. A two-inch (51mm) inlet valve and a standard exhaust valve were used. Another feature was a steeper down-draught angle for the Amal GP carburettor.

Preparation had been held up for various reasons and was not really complete enough for the journey south. Travelling with Alastair King, Bob had to drive overnight to Brands Hatch – through snow and rain – arriving at the Kent circuit with completely new and untried machines. After the first few laps of practice it was found that the front forks, which had been shortened, were not working properly, and the front end was, as Bob described, 'practically solid.' After Brands, Bob (and Alastair) went to Oulton Park and although he managed to improve things 'slightly' he was still in a lot of bother.

On the more positive side, Bob's Easter experiences had not been totally in vain, as he was able to report that the Potts 90mm bore five-hundred Norton engine was 'really flying.' And of course, Alastair King – who scored a 350/500 double at Oulton Park on his standard-framed Manx models – had a most successful outing for the Potts stable.

Next came the annual *Motor Cycling* Silverstone meeting on Saturday 19 April. In contrast to the near arctic conditions over Easter, the day was pleasantly sunny and warm. Although 'still looking rather unhappy on the corners' (*Motor Cycle News)* Bob McIntyre scored second places in both the 350 and 500cc championship races. In the smaller engined event Geoff Duke was the winner, while in the 500 it was Terry Shepherd.

Things improved still further when on Saturday 26 April Bob retained the Scottish 350 and 500cc championship titles, which he had held for the previous two years. For 1958 the venue was Beveridge Park, Kirkcaldy. But unfortunately both class finals were dogged by heavy rain. In fact, as *Motor Cycle News* reported: 'There was a record number of spills on the 1½-mile lap.' *MCN* also said: 'The track was so greasy at the start of the big race (500cc final) that the finalists could hardly find enough grip to push start.'

A hair-raising moment

Bob suffered a hair-raising moment during the 500cc heat at a rain-swept Aintree, the scene of the Red Rose Trophy meeting on Saturday 10 May 1958. The incident came when his streamlined Norton collided with the rear of J.E. Spencer's naked Norton. Bob, trying to overtake in truly appalling conditions, first swung inside, then changed his mind and swung outside again. With the two machines locked, the pair wavered from side to side at around 70mph for

Opening the new premises of Hamilton Brothers of George Street, Paisley. In the background is a specially prepared cutaway BSA twin-cylinder machine.

some 200 yards until they took to the grass still together. Somehow, both stayed on and continued the race (now separated!); the Scot finishing second. Once again it was Alastair King who did most of the winning, with Bob McIntyre runner-up in both the 350 and 500cc finals. In the Handicap he was forced to retire on his three-fifty Norton with a broken clutch cable.

The McIntyre jinx continued when he crossed the Irish Sea to Ulster for the annual North West 200. During practice (on Thursday 14 May), Bob had been quickest on his Potts 500 Norton at 99.49mph. Then, in the race two days later on Saturday 16 May, he smashed the lap record,

Bob riding his Potts AJS 7R at Aintree near Liverpool, September 1958.

going round at a breathtaking 102.042mph. But again the bad luck which had dogged the Scot throughout the start of the 1958 season cut in as he was forced out at Metropole Corner, Portrush. As Billy McMaster said in *Motor Cycle News* 'all the feverish work he could put in failed to get it going.' On stripping the engine it was found to have dropped a valve. This resulted in victory for Jack Brett (Slazenger Norton), while Alastair King took the 350cc class win. Bob's only consolation was in taking the Shields Trophy (for the fastest lap of the meeting).

TT practice begins

For most of the 1958 TT practice week conditions were adjudged nearly ideal. But in this year not only was Bob without the Gilera 'fire engines', but he was also riding in only the Junior (350cc) and Senior (500cc) races – in both cases on Potts Nortons. He headed some of the practice sessions, as on the Tuesday evening on his smaller Norton, going round in 23 minutes 55.5 seconds (94.65mph) and on Thursday morning on his Senior mount in 23 minutes 58 seconds (94.46mph). His motorcycles were conventional Featherbed-framed Manx Nortons (or at least the chassis) after all the problems with the lightweight specials.

All looked fair for Bob to be the main challenger to the MV Agusta four-cylinder bikes of John Surtees and John Hartle. Then came the races. First, on Monday 2 June 1958, the Junior (350cc) event. Heavy rain the night before had followed a day of brilliant sunshine. Then, on race day morning, there was heavy mist at breakfast time in Douglas. And at 10am, an hour before the first man was due to start, the atmosphere of the Grandstand was good – the weather had cleared and as the *Motor Cycle News* report of 4 June was able to reveal, the morning of the race was 'sunny as a Mediterranean summer and the remaining clouds were being rolled away over the farther slopes of the hill by a gentle easterly breeze.' It looked as if weather conditions for the race would be ideal. An original entry of 82 had been reduced to 75. Besides the two Italian MVs the rest of the machinery was British: 44 Nortons, 24 AJSs, three BSAs and two Velocettes.

Numbers 52 and 53 were last year's winner Bob McIntyre (now of course on a Norton instead of his Gilera of 12 months earlier) and MV's new signing John Hartle. By a coincidence, that other speedy Scot, Alastair King (Norton, 61), was followed by the other MV entry, John Surtees.

At the end of the first lap Bob had lapped from a standing start in 24 minutes 13.6 seconds (93.44mph) to put himself second to Surtees. However, that was as good as it got, as on starting the second circuit his Norton's engine 'sounded very flat indeed' (*Motor Cycle News*) and he proceeded no further than the bottom of Bray Hill before deciding the engine had 'tightened up', thus forcing an early retirement. Bob's place was taken by his Potts teammate Alastair King, who then held second place for several laps before finishing sixth, after also being slowed by engine trouble.

It was a similar story in the Senior TT, held on Friday 6 June, when, after putting in the fastest ever lap of the 37.73-mile Mountain circuit by a single-cylinder machine at 99.89mph, Bob was forced out on the third lap when his engine failed (stripped bevel gears). Something of a tribute was made to the Scottish rider in the *Motor Cycle News* race report. When discussing the ultimate winner's performance (John Surtees), the newspaper commented:

> *Few riders can have taken that plunge (Bray Hill) at higher velocity... One who probably has, last year's winner Bob McIntyre, has been trying to get 'Gilera 4' performance out of his production Norton today and now he's paid the penalty: out with engine trouble at Union Mills. Bad luck, Bob – you've really been trying!*

Teammate Alastair King, who lay second on laps 4, 5 and 6 of the Senior TT, crashed on the seventh and final lap, suffering concussion and a broken arm. These injuries put him out of action for several weeks.

Back home

Back home in Scotland on Sunday 14 June 1958, the crowd at Errol Aerodrome saw their favourite, Bob McIntyre, defeated by Englishman Terry Shepherd (Norton) by a matter of inches in the 350cc final. However, Bob got his revenge in the 500cc final and also in the Handicap – where he gave

Shepherd a five-second start and then went on to beat him by over half a mile in the 10 laps! Ray Fay (Norton) was third in both the 350 and 500cc finals.

Six days later, on Saturday 20 June 1958, Bob and Derek Powell finished runners-up in the fourth annual Thruxton marathon for series production sports motorcycles. But for a split fuel tank and a later delay caused by a blocked main jet on their Lawton & Wilson-entered Royal Enfield 692cc Super Meteor, the pairing could have won this prestigious event. As it was, victory went to Mike Hailwood and Dan Shorey, riding a twin carb Triumph Tiger 110. The full story of this and Bob's other Thruxton rides for Syd Lawton is fully charted in Chapter 7.

The following weekend at Charterhall, Berwickshire, Bob took over two spare entries, winning both the 350 and 500cc classes, but could only finish fourth in the Handicap event (on his bigger bike).

With Bob and the popular Terry Shepherd of Liverpool in the entry list, the third annual Southern 100 meeting on the Billown circuit in the south of the Isle of Man on Wednesday and Thursday 9/10 July 1958 proved to be popular with thousands of people on holiday there.

Here's an extract from *Motor Cycle News* dated 16 July 1958:

Wednesday's Junior (350cc) event set the standard of the meeting when McIntyre and Shepherd roared down the straight ahead of the pack. They clung to each other through every corner and along the straights of the five-mile long Billown circuit. The breathtaking sight had the holidaymakers agog with excitement. Mac was the first lap leader, ahead of Shepherd. Then Terry took over for a couple of laps. On the fourth and fifth laps they crossed the line together and chased each other at high speed... When it came to the final lap thousands of spectators were roaring encouragement as Shepherd passed McIntyre near the twisting Malen Church bends. Mac was in his slipstream through the Stadium corner when both riders came upon another competitor pushing his machine to the pits. As Terry braked the Scot slipped out and was first in to the Castletown corner. He kept his lead through the next 100 or so yards to the finishing flag.

The position was reversed the following afternoon when Shepherd took the chequered flag some three yards ahead of Bob.

350cc Southern 100 – 12 laps – 54 miles
1st   R. McIntyre (Norton)
2nd   T.S. Shepherd (Norton)

3rd   G.R. Costain (Norton)
4th   W.A. Smith (AJS)
5th   J.L. Payne (Norton)
6th   J.J. Wood (AJS)

There was no doubt about the star of the Charterhall road races on Sunday 26 July 1958. Bob McIntyre won every race he started in, which included two heats and five finals. There was a 'sensation' (*Motor Cycle News)* when he won the second 250cc race on a borrowed NSU and turned the tables on Jack Murgatroyd (Velocette), who had beaten the NSU's owner Glen Henderson first time out. Bob also pushed the race speed up from 71.8 to 73.2mph. In the larger classes no-one could match his brilliance, including the likes of Alan Shepherd, Louis Carr, Dennis Pratt and Jimmy Buchan.

Back to top form
Bob McIntyre was almost 'unapproachable' said the front page story of *Motor Cycle News* dated 6 August 1958. This was in response to the Scottish star's trio of victories at Oulton Park on Monday 4 August. He not only won the 350 and 500cc finals at the Cheshire circuit, but also the main race of the day, the Les Graham Invitation Trophy over 19 laps (52.5 miles).

With riders of the calibre of Geoff Duke, Dave Chadwick, Bob Anderson, Bob Brown, Terry Shepherd and many more, this was an outstanding performance.

Les Graham Trophy, Oulton Park – 19 laps – 52.5 miles
1st   R. McIntyre (Norton)
2nd   G. Duke (Norton)
3rd   W.A. Holmes (Norton)
4th   R. Anderson (Norton)
5th   K.H. Patrick (Norton)
6th   W.A. Smith (Norton)

Conditions for the 500cc Ulster Grand Prix on Saturday 9 August 1958 were poor, to say the least, with heavy rain and thick mist all around the 7.5-mile Dundrod road circuit, high above Belfast.

And when the 350cc race took place there was 'fine drenching rain' (*Motor Cycle News*). There were 51 starters for this 20-lap, 148.32-mile event, including two official works entries from MV Agusta (John Surtees and John Hartle). Practice performances had put Bob McIntyre (Norton), second fastest to Surtees and Terry Shepherd, a late entry also on a Norton, on the front row

Technique

When interviewed in 1958, Bob McIntyre had this to say about 'what he thought was needed to be successful in motorcycle racing today'. This he said: 'demands two things – a fast and reliable machine and a rider in the prime of physical condition'. Of course, he could – should – have added a third requirement: a rider of the necessary skill level to put one over the opposition. But Bob was at heart a modest man, and even if he thought this, he refrained from saying it.

There is no doubt that Bob McIntyre was a rider gifted with not only the ability to win, but also the iron will to do so. In describing his starting technique, he admitted to

...perhaps being different from most... I begin to push, holding the front brake on with my right hand, as soon as the flag begins to rise. When it drops I let the brake off. This means I don't have to gather myself to push then; I have my weight pushing behind the machine already. Then we get away in a roaring of engines. Up through the gears. I do not use the clutch when changing up. With the superb positive-action, clutch ratio gearboxes of racing motorcycles it is unnecessary and this saves a movement.

In 1962 Bob was quoted as saying:

I eat lunch – a light lunch, of course, but I never go on the bike with an empty stomach. Then it is time for the race. I cannot say honestly that I feel any butterflies in my stomach today. Up to about 1955–56 I would be nervous and worked up, but this does not happen any longer. I suppose it is a case of accumulated experience. I feel something but I think it is just a mental tension and if one were not keyed up to a certain extent I imagine one's racing would lose its edge.

Time and time again the word determination comes to the fore when considering just what made Bob McIntyre such a good rider. And although he was a real gentleman when off his racing bike, on it was an entirely different matter. Bob himself said:

...now it is every man for himself. In short circuit motorcycle racing there are none of the racing motorist's strategies of trying to lure the opponent to blow-up his engine, no carefully planned team tactics. It is a simple matter of going all-out from the start to the chequered flag for the winner.

Bob made a special effort to be as fit as possible – all year round. He saw racing as:

...a job which I take seriously, I make special efforts to keep fit in the winter. Every week I go hill-climbing and swimming and reckon to play badminton at least three times. Badminton quickens the reflexes and strengthens the forearms, as well as

promoting stamina... I used to do weight-lifting, but found it of little value.

He also did wrist exercises as he thought: 'good forearms and wrists are essential'. As for his riding gear, Bob was just as thorough. 'Dress for the job in hand' he thought a sound motto, as 'an incorrectly dressed rider cannot hope to win at road racing'.

The following are what he considered essential:

...one-piece leathers must fit snugly and not be tight. Padding only adds weight and bulk and is useless in a tumble anyway. Boots should have supple uppers so that the ankles may be flexed – the zip-back variety are excellent – and they must have the rubber soles essential to quick push-starting. I'm not fussy about gloves provided they are of wrist length (not gauntlets), have soft leather palms and chamois backs. A cut-away in the neck curtain of the standard ACU helmet (the pudding basin!) allows the head to be craned back when lying right down and I detest face masks, scarves or hankies round the chin. Good goggles, preferably of the Italian racing pattern, last some 1½ seasons and the investment pays dividends; you can't race when you can't see properly.

Bob also believed that: 'without good posture and comfort no rider can give of his best'. So he spent much effort tailoring a motorcycle to fit as he didn't contend that 'a universal riding position' was of much use. Bob said: 'I like to be part of the mount', going on to explain: 'I don't believe in being able to slide about, for I like to become part of my mount. It also allows me to jam myself securely when braking hard and magnifies arm leverage'.

Journalist James Dickson did an excellent profile of Bob in *The Scots Magazine* August 2000 issue. In the course of the feature he interviewed Ewan Haldane, who owned a small motorcycle business in Greenock and had raced against Bob many times. James Dickson described their meeting:

Ewen told me that Bob wasn't just a remarkable rider – he was a terrific mechanic as well, with an instinctive knowledge of how to improve a bike's performance. He would think nothing of stripping down, redesigning and then rebuilding a motorbike to his own specifications. Some of the parts he even manufactured himself. 'Bob knew every nut and bolt of the machines he rode. In fact, he probably tightened most of them!' I asked Ewan what made Bob McIntyre so good. Was it this attention to detail, or did he have a natural balance and a feeling for speed? Ewan's reply was simple. 'I don't know. He was tremendous. That's the only word I can use to describe him'.

At the end of his article, James Dickson said: 'no one I interviewed could give me a definitive answer as to what made Bob McIntyre so good. I suspect he was just a natural'. And I must say that I can only concur with the statement. And as Ewan Haldane says: 'there was only one Bob McIntyre. And you can be sure of this – there will never be another.'

of the grid with them. On the second row came Mike Hailwood (Norton), Geoff Duke (Norton) and Hartle (MV). Other riders included Derek Minter, Luigi Taveri, Bob Brown and Ralph Rensen. At the end Bob McIntyre came home fifth, just behind Geoff Duke.

However, in the 500cc it was a different matter entirely, as Bob rode a superb race to split the MV pair and come home runner-up. And in fact he was so far in front of John Hartle that when Bob followed John Surtees's example and halted for petrol with only two laps to go, the Scot was away before the second MV came into sight!

500cc Ulster GP – 20 laps – 148.32 miles

1st	J. Surtees (MV Agusta)
2nd	R. McIntyre (Norton)
3rd	J. Hartle (MV Agusta)
4th	D. Minter (Norton)
5th	G.E. Duke (Norton)
6th	R.H. Dale (BMW)

Bob then returned to Scotland and just over a week later on Sunday 17 August he was back at Errol, winning the Experts 350 and 500cc races. Even though a new chicane had been introduced which drastically reduced speed, he still managed to average 66mph in the 500cc final which he won by 20 yards from Tom McLeod (Norton). It was a similar scene in the 350cc final, which Bob took charge of from the start, crossing the line in front of Jimmy Buchan, Jack Adam and Gordon Bell (all Nortons).

No news from Gilera

In the 20 August 1958 edition of *Motor Cycle News*, there was a small news story in Mick Woollett's 'Paddock Gossip' column. This is what it said:

> *Thinking about the Gilera business* [rumours continued, wrongly, that they were about to return] *I naturally contacted the man still under contract to the Arcore firm – Bob McIntyre. Bob had heard nothing and had in fact already entered for Silverstone, which means that if they did resume racing he would be in a difficult position for Monza! He would be delighted if Gilera did start again but feels it is extremely unlikely at the moment.*

Another snippet of information from Bob was that he would probably be mounted on a brand new AJS 7R for Silverstone. And he would ride a Norton in the 500cc class. Bob was now concentrating on more standard (but still tuned) bikes, a wise move after all the problems he had suffered for the first part of the season.

The new 7R was delivered at the end of August – and it was intended to debut the bike at Silverstone on 13 September 'if all goes well'. Bob said he was 'very favourably impressed with the speed of the new model'.

As for progress on the modified Porcupine engine that had been scaled down to 350cc, this was 'coming along well' and was in the process of being built up. Bob commented: 'Provided that no more hold ups occur the engine should be undergoing bench tests for power output within a month and if these prove satisfactory the winter will be spent building a frame and getting the handling right.'

Saturday 13 September 1958 saw one of the most thrilling and closely-fought duels ever witnessed at the 2.92-mile Silverstone circuit. Bob and Derek Minter (both Norton mounted) duelled for lap after lap in the Senior Championship race, at the annual Hutchinson 100 meeting. Finally, Bob took victory by a bike's length – both riders sharing a new motorcycle lap record of 97.18mph, the old record having been set up in similar circumstances when John Surtees (Norton) beat Geoff Duke (Gilera) back in 1955, the two sharing the record of 96.45mph.

As one newspaper reported: 'McIntyre was the man of the day.' This was because earlier in the day he had celebrated his return to riding an AJS 7R by winning the 350cc class – and with it the coveted Mellano Trophy – at an average speed that was closer to the existing lap record than any other winner's speed. Just for good measure Bob equalled the 350cc lap record and now shared it with John Surtees.

This was the second time the name McIntyre had been inscribed on the famous trophy – and by a coincidence, his previous success had been in 1954, in one of his last outings on a works 7R!

Bob's main competition, besides Derek Minter, had been from the young Mike Hailwood, plus Phil Read, Bruce Daniels, Jim Redman, Alan Trow, Frank Perris and John Hempleman.

350cc Hutchinson 100 Silverstone – 17 laps – 49.64 miles
1st   R. McIntyre (AJS)
2nd   D.W. Minter (Norton)
3rd   W.A. Holmes (Norton)
4th   B.J. Daniels (Norton)
5th   J.G. Hempleman (Norton)
6th   G. Salt (Norton)

7th   P.W. Read (Norton)
8th   J. Redman (Norton)
9th   R. Fay (Norton)
10th   P. Driver (Norton)

500cc Hutchinson 100 Silverstone – 17 laps – 49.64 miles
1st   R. McIntyre (Norton)
2nd   D.W. Minter (Norton)
3rd   A.J. Trow (Norton)
4th   A.M. Godfrey (Norton)
5th   E.J. Washer (Norton)
6th   J.H.L. Lewis (Norton)
7th   B.J. Daniels (Norton)
8th   J.R. Holder (Norton)
9th   R. Fay (Norton)
10th   F.G. Perris (Norton)

Off song at Scarborough

The 1958 Scarborough International Gold Cup meeting took place over two days, Friday and Saturday 19/20 September. But early on Bob suffered a blow when he retired while leading his heat on his Silverstone-winning AJS 7R. The engine mainshaft nut came loose and the sprocket came off its taper. After winning his heat in the 500cc division, Bob could finish no higher than fourth in the final, the performance of the bike seeming to be well below par. The race was won by George Catlin (Norton) who also set the fastest lap of the meeting. This from a man who had recently announced his retirement only to have second thoughts! The stars at Scarborough included Bob Anderson, Dickie Dale, Geoff Duke, Mike Hailwood, Gary Hocking and many more.

At Scarborough Bob had a Gilera front brake on his Norton. Although he had had the brake for some time, this was its first outing. It was of the four leading shoe type that Gileras had for the first time at the Dutch TT the previous year. The brake was fitted into the normal Manx Norton Roadholder fork, which had been drilled out to accommodate the larger diameter hollow spindle. The rear brake on his Norton was equipped with a large air scoop sticking out into the air-stream, similar to that favoured by several of the Continental sidecar stars. Finally, after Scarborough it was discovered why his Norton had not gone as well as it should – a damaged cambox.

It was also reported that Bob had been offered another year of his Gilera contract. But at the time (late September 1958) he was still thinking about it.

Although Gilera seemed to have no intention of returning to racing at the time, the idea of having Bob on contract was to ensure that they had a world-class rider available should they suddenly decide to return to the sport.

The contract which had been offered was similar to before: it allowed him to ride his own machines. As Bob intended to carry out a similar programme in 1959 as he had done in 1958, this was vital to the Scot.

At Aintree on Saturday 27 September, Bob put in an excellent performance on his 7R in the 350cc race. He led World Champion John Surtees (MV four) at the start, and even though Surtees got past no-one else did. Bob finished runner-up.

350cc Aintree – 15 laps – 45 miles
1st   J. Surtees (MV Agusta)
2nd   R. McIntyre (AJS)
3rd   D. Minter (Norton)
4th   R.H. Anderson (Norton)
5th   G. Hocking (Norton)
6th   G.T. Salt (Norton)

In the 500cc race Bob was fourth behind the MVs of Surtees and Hartle, plus Derek Minter (Norton), with Alan Trow fifth and Mike Hailwood sixth (both Norton mounted).

Race of the Year
The following day, Sunday 28 September 1958, came the Race of the Year at Mallory Park. All roads led to the Leicestershire venue for the much-publicised Mallory Challenge Trophy and the 1.35-mile circuit was packed with an estimated 35,000 spectators. The centre of attraction was the 40-lap Race of the Year. The stars had certainly turned up to contest the prizes.

As the 1 October 1958 issue of *Motor Cycle News* said: 'What a front row on the grid: Surtees, McIntyre, Hailwood… well all the stars except John Hartle who was ready to race but had omitted to send in an entry, and Geoff Duke away on holiday in Italy.'

Surtees (MV Agusta) made the sort of start which wins races, going off the line like a scalded cat! At the end of the first lap he was 100 yards ahead of Bob, Bob Anderson, Bruce Daniels and Tony Godfrey (Nortons). At one stage Bob Mac dropped to fifth, but then fought his way back to fourth, behind John Surtees, Bob Anderson and Bruce Daniels.

It also emerged that two modifications had been made to the new 7R which Bob was now using. Firstly, the frame had been altered where the twin tubes passed under the engine. It had been found that these were prone to ground when the machine was laid over and on Bob's model the frame was narrower by one inch than standard. The petrol tank had also been altered to suit the McIntyre riding stance.

There is no doubt that Bob's success with the motorcycle was to lead others to make a switch from Norton to AJS in the 350cc class; notably the rising young star, Mike Hailwood.

A day and a night of continuous rain prior to the Oulton Park Autumn National meeting on Saturday 4 October turned the paddock into a sea of mud, and as *Motor Cycle News* reported: 'competition among the record entry totalling 480 – for firm ground was keen!'

By the time riders began practicing the rain had at last stopped. And the track was drying out fast when two heats for 250s were held. These resulted in clear cut wins for Bill Smith and Bob McIntyre – both NSU mounted. Next came four heats for 350cc machines, but Bob was forced to pull out from his just before the start, when he discovered that his oil pump had quit.

In the 250cc final Bob and Bill Smith had a tremendous dust up – with the former taking a narrow victory.

250cc Oulton Park – 6 laps – 16.56 miles
1st   R. McIntyre (NSU)
2nd   W.A. Smith (NSU)
3rd   P. Tait (Beesley-Velocette)
4th   C. Bruce (Velocette)

The three 500cc heats were won by John Surtees (MV Agusta), Bill Smith (Norton) and Bob (Norton). The stage was set for an exciting final, held over 10 laps. At the end of the opening lap it was Bob leading, with Surtees on his tail followed by Bob Anderson (Norton). On the second lap the Scot held a slender advantage, but on the third the superior speed of the four-cylinder Italian bike saw Surtees gain a 20-yard lead, which he consolidated into 70 yards by half-distance. The two leaders had by now pulled half a mile from Anderson, who had returned to third place following the retirement of John Hartle (MV Agusta), who had been forced out with a stuck throttle cable soon after displacing Anderson. This position remained at the end of the race, proving that in this company at least, Bob was the only man with a single-cylinder British bike who could stay near the new double (350 and 500cc) World Champion.

500cc Oulton Park – 10 laps – 27.61 miles

1st	J. Surtees (MV Agusta)
2nd	R. McIntyre (Norton)
3rd	R.H.F. Anderson (Norton)
4th	G. Hocking (Norton)
5th	F. Perris (Norton)
6th	A. Godfrey (Norton)
7th	R.N. Brown (Norton)
8th	R.H. Dale (BMW)

And so another racing season came to an end. It has to be said that 1958 was not one of Bob McIntyre's best years. Even so he had some significant achievements to look back on. These included a record lap in the North West 200 (before being forced to retire); winning the 350cc class of the Southern 100; seven race victories in a single day at Charterhall; a 350/500cc double at Oulton Park – and the Les Graham Trophy at the same meeting; second in the 500cc Ulster GP; a double victory at Silverstone – plus the Mellano Trophy and finally finishing second to Surtees/MV at Oulton Park and a victory in the 250cc race on a borrowed NSU at the same event. But, sadly, there were far too many retirements and problems, often from mechanical woes. The determination, skill and dedication were still there, however, and the great days would return in the future. Proof that Bob McIntyre was still a big name with the racing fans came in the *Motor Cycle News* Man of the Year poll from its readership. Bob finished third behind John Surtees (the 1958 double 350/500cc World Champion and MV team leader) and the emerging young star Mike Hailwood who had, thanks in no small part to the money and influence of his millionaire father Stan, made a huge impact in his second season of racing, including winning the 125, 250 and 350 ACU road racing stars.

The new year arrives

And so 1958 passed into 1959 – with Bob once again to compete as a privateer, but with the continued backing and support of his mentor Joe Potts. Alastair King, now fully recovered from his Senior TT crash, would once again also be a member of the Potts équipe.

The Joe Potts establishment was not one to seek publicity. While they simply got on with the job of preparing their bikes for the 1959 season, lots of their competitors told members of the press down south what they were planning. Bob, Alastair, Joe and the rest of the team simply kept quiet.

When the 1959 British racing season began at Mallory Park on Sunday 22 March, this is how *The Motor Cycle* began their report of the meeting:

Just before racing started at Mallory Park last Sunday the public address trumpets summed up the situation eloquently by blaring out the strains of 'The Day the Rains Came Down.' The cold, clammy mist and all-pervading drizzle might well have been sent specially from the Scottish Highlands. But the weather improved as the day wore on and the quality of the riding was so high as to satisfy the most blasé enthusiast.

Bob McIntyre was entered for the 350 and 500cc classes, but in the former he was mounted on a Norton, not an AJS. And he could only finish sixth. The final result was Mike Hailwood, Tony Godfrey, George Salt, Alastair King, Bruce Daniels and Bob Mac.

The 500cc final was what *The Motor Cycle* described as a 'humdinger', with Bob showing his true form, and in the process providing most of the fireworks. Few spectators could have anticipated his success for he was on the last row of the starting grid and nearly half way down the field of 24 after one lap. For the first half of the race it was Alastair King who claimed most attention as he battled first with Bob Brown and then with George Salt to lead the pack at the end of five laps. Behind Brown thundered Mike Hailwood and Bob Anderson; all were on Nortons.

Then Bob really got into his stride. In two laps he disposed of Anderson and Hailwood and closed on Brown. In another lap he passed Brown and next time round he lay in second, in front of Salt. Bob then closed into King's slipstream and for three laps it seemed he was content with that. But with two laps to go, as *The Motor Cycle* described: 'King went the way of all McIntyre's other rivals – behind him – though they crossed the line fairly close.'

500cc Mallory Park – 15 laps – 20.25 miles
1st   R. McIntyre (Norton)
2nd   A. King (Norton)
3rd   R.H. Anderson (Norton)
4th   M. Hailwood (Norton)
5th   B. Brown (Norton)
6th   G. Salt (Norton)

This had been a performance to warn the opposition that when his bike was running well, Bob McIntyre was still the man to beat... a magnificent performance by any standards.

18 April 1959. Bob finished fourth on the AJS 7R – after lying second to race winner John Surtees (MV four) in the 350cc event.

The Easter Holiday weekend

Next came the Easter Holiday weekend, with a comprehensive racing programme for fans to choose from: Brands Hatch (Friday), Snetterton (Sunday) and several on Easter Monday (Crystal Palace, Oulton Park, Thruxton and Cadwell Park). Bob picked Brands and Oulton Park as his starting points. *The Motor Cycle* of 19 March 1959 described Bob as 'incomparable.'

There was also news concerning the Scottish Speed Championships. For 1959 these would be decided on points gained at Beveridge Park, Kirkcaldy (25 April), Charterhall (26 April), Errol (10 May and 14 June) and Edzell (20 June). In the past the championships had been decided solely on the results of one meeting (originally St Andrews and more recently Kirkcaldy).

On Good Friday, 27 March 1959, Bob Mac made one of his rare visits to Brands Hatch in Kent. And as *The Motor Cycle* race report says, he created something of a surprise for the local track specialists:

'Horses for courses' is a pretty sound motto in short-circuit racing. At Brands Hatch, for instance, John Surtees was invincible a few years ago. Then it was Alan Trow, then Derek Minter. All were local riders who took every opportunity to practice on the tricky 1.24-mile circuit. But most generalizations have their exceptions and, on Good Friday, Minter's reputation took a hard knock in three races out of four. In the last and fastest race of the day (1000cc) he was squarely beaten by that brilliant Scot, Bob McIntyre.

In an earlier 1000cc race, Minter had nearly beaten Bob, after what *The Motor Cycle* called: 'McIntyre's persistent challenge.' And in the 350cc race, which had 'begun in vile drizzle and finished in blinding rain', Bob had led by a length or two, before Minter exploited his more intimate knowledge of the track and took over. But the track surface was supremely treacherous and riders tumbled everywhere. Among the leaders Minter was first off – at Clearways – then the Scot lost his front wheel on Druids Hill Bend. The race was won by Bob's friend and travelling partner, Alastair King.

Then it was to Oulton Park for Easter Monday, 30 March. In contrast to the cold, wet weather down south, some 40,000 spectators watched some superb racing at the Cheshire circuit in fine, dry conditions. They also saw some of the most exciting racing served up to that time at the venue. The pick was the 19-lap 500cc battle.

Over the winter months Bob had done around 200 laps at Oulton Park, testing multi-grade oil for BP. So, as *The Motor Cycle* reported: 'He was a hotter favourite than ever.' He started on the back row and was weaving through the pack before the first corner was behind him. Even so, it was a fantastic achievement to be in the lead at Knicker Brook on that first lap. Unfortunately the fates took a hand and on the second lap – with a comfortable lead – Bob was forced to retire with a seized engine. And the day got worse, when in the 350cc race he was forced out when well placed, with lubrication problems. But every cloud has its silver lining, and in this case it was teammate Alastair King's brilliant return to form with three victories.

Another Silverstone shot of Bob, showing the determined stance with the jutting chin.

Everyone expected double World Champion John Surtees to win the main race of the day at Silverstone on Saturday 18 April. But Surtees made a mistake after only two miles and slid off his four-cylinder MV on Club Corner. As *The Motor Cycle* reported in its 23 April issue:

By his one aberration Surtees did much more than prove that the finest riders are fallible: he threw the BMCRC 500cc Championship wide open to privateers… For neither Silverstone nor any other circuit can ever have witnessed a more inspiring four-cornered struggle for supremacy than that which followed. Like a frenzied kaleidoscope, the pattern of the leading quartet (Alastair King, Bob Anderson, Mike Hailwood and Bob McIntyre) changed with dizzy frequency all round the track. The searing pace burnt up the opposition so that even John Hartle, the MV second string, had his work cut out to climb laboriously from tenth to fifth place with never a hope of catching the leaders.

Lap-leading honours went to McIntyre seven times, Anderson five, King four and Hailwood one. At mid-race distance, it appeared that Bob had got the measure of the field. However, back-markers came into the picture and soon the 'shuffle was in full swing'. With three laps to go it was Anderson's turn up front and soon Bob Mac's supporters 'watched their idol inch forward for the last-lap kill they had seen so often.' But they reckoned without the final burst of 'calculated fearlessness' which kept Anderson ahead. McIntyre had to be content with second place and a new motorcycle circuit lap record of 98.26mph.

In the earlier BMCRC 350cc Championship the combination of Surtees and the MV four had raised the class lap record to 93.87 mph. As expected the World Champion led from start to finish and Bob (AJS) was the only other rider who appeared in the same race. Unfortunately his bike's engine faded half a lap from the chequered flag, letting Anderson and King make up the leeway on their Nortons and pip Bob on the run-in, so the record books show he 'only' finished fourth. There was little justice for all the effort he had put in for the vast majority of the 17-lap race.

The battles continue

The next day the battles continued, this time at the picturesque Mallory Park 1.35-mile circuit a few miles north. The same four riders who had thrilled the crowd at Silverstone – Anderson, King, Hailwood and McIntyre – provided some heart stopping moments.

The Motor Cycle sets the scene: 'You could have heard a pin drop just before the start of the 350cc final. These two flying Scotsmen, Bob McIntyre and Alastair King, were expected to continue their furious Silverstone battle with Bob Anderson; Hailwood's gearbox had seized on the third lap of his heat so putting paid to his challenge.'

Bruce Daniels made a cracking start and held an early lead, only to be passed at the end of the first lap by Anderson. McIntyre was third, with King fourth. Then, as *The Motor Cycle* described: 'The two Scots really got their heads down on the second lap and, riding in shattering style, slipped past Daniels. Next Mac saw an opening going into the fast Paddock S and darted inside Anderson to take the lead.' In the closing stages Alastair put in a determined spurt and pulled right up with Bob, in the process setting the fastest lap.

350cc Mallory Park – 15 laps – 20.25 miles

1st	R. McIntyre (AJS)	
2nd	A. King (Norton)	
3rd	R.H.F. Anderson (Norton)	
4th	G. Hocking (Norton)	
5th	R.N. Brown (Norton)	
6th	B.J. Daniels (Norton)	

It was Bob's turn for machine trouble in the 500cc final (after winning his heat with ease) – his Norton refused to start!

Next came meetings at Beveridge Park and Charterhall on 25/26 April respectively. The Kirkcaldy club's annual road race meeting at the Fife coastal town's Beveridge Park was rapidly becoming the most popular in Scotland, and in 1959 reached an all-time high of 267 entries. The event also incorporated the first round of the Scottish Speed Championships. In former years the championships had been decided on the results of a single meeting, but for 1959 they were to be settled on points gained in five meetings. The Beveridge Park circuit could become very treacherous when wet – and wet it was that day – so tumbles were numerous. However, the wet conditions didn't stop Bob McIntyre and Alastair King dominating the proceedings in the larger classes. Bob won the 350cc race and Alastair the 500cc, with the two following each other home.

Organised by the Borders Motor Racing Club, the Charterhall meeting had attracted a large entry from both sides of the border. Weather conditions, although better than the day before, were none too good, there being a stiff, blustery wind which made itself felt on the back leg of the exposed airfield course, both on steering and performance. This meeting incorporated the second round of the Scottish Speed Championships. Again, the honours were shared, with Bob winning the 350cc and Alastair the 500cc race.

There was more wet weather the following Sunday, 3 May, at Mallory Park. But as one commentator summed things up: 'No road race meeting which includes Alastair King, Bob McIntyre and Mike Hailwood in its line-up could ever be dull, whatever the weather.'

In the 350cc race Bob made a terrible start, but battled through to third, behind the winner Mike Hailwood and Alastair King. In the 500cc race the tables were turned, with Bob taking the victory from Alastair and Mike. The Flying Scot also set the fastest lap of the race with a speed of 81mph.

Victory and a lap record in the North West 200

Then came a magnificent victory and a record lap, while taking part in the annual North West 200 international meeting in Northern Ireland on Saturday 9 May 1959. Saved from cancellation by the 11th-hour efforts of the Ulster Centre of the MCUI and the Coleraine Club, the meeting was held over

Bob and Alastair King at Beveridge Park, Kirkcaldy, on Saturday 25 April 1959. After setting the fastest lap in both 350 and 500cc races, the friends shared a victory each, with Bob winning the 350cc and Alastair the 500cc.

the traditional 11-mile 110-yard triangular circuit linking Port Stewart, Coleraine and Portrush, but with the race distance slashed to nine laps, almost 100 miles. Bob completed this distance in 59 minutes 59 seconds, averaging 101.21mph, while his fastest lap was in 6 minutes 28 seconds (102.56mph). Bob's race and lap speeds were course records. Alastair King won the 350cc class.

Fresh from their wins in the North West 200, Bob and Alastair travelled overnight to Errol, where they shared victories in the two main classes the following day. Bob won the 350cc class by 10 seconds and, in the 500cc category, positions were reversed. Quite simply, no one could challenge their Potts-entered machines.

In superb weather at Oulton Park on Saturday 16 May, the blue-faired machines of Bob McIntyre and Alastair King dominated much of the 19-lap, 52.5-mile Les Graham Trophy Race, which for the first time was for a specially invited field of 350cc bikes. The £100 first prize seemed to swing 'like a pendulum' *(The Motor Cycle)* between the two Scotsmen. But with only two laps to go Bob's AJS slowed and on the last lap the engine stopped altogether. And so victory went to Alastair King, and Derek Minter (Norton) was runner-up. As the 350cc race was the last of the day, Bob's only other race was the 500cc final, which he won and also set the fastest lap, with a speed of 86.43mph.

Two days later, on Monday 18 May, records crashed at Blandford, Dorset, the scene of the Blackmore Vale Club's international road races. Because of machine troubles Bob McIntyre was riding a borrowed Reg Dearden Norton in what was undoubtedly the finest race of the day, the 16-lap 500cc final. The race developed into a battle royal between three riders: Alastair King, Bob McIntyre and Derek Minter. It was the latter who eventually came out on top, with Bob second and Alastair third. In the 350cc race it was Alastair, Derek and Bob in that order.

Alastair King pictured during TT practice week, June 1959.

TT practice

Next in the calendar came the Isle of Man TT races. In 1959 Bob was entered in a record four events – the Lightweight (250cc) on an NSU (No.24); the Formula 1 500cc on a Norton (No.6); the Junior (350cc) Norton (No.3) and the Senior (No.1). As was now common practice, he was a favourite for honours with the pundits; the proviso being that his machinery kept going. In fact, in his 'Who Will Win This Year?' column in *The Motor Cycle* Michael Kirk went as far as calling Bob Mac 'one of the greatest racing men of all time.' He went on to say:

> At the end of the first lap of the Senior TT last year Bob McIntyre on his Potts-prepared Norton was – how much slower than Surtees (MV Agusta) think you? Only 4.2 seconds! Indeed, he was probably almost as fast as Surtees, for he had forgotten to open his petrol taps at the start and lost a few seconds when his engine cut out in the first 100 yards.

It seems unlikely that Bob even practiced on the NSU for the Lightweight event. But he certainly made his mark during practice week on his other machines. This is what one press report had to say:

> Last Thursday evening's practice over the Mountain course set the Island alight. Bob McIntyre put in a lap at 99.13mph on his Formula 1 Norton. For hours afterwards boarding houses and hotels buzzed with

excitement. If Bob could do that on a standard Manx model, what might he not do on his Potts Norton in the Senior? All round the course his riding was magnificent. Over the bumps at Hillberry, hardened Island habitués scarcely dared to look. Be he never so fast again, the memory of that terrific lap will live long in the minds of all who saw it.

Earlier in the same day Bill Jakeman had been seen tailoring a new type of light-alloy fairing for Bob's Senior TT mount. Weighing only 7½lb, the fairing had been manufactured in two sections, the lower of which could be detached to leave a small steering-head shroud (for use on short circuits).

During the closing stages of practice, Bob, making a first appearance on his Senior Norton on Friday, was stranded at Crosby during his second lap with a seized engine; and, if the rules were to be applied strictly, that meant that, in spite of his Formula 1 500cc laps, he had to complete his qualifying laps for the Senior TT on Saturday morning. Well, he did – by borrowing Gary Hocking's mount – and completing three laps.

Formula Double Scotch

The Motor Cycle race report dated 4 June 1959 carried the headline: 'Formula Double Scotch.' It went on:

> *Whomsoever Glasgow may belong to on any other Saturday night, last Saturday the Isle of Man belonged to Glasgow! For in the 500 and 350cc Formula 1 events which formed the overture to TT week proper the respective winners – right from flag fall – were Bob McIntyre (Norton) and Alastair King (AJS).*

The two events were run concurrently, and as the first pair of 350cc models roared away from the start line, the 500cc leaders on the road had already rounded Ballacraine and were threading their way through the bends in the leafy Glen Helen valley. Down the long, exhilarating drop to the 13th Milestone sped Bob McIntyre with grid-mate Terry Shepherd already well astern. First into Kirkmichael village was Jimmy Buchan; Bob having already gobbled up all the others, and at Sulby Bridge the gap could be measured in feet only. In the twisty green tunnel of Kerromoar, Buchan was overtaken, and for Bob the road ahead lay gloriously open.

Bob Mac completed the first lap in 23 minutes 0.1 seconds, a speed of 98.35mph. From there he was able to ease the pace, having broken the backs of the opposition. He went on to record a comfortable victory, averaging 97.77mph. Alastair King won the 350cc F1 race.

500cc formula 1 TT – 3 laps – 113.19 miles

1st   R. McIntyre (Norton)

2nd   R.N. Brown (Norton)

3rd   T.S. Shepherd (Norton)

4th   K.T. Kavanagh (Norton)

5th   J. Buchan (Norton)

6th   D.G. Chapman (Norton)

John Surtees (MV Agusta) once again won the Junior TT. But pre-race discussion had centred on Bob. Although programmed from the first as riding a Norton, he had in fact entered on an AJS. He had spent the practice period 'with typical diligence' (*The Motor Cycle*), making repeated comparative tests of handling – AJS v Norton. Initially the AJS had navigated less well but, by making adjustments to the front and rear suspension, he had eventually reached the stage where there was little between them. As for performance, previously the Norton engine had more punch, but it had rather less low-down torque. But things were different now with Jack Williams in charge of the AMC race shop, making changes which made the AJS a better all-round bet than the Norton.

On the basis of this Bob selected the AJS. Early in the race it appeared that the Scot had made the right choice, lying second at the end of the first lap. After two laps he was still runner-up – a position which remained unchanged at the end of lap three. But at the end of lap four he came into his pit to retire.

Exiting Governor's Bridge Dip, lying second at the end of the first lap of the 1959 Junior TT, a position he continued to hold until forced into retirement with serious vibration on the AJS at the end of lap four.

It transpired that he had been fighting vibration from the very start and had decided to accept defeat when a fairing mounting had broken. As *The Motor Cycle* commented: 'Such a disaster after so brilliant a ride paralysed the senses.'

Previously in their race report the magazine had described Bob's efforts thus: 'McIntyre, who aspires to perfection absolute in his riding, was using ten-tenths of the road everywhere and fantastic angles of lean.'

The 1959 Senior TT was postponed, owing to poor visibility, for a day, being run on Saturday 7 June. Then, for six of the seven laps, riders battled against heavy rain in the rerun race. The anticipated duel between the eventual winner John Surtees (MV Agusta) and Bob did not materialise. This was due to the Norton rider suffering clutch trouble. On the third lap Surtees's teammate John Hartle crashed and finally second place went to Alastair King after what *The Motor Cycle* described as 'a most consistent ride.' Australian Bob Brown (Norton) was third – the same position he had enjoyed in the Senior in three successive years. Bob eventually struggled home fifth.

The Scottish ACU, represented by Alastair, Bob and Ewan Haldane (Norton), who finished 14th, won the club team prize. Of the 58 starters only 22 finished, so harsh were the prevailing conditions. Many were frozen to the bone at the finish.

When one considers that Bob spent the equivalent of half a lap at his pits working on his bike (at the end of lap 2) it says something of his riding ability that day, that he dragged himself up to fifth by the end of the race.

The luck returns at Mallory Park

As soon as the race was over there was a general rush to board the Douglas to Liverpool ferry, as many competitors – including Bob – were racing the following day in the Post-TT meeting at Mallory Park, Leicestershire. The luck which had largely deserted Bob in the Isle of Man returned.

On one of only two unfaired bikes taking part in the 350cc event, Bob took his AJS into the lead from the drop of the flag. On his heels for the first two laps was Phil Read, aboard a new Norton. But he was overtaken, first by Alastair King (AJS) and then, on lap six, by Bob Brown (Norton). Bob Mac was clearly in control, also setting the fastest lap with a speed of 84.08mph.

350cc Mallory Park – 15 laps – 20.25 miles

1st   R. McIntyre (AJS)
2nd   R.H. Brown (Norton)
3rd   R.H.F. Anderson (Norton)
4th   J.L. Lewis (Norton)

5th   S.M.B. Hailwood (Norton)

6th   R.H. Dale (AJS)

There were two notable non-starters for the 15-lap final. Dickie Dale dropped his BMW at the hairpin during his heat and Mike Hailwood found the damping on his front forks suspect. So it was Bob who benefited once again – leading from start to finish.

On Saturday 20 June Bob (with co-rider Eric Hinton) took part in the annual Thruxton 500-mile Endurance Race (covered in Chapter 7). But once again, riding a Lawton & Wilson-entered 700cc Royal Enfield was no more successful than in earlier years, and he crashed out after the machine had suffered a broken primary chain and other mechanical woes.

Back to the road circuits

The Isle of Man Southern 100 races were run on Wednesday and Thursday 1/2 July. Riding his AJS 7R, Bob dominated the wet and windy 350cc event from flag to flag. With a lap record of 85mph and a huge lead in the 500cc race, he seemed on course for a double, but a broken valve-spring halted his Potts Norton. Bill Smith went on to win, riding one of the new Matchless G50 machines.

A reflective McIntyre awaits the start of the 1959 350cc Ulster Grand Prix, astride his Potts AJS 7R. But after once again holding second to John Surtees's MV four he was forced to pull out with valve spring trouble.

The same problem befell Bob's AJS during the 350cc Ulster Grand Prix on Saturday 8 August, when he was secure in second position behind race winner John Surtees (MV Agusta). But at least his Norton kept going in the 500cc race and so some form of justice came Bob's way, when as before he ran second to Surtees for the entire 20-lap, 148.32-mile race. What the Ulster events had shown was that except for Surtees and his four-cylinder factory MVs, Bob McIntyre still reigned supreme on genuine road circuits.

500cc Ulster Grand Prix – 20 laps – 148.32 miles

1st   J. Surtees (MV Agusta)

2nd   R. McIntyre (Norton)

3rd   G.E. Duke (Norton)

4th   T.S. Shepherd (Norton)

5th   R.N. Brown (Norton)

6th   A. King (Norton)

Bob with his Norton in the 1959 500cc Ulster. This time his bike didn't let him down and he came home runner-up to Surtees (MV). Third was Geoff Duke.

Double BMCRC Champion

The annual Hutchinson 100 international meeting at Silverstone, held on Saturday 22 August 1959, saw Mike Hailwood win the 125 and 250cc races. But in the 350 and 500cc races even the talented young Oxford rider couldn't keep up with the Flying Scot, Bob McIntyre.

As *The Motor Cycle* said: 'There was a different story in the 350cc Championship which followed. AJS mounted Hailwood met his match.' In fact Bob and Alastair King, also both on 7R AJS models, were dominant. From the start both Scots were nudging John Surtees's lap record. 'Mac seemingly towing his pal with an invisible elastic – sometimes slack, sometimes stretched to 50 yards.'

In the other race, Bob was even more in charge. *The Motor Cycle:* 'With a superb display on one of Joe Potts' Nortons, McIntyre confounded the Formula-1-for-close-racing argument in the 1000cc Championship by increasing his lead on every one of the 15 laps in spite of never being hard pressed.'

Six days later, on Saturday 28 August, Hailwood again had to take a back seat, when Bob was once again victorious in the 350 and 500cc races aboard his AJS and Norton machines. One media headline said it all: 'McIntyre Magnificent.' The only difference between Silverstone and Oulton Park was that this time Bob Mac had *three* wins – adding the Solo Handicap race to his tally for the day.

As *The Motor Cycle* dated 10 September 1959 reported, this winning streak continued upon his return north of the border:

Bob McIntyre, undisputed king of the Scottish road-race circuits, had an easy day at the Dundee and Angus Club's meeting at Errol Airfield last Sunday. Riding Nortons, he had runaway victories in both the 350 and 500cc classes and, without decrying the fine performances of the other riders, it is literally true to say that he had no opponent worthy of his steal.

Getting away from it all. Bob with his future wife Joyce (to Bob's right) and Alastair King's wife Margaret.

Bob also put in the fastest lap of the day, recording 71.29mph.

Things don't always run smoothly for even the best of riders. This point was amply illustrated when, qualifying for the international meeting at Oliver's Mount, Scarborough on Friday 18 September 1959, Bob struck problems. This is how a period race report describes what happened:

In the first 350cc heat on Friday, McIntyre (AJS) went straight into the lead and was 16s ahead of Bob Anderson (Norton) on the third lap… On lap 4 the leader came howling through. But it was Anderson! On the back stretch McIntyre had just dropped to bottom gear when his rear wheel went askew, jammed and threw him off. It was thought that a chain adjuster had broken.

Although Bob's only injury was a bruised hand, it was still enough to keep him out of the following day's racing and so bring to an end the winning sequence he had enjoyed for the previous three meetings, which had resulted in seven straight victories in the main races at Silverstone, Oulton Park and Errol.

End of season meetings

After Scarborough, Bob had entries for three more meetings as the 1959 British racing season came towards its close: Aintree, Mallory Park and Brands Hatch.

Aintree came first on Saturday 26 September. And it showed that his Scarborough mishap had no lasting effect, because Bob won both the 350 and 500cc races – and set the fastest laps in each. There is no doubt that this would have been a triple had he not retired when leading the 34-lap, 102-mile Aintree Century event, when his Norton developed clutch trouble, forcing his retirement.

The following day, Sunday 27 September, Bob was at Mallory Park, where

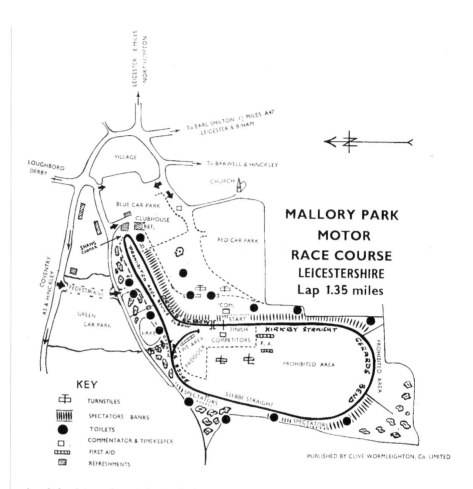

Bob receives a cheque for £300 (from John Surtees, who later drove him around the Mallory Park circuit on a lap of honour). The occasion was the 'Race of the Year' with the top names in racing including Hailwood, Anderson, Brown, Driver, Dale and of course Bob himself, 27 September 1959.

he *did* achieve the triple; including victory in the prestigious Race of the Year. On the grid for the main event (held over 40 laps) were some of the best-known names in the racing world, such as Hailwood, Anderson, Brown, Driver and Dale – plus Bob McIntyre. Even John Surtees was there – to drive the victor on a lap of honour. As *The Motor Cycle* reported:

> *The silence before the start was almost oppressive: hardly anyone in the huge crowd thronging every vantage point dared to breathe. The flag dropped and the riders were away in a snarling, jostling bunch. And as they roared past the start at the end of the first lap an excited murmur ran through the crowd: wonder boy Hailwood (Norton) was in the lead and going like a man possessed. He was closely followed by the two Bobs, Anderson and Brown. McIntyre lay no higher than sixth!*

But Bob Mac had got the urge, for this was no ordinary race; there was too much at stake – the richest prize ever offered for a single race in Great Britain.

And a determined McIntyre was a foe indeed, as the rest of the field were soon to find out. He 'whipped past' two men on the second lap and then set out after the leaders. On the fourth lap, while Bob was attempting to find an opening past Bob Brown, Anderson was also endeavouring to oust Hailwood from top spot.

The fifth lap saw a complete shuffle of the pack. Anderson snatched the lead and Bob slipped past Brown. Not satisfied with third position, the Scot relentlessly closed the gap between himself and Hailwood to a few feet and then managed to scrape through an incredibly small opening. Anderson was the next obstacle and he had no illusion that anyone other than McIntyre was on his tail. As *The Motor Cycle* vividly described in its 1 October issue: 'He spurted but Mac spurted even harder. They drew away from Hailwood and Brown. Then, on the eighth lap, Anderson heard a roar under his right elbow at Shaw's Corner. It was too late! McIntyre had gone by in a burst of acceleration like a jet raising its undercarriage after take-off.' It was all over and from that moment Bob was in command for the rest of the race. And he was in a *very* happy mood when he received his winner's cheque from John Surtees.

Earlier he had displayed his skills by winning both the 350 and 500cc races (and setting the fastest laps). By winning these two races he also clinched his lead on the season-long Mallory Park Championship series. All in all it had been a brilliant display and one which Bob would remember fondly for many a long day.

Then came the season finale at Brands Hatch on Sunday 11 October. In the 350cc class there was what *The Motor Cycle* referred to as 'a wondrous clash.' This saw Mike Hailwood rocket his AJS into Paddock Hill Bend, only to be passed by an 'even quicker rocket, Bob McIntyre, also AJS mounted.' And for many laps these two riders duelled relentlessly, often 'with little more than a coat of paint' between them. Then suddenly Bob eased right off and gradually dropped astern; four laps later he pulled into the paddock nursing an aching right wrist, a memento of his fall at Scarborough three weeks earlier. The effect of this injury also showed in the 500cc race, where he was 'unceremoniously pushed back to fourth place on the last lap by Paddy Driver and Jim Redman, in a race won by Mike Hailwood.' So, in the gathering gloom of an October afternoon, Bob's 1959 season came to an end in something of an anticlimax.

It was one where he had scored some truly notable successes and in the process hoisted himself back up the ladder, after a rather indifferent season the year before.

Closed-season testing

1960 began with news of Bob's continued involvement with the BP oil company, which the Scot had been contracted to for several years. He had been to Oulton Park, where riding a standard Triumph Tiger 110 six-fifty street bike Bob had put in 77 laps of the nearly three-mile Cheshire circuit. The purpose? To prove the worth of BP's new Energol Visco-static multi-grade oil. The idea was to 'drive it as hard as it can be driven round Oulton Park circuit for 200 miles.' And that's exactly what he did, 'using every ounce of power the engine could give.' This was a far more gruelling test than would ever be asked of any normal roadgoing machine. When stripped after the 200-mile high-speed test, vital parts of the engine were examined. The following were the results:

> Piston and rings showed no significant trace of lacquer or other oxidation effects.
>
> The barrel and pistons were perfect.
>
> The cams showed scarcely any wear and no trace whatsoever of scuffing.

This session was all part of Bob's closed season activities. For when he was not working in the Potts Bellshill workshop, he was carrying out testing for trade companies. This involved doing countless laps of a given race circuit, testing products as diverse as lubricants, tyres, spark plugs, electrical components and the like.

By the beginning of March 1960 Bob was already in serious pre-season training at Silverstone, where he had been tyre testing, riding a 500cc Norton.

Like the majority of top British riders his first outing of the year was to be at the BMCRC annual Hutchinson 100 at Silverstone on 9 April. Bob also revealed that the 500 Norton he rode in 1959 was for sale. It had been 'completely rebuilt' and was in 'showroom condition.'

For the TT Bob expected he would ride a 7R AJS in the Junior race – and hoped to do the six laps 'non-stop.' For the Senior he would 'almost certainly be Norton mounted' and would plan to stop for fuel. Towards the end of March Bob was out practicing at Mallory Park – but as circuit owner Clive Wormleighton revealed 'he failed to disturb a gaggle of geese who have settled on the lake during the winter!'

A winning start

Bob McIntyre made a superb start to the 1960 season with two new machines at Silverstone on Saturday 8 April. Sporting home-built frames, these bikes were virtually identical, except for their engine unit – an AJS 7R 350 and a Manx Norton 500 respectively.

Bob won the 350cc class after what *Motor Cycle News* described as: 'The finest race of the day'. From the start Mike Hailwood on another 7R rocketed into a 50-yard lead and at the end of the first lap held this advantage over the Scottish star. Behind the two leaders Tommy Robb (AJS) lay third, closely followed by Phil Read (Norton) and Mike O'Rourke (Norton) with a thundering pack on their heels.

Both Mike and Bob were riding 'brilliantly' (*MCN*) but slowly and surely 'in his relentless style the dour Scot cut Hailwood's lead by ten yards a lap until on the fifth lap – a third of the way – McIntyre was on the tail of the leading AJS.'

On lap six Bob took the lead but Mike didn't give up the struggle and the 'riding from both these aces was superb to see – absolutely 'on the limit' but never once in trouble.'

And so the race unfolded, Bob and Mike simply in a class of their own. Bob couldn't take another inch out of Hailwood but at the same time Mike couldn't gain a centimetre and so they finished, with the Scot half a second ahead. Only windy conditions prevented the 350cc lap record (set by Alastair King the previous year at 94.38mph) being smashed. But it was Bob who got the nearest to this, with a fastest lap of 94.04mph. As one reporter said: 'His ride certainly proved that there's nothing much wrong with his new frames.'

350cc Silverstone – 15 laps – 43.65 miles

1st	R. McIntyre (AJS)
2nd	S.M.B. Hailwood (AJS)
3rd	P.W. Read (Norton)
4th	A. Shepherd (AJS)
5th	J.H.L. Lewis (Norton)
6th	R.E. Rowe (Norton)

In the 500cc event it was Bob McIntyre all the way, riding the second of his new specials, this time with the Norton engine. By the end of the first lap the Flying Scot led by 200 yards. After two laps this advantage had been increased to 500 yards and, as *MCN* said: 'It was obvious that no one could live with the Glaswegian on this form.' And Bob went on to score one of his most impressive ever victories on the British short circuits. Quite simply no one was in the same class. He also set the fastest lap at 97.17mph. The 'specials' are described in Chapter 8.

500cc Silverstone – 15 laps – 43.65 miles

1st	R. McIntyre (Norton)

2nd   S.M.B. Hailwood (Norton)

3rd   F.G. Perris (Norton)

4th   W.A. Smith (Matchless)

5th   R.H.F. Anderson (Norton)

6th   T. Thorp (Norton)

Huge crowds at Oulton Park

Over 50,000 spectators were treated to beautiful spring-like weather with bright sunshine at Oulton Park on Easter Monday, 18 April, to watch the international meeting organised by the Wirral 100 club.

The 500cc race produced a mammoth duel between Bob and Derek Minter, which was only settled when the Scot missed a gear, allowing Minter to gain a 40-yard lead.

Then came the climax to a superb day's racing, the 350cc event. Minter and Bob Mac were at it again, and with Minter inches ahead for most of the way the pair streaked round the Cheshire venue consistently inside the lap record. However, on the last lap, just when it appeared that Minter would complete his double, Bob made a supreme effort and took the lead to win by a length, with Alan Shepherd (AJS) third and Phil Read (Norton) fourth. Minter and Bob also shared the class record lap, with an identical speed of 86.43mph.

Six days later, at the Charterhall circuit in Berwickshire on Sunday 24 April, Bob comfortably completed a 350/500cc double on his AJS and Norton Specials. Among the competiton was Jim Guthrie (499cc BSA), son of the late Jimmie Guthrie, the pre-war Norton star. Another interesting entry was Robin Fitton, later to become a well-known rider of the Continental Circus.

Bob and Mike Hailwood shared the honours when they clashed at Mallory Park on Sunday 31 April, with Mike winning the 500cc scrap (Bob was runner-up). In the 350cc event Bob took his AJS Special to victory with Phil Read (Norton) second.

Bob's day at Beveridge Park

The *Motor Cycle News* headline on the back page of the newspaper's 11 May 1960 issue shouted 'Bob's day at Beveridge Park.' It went on to report: 'At Beveridge Park, Fife, on Saturday a crowd of some five thousand was provided with four and a half hours of almost non-stop racing of the highest standard. The event, organised by the Kirkcaldy and DMC, attracted 118 entries.'

Riding under number 99, Bob was mounted on a pair of Potts Nortons – not his lightweight specials. In fact, this followed a similar plan which had seen Bob use his second string bikes at Scottish meetings for the previous two seasons.

This was also the third round of the 1960 Scottish Speed Championships – Bob having missed the earlier rounds at Errol and Charterhall.

After Beveridge Park came the annual North West 200 on Saturday 14 May. This resulted in what was generally described as the closest finish ever in the event, when, with less than 70 yards to go in the 77-mile 350cc race, Alan Shepherd (AJS) snatched a last second victory from Bob McIntyre, riding his special frame model. The meeting was also notable as, in a marked departure from past practice, the event saw the separation of the 350 and

Bob riding his 7R in the 1960 North West 200. He just missed out on victory, but shared the fastest lap with Alan Shepherd at 93.64mph (150.6kph).

500cc races, which had formerly been combined; thus giving most riders two races instead of one.

Heavy showers before and during the closing stages of the 11-mile, 110-yard Port Stewart–Coleraine–Portrush road circuit put a dampener on the chance of new record speeds. As *Motor Cycle News* reported: 'The mischievous leprechauns which silenced Minter's Norton early in the 350cc race switched their attention to McIntyre's Special Norton when he was leading the 100-mile 500cc race.'

High expectations of recent resurfacing and road improvements were dulled by heavy showers and strong winds throughout race day. The best conditions were experienced by riders in the final race, for 500cc machines, in which three riders lapped at over the ton – Tommy Robb, Derek Minter and Bob. But none of these speeds matched the latter's existing outright lap record of 102.56mph.

So what had gone wrong with our hero's machine? *Motor Cycle News*:

> *Something was wrong with Mac's bike and he swished through the pit area smothered in oil, a trouble he had encountered in practice. That was his 'lot' and, seeing no future in hanging about, McIntyre immediately loaded the bike into his van.*

So Bob was on his way to the Belfast boat and home to Scotland before the race was over!

Bob's next outing was at Silverstone on Saturday 27 May. In the past the international meeting held over the 2.927-mile Northamptonshire circuit had often been marred by poor weather. But not so on this spring day in 1960, when there was a glorious sunrise and good weather thereafter.

The good weather didn't help Bob McIntyre. First, in the 350cc race his AJS engine tightened up and he was forced to retire when right up with the leaders. Then in the 500cc class McIntyre's Norton engine seized solid as he swept round Stowe Corner. The rear wheel locked and the bike skidded across the track. *Motor Cycle News* said: 'Mac was lucky to walk away with bruises and a skinned nose.'

Picking the winners

Next for Bob came the Isle of Man TT races. This year he was only entered in the Junior (350cc) and Senior (500cc) events. The Junior was to be held on Wednesday 15 June over six laps – 226.4 miles.

In *Motor Cycle News* dated 8 June, Mick Woollett in 'Picking the winners' saw John Surtees (MV Agusta) as a certainty to win, saying:

> *I pick Surtees to win but who'll be second? Bob McIntyre was lying second on his AJS last year until vibration got the better of him. Now that he's put the 7R engine in his own frame he's stopped the vibration and with the exception of Silverstone the bike has proved both fast and reliable. Mac is always fantastic in the Island – remember that 99mph lap on the Norton – and so I choose him for second place.*

But this discounted the fact that, just before practice got under way it was announced that MV had re-signed John Hartle – especially for the TT. And it was Hartle – the man MV released from their team earlier that year only to re-sign him for the TT – who emerged the victor of the 1960 Junior TT, with a record class race average speed of 96.70mph. His teammate and reigning World Champion John Surtees was runner-up, with Bob Mac a superb third on his AJS Special (now with five-speed gearbox). Bob's average speed was 95.11mph (compared with Surtees's 95.39mph). But it should be pointed out that John Surtees's bike finished minus first and third gears.

Junior TT – 6 laps – 226.4 miles
1st   J. Hartle (MV Agusta)
2nd   J. Surtees (MV Agusta)
3rd   R. McIntyre (AJS)

Bob resting during TT practice week in 1960. To the far right of the picture, seated on Bob's 499cc Norton, is his mechanic 'Pim' Fleming. The number 4 bike belongs to Mike Hailwood.

4th   D. Minter (Norton)
5th   R.B. Rensen (Norton)
6th   R.H.F. Anderson (Norton)

The cheer which went up for Bob at the Junior prize-giving held in the Villa Marina Ballroom in Douglas on Wednesday evening was 'terrific' (*MCN*). When asked to speak, Bob in his usual modest way said 'I'd sooner do another six laps than this!' and went on to thank all those who had aided him, congratulating the winner and commiserating with John Surtees.

As for the Senior race, Bob was without his Norton special as this had been badly damaged in his Silverstone spill. This meant that he rode a new standard Manx Norton machine. However, this was not the end of his problems, as during the race a misfire started soon after he got under way and got progressively worse. Thinking it was the magneto, Bob retired. But a subsequent post-race test showed the mag to be in perfect working order. It was replaced on the same bike and without further adjustments he was able to ride it to victory only two days later in the 500cc final at Mallory Park! So quite what did cause the misfire remains a mystery.

Mallory's miniature TT

Mallory's miniature TT (more commonly known as the Post-TT) was held on Sunday 19 June 1960. Glorious weather and a top class entry which included the majority of the TT aces attracted a vast crowd to the Leicestershire short circuit.

The first heat of the 350cc race produced a surprise. Riding a brand new standard Manx Norton in place of his AJS lightweight special, Bob lay well back, only coming through towards the end of the race to finish fifth, some way behind the winner Phil Read (Norton). The second heat was won by Mike Hailwood (AJS) and the third, and final one, by Dickie Dale (Norton).

With his 7R fitted with coil ignition (a post-TT modification), Hailwood shot into the lead in the 20-lap 350cc final. At the end of the opening lap he led by 20 yards from Phil Read, Bruce Daniels (Norton) and Bob – whose standard Norton was cloaked in an unfamiliar – for Mac – red streamlining (his more familiar lightweight 500 Norton usually had a blue fairing).

On the second lap Bob was up to third (in front of Daniels) and soon he was past Read to hopefully mount a challenge to the flying Hailwood. But in the end he finished runner-up; an excellent result considering the newness of his machine.

The 500cc final was even better for the Scot. From the drop of the flag Hailwood again made a superb start, as did Phil Read (both riding Nortons), followed by Bob. At the end of the lap Mike still led, but only by a wheel from McIntyre. On the second lap Bob took the lead from Hailwood. What followed was a close-fought battle, but by the 10th lap Bob had pulled a 50-yard lead over Hailwood and Ron Langston (Matchless), the latter having come through the field to take third position. With a lap to go the leaders – McIntyre, Hailwood, Langston and Read – were well spread out and Mac came home to win a popular victory. Bob and Mike shared the fastest lap, with a speed of 87.73 mph.

500cc Post-TT Mallory Park – 20 laps – 27 miles
1st   R. McIntyre (Norton)
2nd   S.M.B. Hailwood (AJS)
3rd   R. Langston (Matchless)
4th   P. Read (Norton)
5th   P. Driver (Norton)
6th   R.H. Dale (Norton)

On Saturday 25 June Bob was in action at Thruxton, the scene of the annual 500-miler – and, as covered in Chapter 7, he ended up experiencing problems with the Syd Lawton-entered Royal Enfield, before crashing out of the event for the second year running.

Disqualified
'Poor old Bob!' said *Motor Cycle News* in the newspaper's 13 July 1960 issue. Why? Well, in the 350cc race of the sixth Southern 100 meeting in the Isle of Man on Wednesday 6 June, Bob was beaten by Ron Langston (AJS) by a mere five yards. And the following day, after scoring what was generally viewed as a brilliant 500cc victory, in which he broke the course and lap records, the Flying Scot was disqualified for ignoring a rule which forbade refuelling during the race. Thus, for the second time in 24 hours Ron Langston (Matchless) was again the winner.

Bob was using a three-gallon short circuit tank on his unfaired Norton and pulled into his pit as he began his 22nd lap of the 4.277-mile Billown road circuit. With only two laps to go, he was well ahead of the field and had lapped all but the next three men: Langston, plus Bill Smith (Matchless) and Peter Middleton (Norton).

On his sixth lap, when he had broken away from Langston, Bob had raised the lap record to 85.28mph.

The dramatic exclusion was announced shortly after he had been cheered in the winner's enclosure and Bob accepted the officials' decision with typical

McIntyre quiet, dignified sportsmanship, simply saying: 'I should have read the regulations.'

Prior to the Southern 100, Bob had decided to spend 'a quiet weekend' on the Isle of Man; hence his non-entry for the first race over the extended 2.65-mile Grand Prix circuit at Brands Hatch the following weekend.

Putting the disappointment of the Southern 100 behind him, Bob made a victorious comeback at Mallory Park on Sunday 17 July 1960. Four of the five finals at this national status meeting resulted in tremendous duels which were only resolved in the closing laps. Bob, riding his AJS special, passed Terry Shepherd, riding Francis Beart's 7R, on the last lap to win the 350cc final, the only race to be run on a wet track.

In the 500cc final it was McIntyre (Norton special) who got passed, by Mike Hailwood (Norton). Mike rode in Bob Mac's slipstream for the entire race, pulling out to win by a few lengths in the closing stages. Bob and Mike shared the fastest lap of 87.41mph.

Double British Champion

It was Bob McIntyre's day at Oulton Park on Bank Holiday Monday 1 August, when he won both the 1960 350 and 500cc British Championship titles on his AJS and Norton-engined specials. To confirm his mastery he ended the day by winning the Les Graham Memorial Trophy race, although Mike Hailwood (Norton) made him fight every inch of the way, just as he had in the 500cc Championship race. Bob also set the fastest laps – 350cc: 86.28mph; 500cc: 88.59mph.

350cc British Championship Race Oulton Park – 30 laps – 82.83 miles
1st   R. McIntyre (AJS)
2nd   A. Shepherd (AJS)
3rd   R.H. Dale (Norton)
4th   T.S. Shepherd (AJS)
5th   F. Stevens (Norton)
6th   R. Fay (Norton)

500cc British Championship Race Oulton Park – 30 laps – 82.83 miles
1st   R. McIntyre (Norton)
2nd   S.M.B. Hailwood (Norton)
3rd   A. Shepherd (Matchless)
4th   J. Hartle (Norton)
5th   F. Stevens (Norton)
6th   R. Fay (Norton)

After the Ulster GP in early August 1960, Bob didn't race again until the end of September. The reason? He married Joyce Campbell and the happy couple had something of an extended honeymoon. They then settled into their new home in Bearsden, on the north-west fringes of Glasgow.

The Les Graham Memorial Trophy race over 10 laps was a fitting climax to what had been a fine day's sport – and a highly successful one for Bob. John Hartle (Norton) led for the first four laps until a footrest dropped off and with it went the gear change controls. This slip let Bob through and with Mike Hailwood on his tail they began a ding-dong struggle which only ended when Bob took the chequered flag half a wheel ahead.

Then it was across the Irish Sea to Dundrod for the Ulster Grand Prix on Saturday 6 August – Bob's favourite circuit. Sadly, 1960 was not to be the Scot's year for success in this event. First he was forced out in the 350cc race, retiring at his pit early in the race. Then, in the 500cc event, he built up a commanding lead, only to have victory snatched from his grasp after suffering 'violent vibration' on his Norton special on the 11th lap of the 20-lap, 148-mile race. At the finish it was John Hartle (Norton) who won from John Surtees (MV Agusta), the latter having to pit early in the race to rectify a broken gear lever on his Italian four-cylinder machine.

Even though Bob's luck had been out in Ulster, good fortune came later that month, when he married Joyce Campbell. And the happy couple had something of an extended honeymoon, as Bob did not race for some six weeks until late September. Bob and Joyce settled into their new family home in Ballater Drive, Bearsden, on the north-west fringes of Glasgow.

A move to Honda?

In *Motor Cycle News* there was a front page story saying that Bob would ride 125 and 250cc works Hondas at Aintree if the Japanese factory provided the machines. The entries were listed in the programme and Bob commented: 'If they are there I will ride them.' He added: 'My Gilera contract expires at the end of this year and I'm on the market for next season. If I can get a competitive machine I'll ride in the World Championship series, but there's no point in travelling if I can't win.'

Mick Woollett said he was 'a little surprised' when Bob told him he was in the market for a works ride in the Grand Prix in 1961. Mick was 'under the impression that Bob had settled down to race only in the British Isles as he has for the past three seasons.' Bob did however point out that 'at eleven and a half stone stripped' he was a 'bit on the heavy side for the tiddlers.'

And, yes, as fully covered in Chapter 9, Bob did make his Honda debut at Aintree on Saturday 24 September 1960. And a winning debut it was too, beating Mike Hailwood (FB Mondial) in the process.

But he also turned out on his Potts-entered British bikes in the 350 and 500cc events at the Liverpool circuit, finishing second (behind John Hartle – Norton) in the 350cc on his AJS special, while in the 500cc he was third

(behind Hartle and Mike Hailwood – both Norton mounted). But in truth it would be fair to say that he was concentrating his mind on the Honda ride. He also crashed out of the 21-lap Aintree Century, the last race of the day, in a shower of sparks, when disputing the lead on his 499cc Potts Norton with John Hartle.

Success and disappointment at Mallory

The following day, Sunday 25 September, Bob won both the 350 and 500cc finals and with these wins clinched both Mallory Park Championships for 1960. However, he was to suffer a bitter disappointment, when as favourite to take home *The Race of the Year* title and the £1,000 first prize – witnessed by the largest crowd ever to attend a Mallory Park meeting – he was forced out of the 40-lap race with engine trouble while challenging for the lead.

The final weekend of the British 1960 season came on 8/9 October. As *Motor Cycle News* reported:

> *Conditions for the final Oulton Park meeting of the year on Saturday – a national event organised by the Chester MC – were just about as bad as they could be with drizzling rain alternating with heavy showers combining to turn the near three mile circuit into a skating rink that got steadily worse as the day wore on and the light faded.*

As if sensing the conditions, the top stars, including Derek Minter, Phil Read and Bob McIntyre, were 'non-arrivals'. Conditions were little better the following day at Brands Hatch – where again Bob took no part.

And so another racing season came to an end. But unlike recent years, 1960 had given the promise that Bob McIntyre just might be returning to the big time and the Grand Prix life.

When Bob and Alastair King travelled south for the annual Mallory Park dinner at the beginning of November, Bob told journalists that he had 'not heard a word' from Honda since he won the 250cc race riding a works four-cylinder machine at Aintree in September.

As 1960 became 1961, there was still no word as to what Bob McIntyre would be riding in the new season. Rumour and counter rumour linked him with Honda, MZ and Gilera, among others. But Bob said: 'none of them have been in touch; maybe they think I'm past it!' As the following chapters reveal, Mr McIntyre was to make a dramatic return to the big time during 1961.

Chapter 7

Endurance racing at Thruxton

F OR FIVE years (1956, 1958, 1959, 1960 and 1961), Bob McIntyre attempted to win the annual Thruxton endurance race for series production machines. The highest position he achieved was runner-up in 1958 (co-rider Derek Powell). However, more often than not he was favourite to win the event, but as was often typical in the Bob Mac story, mechanical failure and bad luck dogged his efforts. So certain was one leading figure in the sport that a McIntyre entry was likely to win that Mac was offered a bribe to throw the race; but in typical fashion he rejected this offer out of hand. Quite simply he rode to win, not for pure financial gain!

How it all began
The idea of holding a long-distance race for standard production machines in Great Britain came about in late 1954. Originally, a 24-hour or 12-hour race length was envisaged, part of which would be run in darkness, like the famous French Bol d'Or event. However, the promoters, the Ashton Combine, finally decided that for the first venture, at any rate, nine hours would suffice.

And so the first 'Thruxton Nine Hours' was held on Saturday 25 June 1955 over the 2.76-mile Thruxton airfield circuit near Andover in rural Hampshire. The rules stated that two riders for each machine would be allowed and the winning team would be the one which had completed the most laps after the ninth hour. No one rider was permitted to continue for more than two hours at a stretch.

As events transpired, for most competitors nine hours was just about long enough. And, amazingly, the real problem which reared its ugly head in this first year was not rider fatigue or mechanical failure, but tyre wear. The surface at Thruxton in those days was extremely coarse, so that abrasion on corners was considerable. Front tyres suffered more than rear ones, and some of the riders were finding canvas showing before half distance! This situation was soon to cause a state of near panic as very few teams had come prepared with spare tyres or, better still, spare wheels and tyres. Countless SOS calls were relayed over the public address system. Helpers and spectators lent tyres from their roadsters, while mechanics were sent scurrying to scour nearby Andover. And remember, tyres in those days were of a much, much harder compound than the super sticky, but exceedingly soft tyres of today.

Although the meeting received considerable press coverage prior to the actual race – and it was staged under a national status permit – few riders entered. Of the 45 teams whose entries had been accepted, 43 came to the line for the start at noon.

Bob McIntyre (700 Royal Enfield) overtaking the Velocette Venom of D. Hamilton, Thruxton, 20 June 1959.

Bob McIntyre was the godfather of Syd Lawton's youngest son Ian. He was highly regarded by the entire Lawton family.

Favourites were Eddie Dow and Eddie Crooks with a 499cc BSA Gold Star. Others in contention included the Perris/Williams Triumph Tiger 110 and the James/Lloyd three-fifty Gold Star. Other 'name' riders were Ron Langston and Derek Powell, while Southampton dealer and former works Norton racer

Syd Lawton first displayed his talents as a team manager with some efficient pit work.

After the end of the nine hours the Dow/Crooks BSA which crossed the line with the most laps – 221 (610 miles) was declared the winner; the runner-up spot went to James/Lloyd and third to Williams/Shekell on a Triumph Tiger 100. The Perris/Williams Tiger 110 had led for a considerable section of the race but first an accident and then slipped timing put paid to their challenge. There were a total of 14 retirements for various reasons.

A bigger entry and Bob's debut

A year later, now organised by the Southampton Club, the Thruxton Marathon, as it was labelled in those days, was a much bigger affair, with several well-known competitors among its 60-team entry. Bob McIntyre (with co-rider Alastair King) made his debut. Other riders included Geoff Tanner, Roy Ingram, Tony Godfrey, Eddie Crooks, Bernard Codd, Percy Tait and Rex Avery. Bob and Alastair (No.40) were mounted on one of the latest BSA DB34 Gold Star five-hundreds.

Saturday 23 June 1956 'dawned grey and with a cumulus-broken sky. A drizzle early would have caused no surprise. As the day wore on so the light increased. The sun shone and alternated with overcast during the greater part of the race period' (*The Motor Cycle*).

The single carburettor Super Meteor engine, as used by Bob McIntyre in the 1958 Thruxton marathon. Together with Derek Powell, the Lawton-entered machine finished runner-up behind the Triumph Tiger 110 of Hailwood and Shorey.

At noon the flag went up, and upon its fall the field swept away with exhaust blending with exhaust into Club Corner. The snarling pack was headed by Ron Jerrard (runner-up in that year's 500 Clubman's TT) and Bob McIntyre 'at such a knottage as to suggest a sprint rather than a marathon.'

However, the Jerrard-McIntyre duel was to be short-lived. At Windy Corner, with only 2½ miles completed, Jerrard (BSA Gold Star) fell, with Bob running into his machine. This caused Bob to fall too and both riders were left injured. As outlined in Chapter 4, these injuries were to keep Bob out of action for several weeks. For the record, the race was eventually won by Ken James and Ivor Lloyd on a three-fifty BSA Gold Star; the pair covering 236 laps (651.36 miles) at an average speed of 72.3mph.

Because of his Gilera commitments, Bob didn't compete in the Thruxton event during 1957. But that year another BSA Gold Star three-fifty was victorious (Rex Avery and Fred Webber); in third place a 692cc Royal Enfield Super Meteor had shown that it was the fastest bike on the circuit. However,

Royal Enfield 700 Twin

At the beginning of November 1948, the Redditch-based Royal Enfield concern announced a brand new twin. The work of Ted Pardoe, and to a lesser extent Tony Wilson-Jones, the newcomer was Enfield's interpretation of the then-popular British vertical twin, a fashion sparked off by the great success achieved by the arrival of Edward Turner's ground-breaking Triumph Speed Twin of the late 1930s.

Like Turner's creation, the Enfield twin was a five-hundred (496cc – 64x77 mm), but here, except for its general configuration, overhead valves and vertical cylinders, the resemblance ended.

Unlike the other twins by then emerging from other British factories, there were two separate cast-iron cylinder barrels (only AMC followed this route). Each featured its own light alloy cylinder head and integral rocker box. Another Enfield feature was that the skirts of the barrels were sunk very deeply (by over half their length) into the mouth of the crankcases.

Another familiar Enfield trademark was the arrangement of the oil compartment, cast into the crankcase assembly. While this was not a wet sump system, it did mean there was, unlike all the other British four-stroke parallel twins of the era, no separate oil tank attached to the frame and separate from the engine. The oil pump was located in the timing cover. Both these features copied the company's Bullet single.

Other technical details included two main bearings; vertically-split crankcases; one-piece crankshaft, with plain split big-end bearings; two separate crankcases; an Albion-supplied four-speed gearbox and duplex primary chain. The oil-damped telescopic fork and twin shock, swinging arm rear suspension also followed the latest Bullet single. At the time, the new Enfield twin was seen very much as a tourer, rather than a sportster.

The 692cc Royal Enfield Constellation, itself developed from the earlier Meteor and Super Meteor models.

A new 692cc version of the twin (using the 70 x 90mm bore and stroke dimensions of the three-fifty Bullet single) was launched at the London Earls Court Show in November 1952. For its day, the newcomer, named the Meteor, was considered a sports/tourer capable of quite high performance – and was the biggest British vertical twin at the time. Heavier than the well-proven 500 Twin by a mere 10lb (4.5kg), the larger engine had plenty of flexible muscle. Although based largely on the 500, the 700 had several changes aimed at coping with the additional power output (36bhp at

R.A. (Tony) Jones, the
designer of the
Constellation.

6,000rpm), to both the engine and the clutch.
The chassis was also beefed up, while the
development team saw fit to provide a dual
front brake.

In September 1955, a new higher
performance 700 was announced; known as
the Super Meteor, this was a considerably
modified version of the Meteor, which it
replaced. Development of the 692cc engine
had resulted in an increase of both power
and torque – with the added advantage of a
slight reduction of the engine speed at which
peak power was generated. The new unit put
out 40bhp at 5,500rpm. This gave the 700 Enfield a 100mph (161kph)
potential for the first time – thus opening the way to its use in sporting
events. To withstand the additional grunt the following changes had been
made: stiffened crankshaft; increased fining of the barrels and heads; valve
gear improvements; automatic advance and retard for the Lucas magneto
and a new frame.

In spring 1958 Royal Enfield introduced an even hotter bike, the
Constellation. This still used the same engine displacement, but with much
more power (51bhp at 6,250rpm). On the original Constellation there was
a single Amal TT9 racing carburettor of 1³⁄₁₆in (30mm), this was later
replaced by a pair of Monoblocs from the same source. Also, to provide
the additional zap, there were higher lift camshafts, 8:1 compression ratio
and siamesed exhaust system.

At the time of its arrival, the Constellation was the most powerful
British series production roadster in production. And it is little wonder that
examples were raced in the long-distance sports machine races of the day;
notably at Thruxton Airfield near Andover, Hampshire.

As related elsewhere, the team of Syd Lawton and rider Bob McIntyre
usually led the Thruxton 500 mile race, but for various reasons never won
it. Not because of any fault of the team or its riders, but quite simply the
Enfield 700 twin had too *much* power and was prone to self-destruction –
thanks largely to a combination of all this power and the effects of the
vibration this caused.

Geoffrey Brown taking
part in the 1962 Thruxton
500-mile endurance race
on his 692cc Constellation.

the Enfield had not been without problems, severe vibration causing a split fuel tank.

A name change

For the 1958 event, the name was changed to the Thruxton 500-Mile Race, and this coincided with new levels of interest from both spectators and the trade. Also a speed comparison with earlier years was of no use, because a new 2.275-mile lap (first used at the Easter meeting earlier that year) was in operation.

The machine Bob McIntyre rode in the 1958 500-Mile was Syd Lawton's Royal Enfield Super Meteor (now updated to Constellation specification), which had been ridden by Brian Newman and Derek Powell to third place the year before, Syd having nominated Derek Powell to partner the Scottish star.

From first to last the duel between the Royal Enfield mounted McIntyre/Powell pairing and Mike Hailwood/Dan Shorey (649cc Triumph Tiger 110 – but with two carburettors!) was, as *The Motor Cycle* commented, conducted 'almost as closely contested as a sprint'. If it had simply been a case of speed and riding ability, it is certain the Royal Enfield team would have come out on top. But the race was most certainly won in the pits and also upon reliability. This is how *The Motor Cycle* race report viewed what happened:

> *The Hailwood-Shorey Triumph made four stops for fuel and rider change. Stan Hailwood, Mike's father, controlled these stops to a split second. Petrol and oil went into their respective tanks simultaneously; at the same time brake adjustments were made and the fresh rider pulled the model back on compression. On average he was away within 25s of his partner's pulling in, discounting extra time spent in the pit changing a leaking fuel tank and tracking down a subsequent misfire, a change-over on the McIntyre/Powell Royal Enfield took two or three times as long. The two differences on four stops was more than the winner's advantage at the finish ... And though the Royal Enfield's troubles were of a trivial nature, the tank change stretched the second stop to 3m 15s and both sparking plugs and the magneto rotor arm were changed before the misfire was traced to swarf in the jet well – swarf, possibly, introduced into the fuel line when the tank was changed?*

As one commentator said: 'In his second and third stints McIntyre rode at his brilliant best and often pulled back 3 or 4 seconds a lap from Hailwood.'

But in the end these efforts were 'unavailing against the trouble-free Triumph pair and Stan Hailwood's masterly organisation' (*The Motor Cycle)*.

It is sad to say that, prior to the race, Stan Hailwood had tried to buy Bob McIntyre off. Bob's reply was quite simple: 'On your bike Mr Hailwood!'

Thruxton 500-Mile Race – 219 laps – 498.22 miles

1st	S.M.B. Hailwood/D. Shorey (649cc Triumph Tiger 110)	219 laps
2nd	R. McIntyre/D.T. Powell (692cc Royal Enfield Super Meteor)	219 laps
3rd	K.W. James/B. Newman (692cc Royal Enfield Super Meteor)	216 laps
4th	J.H. Lewis/P.B. James (595cc BMW R69)	215 laps
5th	P.H. Tait/D. Peacock (649cc Triumph Tiger 110)	212 laps
6th	H. German/C.A. Rowe (597cc Norton Dominator 99)	208 laps

Crashing out – again

The 1959 500-Miler saw a BMW R69 take a surprise victory. The initial leaders had been Bob and his Australian co-rider Eric Hinton on a Royal Enfield Constellation, entered by Lawton & Wilson of Southampton.

But this bid came to an end after first the primary chaincase shed its oil, the chain snapped and, after repairs which took 20 minutes, Bob subsequently spilled at Anchor Corner while attempting to make up lost time. The lead then went to one of the newly released Triumph Bonnevilles ridden by Tony Godfrey/Brian Holder, but seven minutes in their pits at the 350-mile stage to fix a loose dynamo cost them the race. And so the final victory went to the BMW, which was ridden by John Lewis and Bruce Daniels (entered by the London-based MLG concern).

The 1960 Thruxton marathon was run on Saturday 25 June. By now the event was a most closely-fought contest, with works machinery making its presence known via the leading dealers of the land. The successes of the machines concerned were publicised by the press and in the manufacturers' own brochures. A victory at Thruxton was now a major weapon for sales and would be even more important as sales declined over the next few years.

Once again Bob McIntyre 'fell under the irrational hammer of fate' (*The Motor Cycle)*, continuing:

> *The lion-hearted Scot is patently destined never to finish in a 500-miler.* [Actually not entirely true, as of course he was runner-up in 1958]. *The story is annually reported. Royal Enfield Constellation-mounted, Bob rushes round the tricky 2.275-mile lap as though making a study in space-flight technology. Then, inevitably, something happens.*

Syd Lawton (second from left) after winning the 500cc class of the international North West 200 race in Northern Ireland, May 1953. Also in the picture are Bob (350cc winner), Arthur Wheeler (250cc winner) and Irish Gilera works rider Reg Armstrong (far right).

Syd Lawton

Syd Lawton was born on 20 December 1913, in Tunstall, Stoke-on-Trent, Staffordshire, but moved to Colwyn Bay, North Wales, in 1925, where his parents subsequently ran a boarding house. He was the first son of an engine winder operating the lift cage to take miners to and from the coalface. His mother was a school teacher. At 17, Syd became a pharmaceutical apprentice and after five years he made a career change, joining the Prudential Assurance Company as a sales representative. However, neither of these careers appealed, so in 1937 he joined the Sheffield branch of the nationwide chain of motorcycle dealerships, Grays, as a salesman/mechanic. Proof of his aptitude came in a matter of weeks, when he was promoted to manager of the branch in Manchester. Then, in September 1938, Syd was moved to Southampton, where he stayed with Grays until the war broke out. Then, due to his mechanical knowledge, he was recruited into the aircraft industry as a fitter.

The end of the war did not signify an immediate return to the motorcycle industry, but eventually Syd managed to take up the threads of the game he loved. The Southampton branch of Grays had closed at the outbreak of war, so Syd became a salesman for a rival firm. At this time, Syd was a Rudge enthusiast and so when he heard of a job lot of spares for the marque going for sale, he snapped them up. Initially, it has to be said, these were for his own use, but the Rudge spares stock served as the nucleus of his own business, which slowly developed over the next few months, virtually as a hobby.

In 1947, having become restless at his official workplace, Syd took over a small garage in Freemantle, Southampton, in partnership with a friend, Pat Wilson. There, the two men initially concentrated on repair work, rather than sales.

The acquisition of their local Vincent agency in 1951 was, as Syd was later to recall, 'largely for Pat's benefit, he was a Vincent enthusiast, but I never really had much interest in them'. But two other aspects of Syd's life had by then become really important. One was racing. After witnessing his first Isle of Man TT in 1934 Syd had caught the racing bug, and even bought one of Harold Daniell's Nortons in 1939. His first race was in a scramble – on a 1928 Rudge with hand gear change. Syd first rode in the TT in 1948, gaining a silver replica in a Junior race on an AJS 7R loaned to him via Southampton dealers Jenkin and Purser. He made his Island debut the previous September in the Manx Grand Prix, but a split oil tank caused his retirement.

The other love of Syd's life was Beryl, whom he had married in Shirley, Southampton, on 9 April 1941. The couple had six children, the eldest, John, born in 1942. Then came Pamela, Barry, Sheila (sadly to die at only 34 in a car crash on 25 November 1986), Christine and finally the youngest, Ian, in 1958. Bob McIntyre was godfather to Ian Lawton, due to the friendship shared by Bob and Syd.

Syd joined up with Tommy Woods in 1952, the latter having been suspended for six months by the FIM, so Syd rode Tommy's bikes, including a very fast Moto Guzzi 250. Syd's performances that year were so good that he was signed by Joe Craig for the works Norton team. However, practicing for the 1953 TT, Syd crashed heavily at Creg-ny-Baa, breaking 37 bones. He spent five months in Noble's Hospital, not helped by gangrene setting in on his heel, bringing him close to death at one stage. And so, with his racing career at an end, he returned to Southampton, determined to throw everything into the business. 'Let's forget all that competition stuff, we'll just concentrate on bread and butter bikes from now on,' Syd told Pat Wilson. He agreed and the business went from strength to strength.

Eighteen months later they purchased an old malt-house for £6,000, a site which was to remain the Lawton and Wilson headquarters, even though expansion took place elsewhere.

After Vincent closed in 1955, Lawton and Wilson took on the Royal Enfield agency. Sporting involvement included the Rickman brothers riding Bullet 500 scramblers and participation with Royal Enfield Twins in the Thruxton 500-Mile race from 1957 onwards. Earlier, in 1955 and 1956, Syd had prepared Norton 88 Dominators for the Thruxton nine-hour race.

On the Enfields (from 1957 through to 1961) Bob McIntyre, Derek Powell and others had often led the race, only to strike trouble.

Then, in 1962, two important things happened to Syd. He changed from Royal Enfield to Norton for the 500-miler and promptly won with the newly released 650SS model ridden by Phil Read and Brian Setchell. The team then went on to a further two victories, making it three out of three between 1962 and 1964. Switching to Triumph for 1965, the success continued.

Also in 1962, Syd had purchased a new Aermacchi for son Barry to race. This was to lead to an involvement of over 30 years with the Italian marque. Later in 1962, he became southern distributor, and then in May 1963, after the sudden death of Bill Webster at Mallory Park in April, Syd bought the Aermacchi UK concession from his estate. And so on 27 May he reported: 'I have purchased the entire stock of spares and machines, both touring and racing. An agreement in principle, for my firm to be the official concessionaires, has been reached with the Italian factory and only

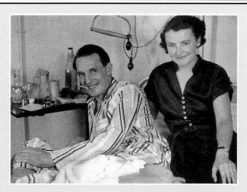

remains to be formally ratified. I shall be taking racing spares to the Island and shall be staying at the Douglas Bay Hotel.'

For the remainder of the 1960s Syd was deeply involved in sponsoring a long list of riders on Aermacchi machinery, including Dave Degens, Rex Butcher, Phil Read, John Hartle and Alan Barnett. Later, from the end of the 1970s, Syd was to re-enter racing via the classic movement with the likes of the late Richard Swallow to bring yet more successes during the 1980s. Then in the mid-1990s, Syd's health deteriorated, and he finally passed away on 17 January 1997, aged 85.

Syd recovering after the accident (his wife Beryl is also shown here) which ended his racing career, in the Isle of Man, June 1953. He fought back to become not only a leading dealer (Lawton and Wilson of Southampton), but also a top entrant and tuner and, later still, in the 1960s the British Aermacchi importer.

And of course 1960 was no exception! Bob had taken that first spell and, within one hour, had built up a lead of two laps (over five miles!). He then came in, to hand over to his co-rider Alan Rutherford, and soon afterwards the commanding lead had been transformed into a disappointing half-lap deficit. The cause? The silencer had broken and the exhaust system had to be wired up. At the end of Rutherford's spell Bob 'was at it again and proceeded to give a performance that held the crowd in a cyclone of excitement.'

Then the nipple pulled off the bottom end of the clutch cable and the Scot was forced to carry on with no clutch. Unfortunately, a few laps later and the rear wheel locked up (possibly caused by the offending nipple becoming jammed with the primary chain and its sprockets), and Bob was cast off at Club Corner. He was undamaged, but the Royal Enfield's racing for that day was over.

Eventually, after many other incidents, Ron Langston and Don Chapman emerged as the winners on a 646cc AJS CSR Sports Twin, entered by Monty & Ward. They completed 220 laps, averaging 68.48mph.

Bob and Alastair get back together

On Saturday 8 July 1961, Bob got back together with Alastair King to share the riding duties at Thruxton. Once again there was an oversubscribed entry. As Vic Willoughby wrote in *The Motor Cycle* race report:

> A mixed bunch of pure talent in top-liners such as Bob McIntyre, Alastair King, John Hartle and Phil Read; lesser stars of every

Bob about to leave his pit during the 1960 Thruxton event. He was later to crash, trying to make up time lost to mechanical problems.

magnitude; unsung but dyed-in-the-wool privateers; and even ex world champions unable to resist the call of the track.

There were even men such as trials expert Sammy Miller and Tommy Price, the former Speedway World Champion.

Vic Willoughby also commented:

One rider, though, has cause and more to raise a cynical eyebrow at my mention of fun, he's Bob McIntyre, potential winner with his bosom pal Alastair King but year after year marked down by fate for her cruellest blow. In driving rain on Saturday, Alastair took the first spell and had their 692cc Royal Enfield Constellation in the lead when he handed over. On a drying track Mac settled down to reeling off the slickest laps of the day – until one of the connecting rods poked its way through the crankcase and pitched him off at 110mph. Fortunately, Mac's torso is as tough as Scottish granite.

With the McIntyre/King partnership on the sidelines, leadership of the race was taken over by Tony Godfrey and John Holder (entered by Alec Bennett). They completed the race and won, the precise statistics being 220 laps at an average speed of 67.29mph.

1961 was also the first year that two long-distance events were held in Britain, as the BMCRC (British Motor Cycle Racing Club) also ran the rival 1000 Kilometres at Silverstone in May that year. However, neither Bob McIntyre nor Alastair King rode in that event.

The 1961 Thruxton outing was the last Bob undertook on a production-based machine. Generally, it had been a most unrewarding experience. The only really bright spot was the friendship that had grown over the years with his entrant for these events – Southampton dealer Syd Lawton (see separate boxed section within this chapter).

In his 1962 book *Motor Cycling Today*, Bob's problems on production-based machinery show in his advice to would-be novices to road racing:

One may decide to confine oneself to Clubman's races where a wide range of less highly-developed machines are used. Personally, I am not very keen on Clubman's events. The machines are comparatively cheap; the racing helps manufacturers develop touring machines. But I do not think it is a good thing to race motorcycles not designed for racing... A professional racer would break a Clubman's machine; they are just not designed to race the way we race. So I think it better to try to procure machines designed for racing rather than compromise machines.

And of course he was speaking from his own personal experience!

Chapter 8

Bianchi

THERE was no hint of what was to come when *Motor Cycle News* spoke to Bob in mid-January 1961, with him commenting: 'Gilera will definitely not be racing in 1961.' He went on to say that he hoped 'to get over to Italy for a purely friendly visit to Gilera's sometime soon,' although no definite arrangements had been made.

When asked by *MCN* journalist Mick Woollett if he had heard from any of the works teams yet, Bob replied: 'Not a word – it seems they're not interested in me so it looks as though I'll be riding AJS and Norton unless someone comes up with a better offer.'

Regarding rumours that had been circulating during the closed season that he intended to cut down his racing programme in the coming year, Bob said: 'I'll be doing the races that suit me but you must remember that it's a round trip of eight hundred miles from Glasgow to southern circuits and it's a very expensive business,' but he added that he would be 'a regular visitor to Mallory Park'.

And as for another story which had its origins in the Border Motor Racing Club's journal, Bob was *not* taking an interest in car racing. The rumour had begun when he was seen at Oulton Park when a car was being tested, but he was at the Cheshire circuit trying a bike out.

A Bianchi offer?

A mere seven days after the *Motor Cycle News* story, the same newspaper splashed the following headline across their issue dated 25 January 1961: 'Works Bianchi Offer to Bob McIntyre'. The story went on to say: '*MCN*'s Italian correspondent, Carlo Perelli, reports that Bianchi have invited Bob McIntyre to join their works team for the 1961 season.'

When *MCN* tried to contact Bob by telephone just before going to press, to find out whether he had received the Bianchi invitation or not, it was discovered that Bob had left Glasgow for the Continent with Shell and BP competitions manager Lew Ellis for the Monte Carlo Rally. As *MCN* went on

Bianchi dohc twins

Although Bob McIntyre only rode the Bianchi three-fifty twin, this had been developed from the earlier two-fifty, the latter being announced on 31 March 1960, when the Milanese company held a dinner for members of the press. It was here that something of a bombshell was dropped, when the compère announced 'a major push for Grand Prix honours.' This was to be made with a works team mounted on a brand-new 249.45cc double overhead camshaft vertical twin, which the spokesman claimed produced 34bhp at 11,500rpm.

The new machine, designed by Ing. Lino Tonti (formally of Aermacchi, Benelli and FB Mondial) and constructed over the preceding months, comprised an impressive looking engine built in unit with a six-speed gearbox and mounted in a 9kg (20lb) welded duplex frame. The latter featured extensive triangulation.

Supported in two ball and two roller bearings, the built-up crankshaft assembly included four flywheel discs. Between the inner pair was a pinion, from which both transmission and valve gear were driven. The pinion meshed with a gear on an intermediate shaft, at the nearside end of which was another gear driving the exposed dry clutch; the final drive being taken from the offside of the unit. A train of gears, housed in an upward extension of the crankcase between the cylinders, transferred the drive from the intermediate gear to the inlet camshaft, while a further train led forward from there to the exhaust camshaft.

Electron alloy was employed for the cam boxes, clutch housing and integral 2.25-litre (½ gallon) sump; the vertically-split crankcases, cylinder barrels and heads were in aluminium alloy. Each head featured dual 12mm spark plugs, which fired simultaneously courtesy of a pair of Bosch six-volt, double-ended coils, which were mounted just aft of the steering head.

There was a total of four contact-breakers, which were driven by the offside end of the crankshaft. With a bore and stroke of 55x52.5mm, the engine was slightly oversquare. Twin 27mm Dell'Orto carburettors employed separate float chambers. Two oil pumps were used; one fed the crankshaft beatings, the other the valve gear.

There was a strong family resemblance between the frame and that of the successful motocross models. However, some of the triangulated tubes on the racer were smaller in diameter, while there was an additional, oval-sectioned tube crossing the top of the steering head to a crossmember at the seat nose.

Equipped with a quick-release cap and twin large-bore taps, the 14-

Designed by Lino Tonti, the first dohc twin-cylinder Bianchi was the 250cc, which debuted in spring 1960 and was subsequently developed into a 348.4cc (65x52.5mm) version, as raced by Bob McIntyre in 1961.

litre (3 gallon) fuel tank was a superbly-crafted affair in aluminium alloy. The Bianchi motif was proudly displayed on its sides.

The front forks were specially commissioned and were interesting in two respects. Firstly, the top and bottom yokes were made of light alloy; secondly, the wheel spindle was mounted in lugs extending forwards from the sliders (this arrangement permitted straighter, stiffer yokes). Both front and rear suspension assemblies were manufactured for Bianchi by the Ceriani company.

Other details included 18in wheels, Oldani 2LS full-width drum brakes, with a diameter of 200mm, and a purpose-built aluminium dolphin fairing, which had several bonded-rubber attachments riveted in place. Dry weight was 127kg (280lb).

Riders signed to race the Bianchi 250 twin were Derek Minter, Osvaldo Perfetti and Gianfranco Muscio. Much was expected, but due to a series of mechanical failures, which centred around the caged-roller big-end bearings and gearbox, finishes, let alone results, were at a premium. However, this did not prevent Tonti from proceeding apace with development. And by the time the Italian Grand Prix took place at Monza in September 1960, a 348.42cc (65x52.5mm) version made its debut. Ridden by Muscio and Ernesto Brambilla, the larger Bianchi twins really harried the four-cylinder MVs in the early laps, before engine vibration put paid to Brambilla's chances, while a broken oil pipe sidelined Muscio.

As related in the main text, Bob McIntyre visited Bianchi in January 1961 and after testing the 350 was interested enough to return to Italy in March for a longer, more serious test session at Monza, after which the Scot signed on the dotted line to race the Bianchi in the upcoming season. As explained elsewhere, Bob had both success and disappointment in equal measure in his Bianchi rides. But while the bike kept going he was usually right up there with the leaders,

Later, after Bob had left the team, not only did reliability improve, but the engine was progressively enlarged (starting with a displacement of 386cc in late 1961, until it was finally up to 498cc some two years later).

Whereas the 350 as ridden by Bob McIntyre put out almost 50bhp, the ultimate 500 of 1964 was producing over 70bhp and by now featured a much stronger gearbox – plus uprated brakes, improved frame and central-axle front forks.

It is worth noting that the Italian veteran Remo Venturi won both the 350 and 500cc Italian Senior Road Racing Championship titles in 1964, after which official factory interest at Bianchi ceased, although Silvio Grassetti rode as a privateer on the machines in 1965.

Besides its small diameter tubing the Bianchi 250/350 twin also featured an oval section brace from the top of the steering head down to the centre section of the frame.

to say: 'It's a short step from Monaco to Italy and it seems highly likely that Bob and Lew will slip across the border to Italy after the Monte Carlo Rally is over.'

Bob had made no secret of the fact that now his Gilera contract had finally expired he was very keen to join a works team. His only proviso was that the factory team he joined must have bikes which would give him a reasonable chance of success in the World Championships and that he would prefer to ride in the bigger classes, due to his weight.

After travelling to Italy with his friend Lew Ellis (the competition manager for Shell and BP) towards the end of January 1961, Bob eventually signed for the Bianchi factory in March that year – to ride the 350 dohc twin in the world championship.

As *MCN* reported: 'The works Bianchis would seem to fill the bill admirably.' At Monza in September 1960 an example ridden by Ernesto Brambilla showed more than a fair turn of speed and was as quick, if not quicker, than the MV fours of John Surtees and Gary Hocking – until the filler cap on Brambilla's machine popped open, drenching the unfortunate Italian in fuel and forcing him to make a pit stop which effectively put him out of the running.

MCN finished by saying: 'The combination of Bob McIntyre and works Bianchis would put back into international road racing much of the glamour lost by the retirement of MV and John Surtees.' Not only had John Surtees quit two wheels for four at the end of 1960, but Count Domenico Agusta had also announced that MV Agusta were quitting. However, this latter part of the story was to prove incorrect as MV Agusta did field works bikes in 1961. Riders such as Gary Hocking were entered under the 'Private MV' banner… but they were still works bikes with the same back-up and team of mechanics as before.

Although Bob had not ridden factory bikes since 1957 there is little doubt that deep down he still dreamed of doing just that. Mick Woollett also revealed: 'When I rang him before the reported Bianchi offer regarding a works ride Bob replied: "Well there's a remote possibility that I might… you never know. I'll have to find out exactly what MV are up to before I make up my mind… the thought of winning a World Championship is very interesting".'

Back in Glasgow

In their 1 February 1961 issue *Motor Cycle News* were able to report: 'Bianchi impresses Mac.' He then admitted that he had visited Italy at the

Bianchi

Founded by Eduardo Bianchi in Milan, during 1885, the company which bore his name was destined to become the very first to manufacture motorcycles in Italy. Versatility was its keynote in those early days; first came surgical instruments, then bicycles, trikes and finally, in 1897, motorcycles.

However, it was not until 1920 that the Milanese company began to take a serious interest in speed events. It was in that year that Carlo Maffeis, riding a 500cc ohv V-twin Bianchi, established a new flying kilometre world record at 77.6mph, on a stretch of road near Gallarate (later the home of the legendary MV Agusta marque). Even then, it was not a full works effort, as the engine had been prepared by Carlo and his brothers, Miro and Nando, who later marketed their own Maffeis machine powered by British JAP or Blackburne engines. Riding his record-breaking Bianchi V-twin in the following year's Brescia road race, Carlo Maffeis crashed heavily and died of his injuries.

The Bianchi factory team at the 1928 Italian Grand Prix held at Monza. Left to right: Tazio Nuvolari, Zanchetta and Amilcare Moretti.

Following this tragedy, Bianchi took no further part in racing until 1925, when it became necessary to counter the challenge being made to its sales by the likes of Moto Guzzi and Garelli. Both companies were winning races and thus gaining valuable publicity, which, of course, was being denied by Bianchi. Initially, Bianchi chose to dispute the 350cc class which, in Italy, was dominated by the all-conquering Garelli split-single two-stroke.

The new machine was designed by Ing. Mario Baldi and incorporated several innovative features. Featuring double overhead camshafts, the Bianchi displaced 348cc (74x81mm). A rarity in those days was that the camshaft and valve springs were enclosed in an oil-tight compartment.

Named the *Frecia Celeste*, this machine proved both fast and reliable and was ridden to many victories by the likes of Achille Varzi and the great

Tazio Nuvolari. But by the end of 1930, the *Frecia Celeste* had had its day. After its run of success, Bianchi had no desire to quit racing, so Baldi went back to his drawing office and, in 1932, a new 500cc dohc single made its bow. The larger machine was not as successful as its smaller brother, even though it won the 1933 Milano-Napoli and 1934 Lario races. However, in full GP events it was not fast enough against the latest Norton singles or Moto Guzzi's new V-twin.

Against this background, Bianchi instructed Ing. Baldi to design a brand-new multi-cylinder machine. The result was the breathtaking, supercharged 492.7cc four, which first

appeared towards the end of 1939. Developing around 75bhp at 9,000rpm, this machine would have been a true competitor to the Gilera fours and BMW twins which had dominated international racing in the months leading up to the outbreak of war in September 1939.

Sadly it was not to be, and by the end of the conflict in 1945 Baldi was dead and the FIM banned supercharging.

During the late 1940s and early 1950s Bianchi concentrated its efforts purely on series production roadsters. However, by the mid-1950s the factory was back in the sport, with several successes in the Milano-Taranto, the *Giro d'Italia* (Tour of Italy) and the Italian Moto Cross Championship title in 1958, 1959 and 1960. In addition, during November 1957 Bianchi had gained considerable publicity, breaking a number of speed records at Monza, with a fully streamlined machine derived from the production 175 ohc Tonale.

In mid-1958 Ing. Lino Tonti became head of the Bianchi racing and development department. He was responsible for the Moto Cross bikes and for a return to Grand Prix type road racing events. At first the road racers employed 174 and 248cc single-cylinder engines based on the dirt bike power units.

Then, in March 1960, came news of a brand new dohc two-fifty twin. This design, also the work of Ing. Tonti, was to be developed into a three-fifty; which was to be ridden in the 1961 World Championship series by Bob McIntyre.

Bianchi ceased motorcycle production during the mid-1960s but continued both as a pedal cycle manufacturer and building cars. Today the famous name survives as a major cycle producer, building both roadster and racing models. But Bianchi's days of being a major motorcycle marque are long over.

Born in July 1865, Eduardo Bianchi was brought up in a Milan orphanage, but his engineering genius saw him build up one of Italy's largest industrial empires.

The designer of the 350 Bianchi twin, Lino Tonti (right), with motocross star Emilio Ostorero at the Bianchi factory in late 1960.

invitation of the Bianchi factory to test ride their works machines. Speaking to Mick Woollett Bob said: 'I rode the 350cc twin and it was very good... I was very impressed, it's certainly faster than any British 350 but like anything Italian it's rather temperamental.'

The tests took place at the Modena Autodrome near Bologna as there were icy patches on the Monza circuit. Bob went on to explain:

I want to make it clear that I've not made any definite plans. I haven't signed anything. I only tried the 350cc Bianchi (the company also have 250cc twins, plus an overbored experimental model which might be raced in the 500cc class) out and until I've been out to Italy again and had a talk with the Gilera people I don't know what my plans for 1961 will be but I will certainly be trying the Bianchi again.

Asked for his impressions of the machine Bob replied: 'Well, it had plenty of speed although it was temperamental. The steering was reasonable and the gearboxes – five and six-speed – were good... I never missed a gear in all the laps I did at Modena.' He summed up the works Bianchis: 'They appear to have the makings of a good racing motorcycle... they need a general clean up but it wouldn't take a lot to make them really raceworthy.' The Bianchi factory staff from directors to mechanics made a 'very favourable' impression on Bob during his visit, in particular Lino Tonti, the engineer responsible for the design and development of the new twin cylinder dohc Bianchi racers.

Following the Modena test session, Bob advised the factory technicians on how he considered the machines could be improved. *MCN* went on to say: 'If the Italians follow his advice and if Gilera have no surprise plans in mind then it very much looks as though Bob will be Bianchi mounted in the 350cc class of the World Championships, but he said they mentioned nothing about a 500cc mount.' Bob finished by saying: 'That's the full story – now you know as much as I do!'

In the 22 February 1961 issue of *Motor Cycle News* it was reported that Bob still had no definite date to go to Italy to test the Bianchis for the second time. From what Bob said it seemed just about certain that he would ride the Bianchi in the 350cc World Championship series – provided they had made the changes Bob recommended on his earlier visit.

It also seemed that at long last he had finally given up all hope of a Gilera return – one which, in effect, had put his world title hopes on hold for the last 3½ years since Gilera had quit at the end of the 1957 season.

If he was to sign for Bianchi, Bob would still ride his own bikes in British events. He said: 'I've no intention of tying myself down to one make and they'll

The 348.4cc Bianchi dohc twin made its debut at the Italian GP at Monza in September 1960. Features included a six-speed gearbox, hairpin valve springs, roller bearing big ends and a dry multi-plate clutch.

have to accept me on those terms if they want me to ride for them in the big races.'

It also transpired that a new frame of revolutionary design was being constructed at Joe Potts's Glasgow emporium to house the 350cc AJS 7R engine, and, if it proved successful, a similar frame was to be made for a 500cc Norton engine. Later still, as covered in a separate boxed section within this chapter, this was to be fitted with a Matchless G50 engine and raced successfully by the Australian Jack Findlay during the late 1960s.

In the 16 February 1961 issue of *The Motor Cycle* there was a three-page feature on Bob's latest plans entitled 'The Tartan Banner Unfurls!' Written by George Wilson, this began by saying:

> *That three-fifty Bianchi or no, Bob McIntyre goes classic (World Series) racing this year. Since the Agusta withdrawal last month, one vast question mark has hung suspended over the name of that tough, dour, dynamic veteran from north of the border. Would Bob, now that the impregnable Italian fortress had crumbled, again be tempted to leave his eyrie in the northern slopes of Glasgow for the great European classic road-race circuits? The answer is yes!*

George Wilson then set the question: 'Who, did you ask, is Bob McIntyre anyway?' he went on to list Bob's main achievements:

> *He was the first to lap the Isle of Man Mountain course at over 100mph; winner on a Gilera of the Senior and Junior TT races in 1957 when that momentous 100mph plus lap was achieved; he hoisted the world's hour record to over 141mph in November that year – with a three-fifty! He is the man who split the Surtees-Hartle (MV) duo in the 1958 Senior before the Norton's camshaft bevels decided they'd had enough; he is the man who, that same year, lay second to Surtees for the opening lap of the Junior TT in spite of the handicap of periodic piston grabbing. In the Junior 12 months later Bob kept the MVs apart until vibration put him out, and in that never-to-be-forgotten gale-lashed Senior he finished 12½m down on Surtees after he had lost 12½m trying to get his clutch to free. Last year the Scot rode his AJS into third berth in the Junior behind the MVs and was set to repeat the performance in the Senior until the sparks gave out. That's who Bob Mac is. And news that he is to contest the World Championships is in itself enough to cast a vast effervescent bombshell into this year's series.*

Bob, together with his mentor Joe Potts, flew to Italy on Friday 3 March, the object being to visit the Bianchi factory and to test ride the 350cc dohc twin GP bike. Whether the Scot signed to race the Italian bike would depend upon these talks and tests.

Signing the Bianchi contract

Motor Cycle News, dated 15 March 1961, carried a front-page story with the headline: 'Mac Signs Bianchi Contract'. It went on to say:

> *Bob McIntyre has signed to ride works Bianchi machines in the 350cc class of this year's World Championship road races. This news – which will do a great deal to create new interest in the TT and the other 'classic' grands prix which stage a 350cc class – followed Bob's second visit to test ride the Bianchi at Monza.*

As reported in *MCN* the previous week, Bob was accompanied by Joe Potts and the try-out was held at Monza on Tuesday 7 March. It didn't take Bob long to make up his mind, for that same evening he and Joe Potts flew home after signing the official contract.

On Friday 10 March, Mick Woollett (*MCN*'s racing correspondent) tracked Bob down to the Mallory Park circuit where he was getting into shape for the forthcoming season, practising on a standard Norton. Bob confirmed to Mick that his contract with Bianchi was for the 350cc class only. It set out that he would ride the Italian bike in six World Championship events – German GP, Isle of Man TT, Dutch TT, Ulster GP, Italian GP and Swedish GP – plus one other event. This 'other' event would, in fact, be the international pre-season meeting to be held at Imola on Sunday 16 April, which would serve as a 'warming up' exercise for the world championship rounds.

Under the terms of the contract Bob was to be allowed to ride what he liked, when he was not required by Bianchi for the events named in the contract. This meant that home fans would still be seeing a lot of their idol riding Joe Potts machinery, beginning with the Oulton Park international on Easter Monday, 3 April.

Asked if readers could expect to see him riding the Bianchi in British short circuit events Bob replied: 'I'm not interested in riding the Bianchi in England. I don't believe in bringing foreign works bikes to race against the lads on AJS, Matchless and Norton machines.'

Bob also went on to reveal that he would be supported by Ernesto Brambilla, who rode the Bianchi in 1960. As far as he knew there would be just two of them – no mention having been made at the factory of a third rider

– and due to the relatively small size of the Bianchi racing department and staff Bob thought it unlikely that the team would be enlarged.

Commenting on the machine he rode at Monza Bob said: 'It went very well indeed. It's a good engine, the bike steers well and the brakes are quite good. In fact it could be raced as it is but the factory intend to clean it up still further before the season starts.' The modifications were to include a switch to magneto ignition – in place of the existing coil arrangement – and suspension changes to improve the handling on rough surfaces.

Problems at Oulton Park

Bob, as planned, made his 1961 racing debut at Oulton Park on Easter Monday, 3 April. However, it certainly wasn't the debut he had hoped for. In the 19-lap 500cc race he eventually retired after dropping back down the field on his Potts Norton. Then came news that he would be a non-starter for the 350cc event. The reason? His AJS 7R had been 'lost' by British Railways somewhere between Glasgow and Chester!

Only five days later Bob was back in action at the international Silverstone meeting. His best position was runner-up to John Hartle (Norton) in the 500cc event. Earlier in the 350cc race Bob could manage no higher than fifth – but at least his AJS had been 'found' safely.

The following day, 9 April, Bob was beaten into second place in the 350cc final at Mallory Park by the up-and-coming Phil Read (Norton), while on his Norton he was third, behind Mike Hailwood and Dickie Dale (also both Norton-mounted) in the 500cc final.

The racing at all three meetings so far held had been 'keener than ever with results being decided by inches rather than yards' (*The Motor Cycle)*. The same journal also commented:

> *The surprising thing is that most of the winning machines outwardly appear quite standard. Even Bob McIntyre, who used a brace of very successful Specials last year, appeared at the Hutchinson 100 meeting on Saturday with two fairly ordinary-looking models – a 7R AJS and a five-hundred Manx Norton.*

However, in typical McIntyre fashion, there were subtle changes. For example, on the five-hundred there was an oil supply by external pipes to the cam spindles 'to provide cooler oil where it is needed.' Bob's new lightweight framed 7R had not yet been used.

Explosive news broke from Dublin on Monday evening 11 April – Bob McIntyre was to ride a two-fifty Honda four entered by 1952 Senior TT

Welcome
To
Mallory Park
Meeting organised by

THE LEICESTER QUERY
M C
?

In conjunction with
EAST MIDLAND CENTRE AUTO CYCLE UNION

winner Reg Armstrong of Dublin, in world championship events. The full story of Bob's Honda involvement is charted in Chapter 9, but suffice it to say this was big news indeed. And with a Honda four in the 250cc class, the Bianchi three-fifty and Joe Potts five-hundred Norton, it looked as if the brilliant Scot was to have a grand but varied time. As *The Motor Cycle* said: 'Stand clear of the sparks!'

Hocking and MV

As *Motor Cycle News* dated 19 April 1961 reported, there was 'A bombshell from Imola!'. Everyone – including Bob Mac – had expected MV to not be present in any capacity during 1961, but Gary Hocking rode one of the works four-cylinder models to victory at the international Gold Cup meeting at Imola on Sunday 16 April. And to add to Bob's problems all three 350cc Bianchi twins entered (they raced in the 500cc event, as there was no 350cc class) went out of the race, all suffering from mechanical failures. It was later revealed that the bike Bob rode at Imola actually displaced 386cc.

The first round of the World Championship series took place the following weekend in Spain. However, Bob was not there – as there was no 350cc class and it had been decided not to race the Honda four at Barcelona by Reg Armstrong – even though the official Honda team was represented.

Breaking records in Ulster

After an indifferent start to the season, everything came together for Bob in early May, when he not only scored a double 350/500cc victory but also set a new outright lap record during the 500cc race in the North West 200 meeting. As Billy McMaster reported for *Motor Cycle News*: 'The Port Stewart circuit enjoyed real summer weather, for both practices and racing, and quickly recovered from such rain as did fall during the non-racing periods and, more important still, that racing was the best ever seen and was also the fastest ever seen in Britain.'

The *MCN* report continued: 'During the practice period on the Thursday evening, Bob McIntyre had pointed to what lay ahead. On his AJS he had touched the fringe of 100mph and lapping on his 500 Norton he had indicated that his own 1959 lap record of 102.56mph had not much longer to stand.'

The first race, on Saturday 6 May, was the 350cc. Bob Mac opened by leading the 37 starters round the opening lap at an average speed of 98.02mph – just one second outside the 1959 class record set by

In May 1961 Bob scored brilliant double victories at the Irish North West 200. He is seen here with the Potts 499cc Norton, setting a new lap record of 106.89mph (172kph).

Alastair King. Behind him, Fred Neville (AJS) was riding superbly, with Alastair King and Derek Minter (both riding Nortons) locked in a wheel-to-wheel battle.

Then Bob carved his own little place in the history books, when he sent the lap record tumbling with a round of 101.06mph. It was at this point that a new name came onto the leaderboard in the shape of Phil Read. And although Bob went on to win quite comfortably, Read stormed through to finish runner-up and also raise the lap record to 101.78mph.

Read also finished runner-up to Bob in the 500cc race. But what a race Bob rode that day. Of the 34 starters, he was to suffer an awful start. 'Poor McIntyre pushed desperately at a sluggish Norton and, before it fired, was hemmed in by the pack.' He was down in around 20th place as the pack of riders shot down towards Port Stewart promenade. *MCN* takes up the story again:

> *Those who watched the race from the Drumslade straight, leading to Coleraine, watched in awe as the Scot thundered the Norton through the weaving pack, mopping-up the leaders one by one until, at Millburn, he was into the place he had always hoped he would be in – the lead.*

But that was only the start, for on the second lap Bob was, in McMaster's words, 'fantastic', electrifying the spectators by cutting an incredible *13 seconds* off the old lap record and recorded a lap at no less than a pulsating 106.12mph. But not content with this, he later upped it to 106.86mph.

500cc North West 200 – 9 laps – 100 miles

1st	R. McIntyre (Norton)
2nd	P. Read (Norton)
3rd	F. Neville (Matchless)
4th	A. King (Norton)
5th	E. Boyce (Norton)
6th	P.D. Chatterton (Norton)

After the North West, Bob left for Germany to ride in the German GP. He didn't take any machines with him so he would not be contesting the 500cc class on the Joe Potts Norton which had proved so phenomenally fast in the North West 200. The plan was to race a works Bianchi in the 350cc (and a Honda four in the 250cc race – if one of the latter was available for him).

The 1961 German GP was held on Sunday 14 May over the super-fast

four-mile Hockenheim circuit, near the ancient university town of Heidelberg. Although there was no Honda available, Bob did ride the Bianchi in the 350cc race.

Fastest lap in practice had been put up by the Czech Frantisek Stastny (Jawa), ahead of teammate Gustav Havel, then came Bob and his Bianchi partner Ernesto Brambilla.

In the race, Stastny and Bob fought a tight battle out at the front of the field. And as *Motor Cycle News* reported: 'While it went Bob McIntyre's Bianchi proved fast.' Unfortunately, neither of the two Bianchis kept going – both being sidelined by piston failure.

Scottish interlude

Between the German GP and the Isle of Man TT came a Scottish interlude. Bob returned to his roots, racing at Beveridge Park, Kirkcaldy, on Saturday 20 May and Charterhall, Berwickshire, the following day.

At Beveridge Park he clashed with Alastair King – the pair sharing the spoils in the larger classes, Bob taking the 350cc race on his AJS, Alastair the

Beveridge Park, Saturday 20 May 1961 – Bob's pair of immaculate 'standard' Nortons. It was common for him to use 'specials' for the big races, and new standard bikes for lesser events. The new bikes would then be developed for the next season, whereas the specials would be sold off at the end of the season.

500cc on a Norton. Bob also made a debut on an Aermacchi (loaned by Syd Lawton) in the 250cc class, but after winning his heat suffered mechanical problems in the final and was forced to retire on the Italian ohv horizontal single.

At Charterhall it was a McIntyre double. *Motor Cycle News* reported:

Five hours of fast, exciting racing at Charterhall on Sunday gave Scottish enthusiasts something to talk about as they left the Berwickshire circuit, having seen over 300 riders from all parts of Great Britain taking part in the scrapping. Bob McIntyre, in sparkling form, ran away with the 350cc and 500cc Allcomers races but broke the race-record average speed in both events despite the fact that in the heats and finals he was never headed.

The TT

Next came the Isle of Man TT. Bianchi had promised Bob no fewer than three machines for TT practice. From them he would be able to select his race mount. The Italian company were also reported as sending another two bikes for Alastair King (who was a late entry on one of the Bianchis for the Junior TT). Bob was also to have his first outing since Aintree the previous year on a Honda four in the 250cc Lightweight event, but this is covered in Chapter 9.

Bianchi was late in getting the bikes over to the Isle of Man and when they did finally arrive not only had Bob missed several practice sessions, but in the remainder he had very little luck and failed to get on the final leader board for the 350cc class (in contrast to the 250cc where he was the fastest – on the Honda).

Working on the Syd Lawton Aermacchi two-fifty at Beveridge Park. After winning his heat Bob suffered mechanical problems in the final and was forced to retire the Italian horizontal single.

As for the race, Bob and Alastair were early retirements, both with broken gearbox layshafts – neither completing a single lap! But early in the proceedings Bob had led the race for the first part of the lap before his gearbox gremlins. So the whole Bianchi episode to date had proved a huge disaster. The potential was not matched by any form of reliability.

In the other two races he was entered in Bob showed up much, much better. First in the Lightweight (250cc) he had led for almost the entire

distance on the Honda, only to retire near the end – and set a new class record lap at an amazing 99.58mph – nearly 100mph on a two-fifty!

1961 is remembered as the year in which Mike Hailwood set a new record by winning three TTs in a week. But although Bob would have beaten the young Oxford rider had his Honda not expired in the Lightweight event, Mike took a deserved victory in the Senior race, which ended the TT proceedings on Friday 16 June. However, Bob was good enough to beat everyone else that day on his Potts Norton. The Norton with which the Australian Tom Phillis finished in third position was an experimental works Norton with a tuned Dominator ohv twin-cylinder engine. The lone MV Agusta of Gary Hocking retired on the fourth lap. Bob's average speed for the race was 99.20mph, Hailwood's 100.60mph.

500cc Senior TT – 6 laps – 226.4 miles
1st   S.M.B. Hailwood (Norton)
2nd   R. McIntyre (Norton)
3rd   T. Phillis (Norton twin)
4th   A. King (Norton)
5th   R.J. Langston (Matchless)
6th   T. Godfrey (Norton)

Screaming the Bianchi twin past the pits during practice for the 1961 Junior TT, but again retirement beckoned, this time with a broken gearbox layshaft on the first lap of the race. His Honda four also broke after he had lapped at almost 100mph in the 250cc race.

There was much better news in the Senior (500cc) race when he took his Norton to runner-up position, behind race winner Mike Hailwood. Here Bob takes to the air over Ballaugh Bridge on his Norton.

The first three finishers in the 1961 Senior TT. Left to right: Tom Phillis (third), a Norton mechanic, Doug Hele (Norton designer), Pamela Lawton, Mike Hailwood, Stan Hailwood (with white coat), Rem Fowler (winner of the 1907 Twin Cylinder TT), Reg Armstrong, Pim Fleming (in white overalls), Lew Ellis and Bob McIntyre.

Bob negotiates Parliament Square, Ramsey, on his way to second in the 1961 Senior TT with his Potts Norton.

McIntyre's Mallory

After a disappointing week in the Isle of Man, Bob's luck returned at the Post-TT meeting at Mallory Park on Sunday 18 June, where in perfect conditions of summer sunshine, he, 'well and truly beat TT winners Mike Hailwood and Phil Read to win both the 350 and 500cc finals, riding AJS and Norton machines.' The *MCN* report continued: 'Hailwood in fact didn't win a race –

The McIntyre Specials

The first of the McIntyre Specials using either 350 or 500cc AMC or Norton engines was built in the winter of 1957/58. Bob had returned to his mentor Joe Potts in Bellshill, Glasgow, after Gilera quit racing at the end of 1957.

The original frame made its debut at Oulton Park on 7 April 1958 (with a Norton engine). It was very light, with a single front down-tube. However, it was not a success and was soon dropped. The next idea came from a late evening session in the Potts workshop, where together with Alex Crummie and Pim Fleming, a frame was conceived which actually enclosed the engine unit. However, this made engine removal/replacement difficult, hence modified versions were to appear over the next few years.

Talking in the spring of 1960, Bob had this to say: 'there were two reasons why we built these two machines [by then there were models powered by AJS 7R and Manx Norton engines – the 350 and 500cc classes respectively]. The first had been to decrease vibration and the second was to have two identical sets of frames and their component parts'. He went on: 'I dislike swapping from one type of frame to another.' Bob went on to reveal that weight was the last consideration and that the models were 'built to handle.' In fact, the weight was certainly no lower than the respective production 7R and Manx. Bob even thought they might have been 'a shade heavier'.

Bob McIntyre pictured in February 1962 with the lightweight Matchless G50-engined special. The other man in the photograph is frame builder Alex Crummie.

Bob continued: 'we took what we felt were the best engines in the two classes – a 350cc 7R and 500cc Manx'. The frames were built in Joe Potts's workshop, the front section of the frame being similar to the Manx Norton (the first prototype was actually a section removed from a Norton frame) while the rear differed quite considerably. Front forks were Norton

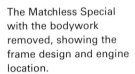

The Matchless Special with the bodywork removed, showing the frame design and engine location.

Roadholder (genuine Manx components), while the front hubs were Gilera with 2LS operation (of the same type used by Bob in 1957). The fuel and oil tanks were of aluminium construction, the latter being mounted in the orthodox position, but were slab-sided and mounted to give the maximum space for the carburettor intake. There was also a large aluminium shield at the front and side of the carb.

A five-speed gearbox, one of a small batch manufactured by Harold Daniell, was fitted to the 7R-engined machine, whereas the 500cc Manx Norton bike relied on the standard AMC four-speeder. The rear swinging arm and rear brake hub assemblies were both 7R components. Much of the original testing, including actual racing with the original prototype chassis, was undertaken in Scotland at venues such as Charterhall and Beveridge Park, Kirkcaldy, during 1959.

Development of the McIntyre specials continued throughout much of 1960, and by early 1961 *The Motor Cycle* was able to publish a comprehensive feature about Bob McIntyre's hopes for the coming season. The headlines read 'The tartan banner unfurls!' and the article went on:

> *Bob McIntyre, most formidable racing man of the present day, decides to contest the World's Championships. It seems probable that Bob will be riding a works Bianchi 350cc twin in the world championships. But even if this doesn't occur he has another string to his bow, in the shape of a new lightweight 7R special. So if the Bianchi comes to nought then Bob can still take part using the 7R (and a five-hundred Manx Norton).*

By the end of 1961 priorities had changed somewhat 'to reduce weight and provide greater rigidity' as Bob said when interviewed by *The Motor Cycle.*

The latest development of the McIntyre special was the joint work of Bob and Alex Crummie, and was again constructed at Joe Potts's Glasgow premises. And for the first time a more detailed specification was released for public consumption. This revealed that frame tubing consisted of 1½in outside diameter by 17-gauge, with all the members being as straight as possible. From the base of the steering head (a Manx Norton component) twin tubes ran downwards and out to a loop, or cradle, encircling the engine. At the back end of the cradle a 2½in outside diameter tube formed a housing for the rear swinging arm pivot. From the top of the steering head twin tubes extended downwards and rearwards to pick up to the pivot tube.

Rear engine plates surrounded the AMC close ratio gearbox, making a form of semi-unit construction. Mounting to the frame was by lugs brazed to the main cradle tube forward of the crankcase, to a cross tube above the gearbox and to the swinging arm pivot shaft. The engine sat deep inside the frame. Indeed, the engine's crankshaft was some 1½in below the cradle centre line. Weight reduction overall was around 1½lb and the weight was some two-thirds of the standard AMC frame.

A sub-frame was manufactured in ½in outside diameter, 17-gauge tube. Front suspension was taken care of by a pair of Manx Norton Roadholder forks, shortened by 1in, a standard Manx swinging arm pivoted on a pair of Oilite bushes, the rear shock absorbers being of Girling manufacture. At that time the wheel size had yet to be determined (either 18 or 19in), with Norton brakes.

After Bob's death, and fitted with a 496cc Matchless G50 engine, the bike sprang to fame in the hands of the Australian Continental Circus rider Jack Findlay during the late 1960s, particularly after Findlay used it to secure runner-up (to Giacomo Agostini's MV Agusta) in the 1968 500cc World Championship series. Today this motorcycle is owned and raced in historic events by Northampton Norton specialist Mick Hemmings.

Drawing of the special, circa 1962. After Bob's death the machine eventually passed to the Australian Jack Findlay, who took it to runner-up position in the 1968 500cc world championship, behind Giacomo Agostini's MV.

Bob and Mike Hailwood sharing a quiet moment between races, summer 1961.

and that's new in itself! – for in the 250cc race his Honda wasn't available and, riding his Mondial, he couldn't catch Tom Phillis and Jim Redman on the Japanese "fours".'

From the start of the 350cc final Phil Read (Norton) and Bob streaked away into the lead, side by side, with the Scot swooping ahead as they peeled off for the long, sweeping Gerard's Bend. Not to be outdone, Read slipped past at the esses and hung on to lead the field at the end of the first lap, closely tailed by Bob, Fred Neville (AJS) and Hailwood (AJS).

On the second lap, Bob again took charge and with Read in his slipstream the pair of them began to pull away from the pack. On the third lap, Neville retired, leaving Hailwood to pursue the two leaders. Relentlessly, Bob shook off Phil Read so that after 10 laps the Scot led the race by 100 yards, with Hailwood a further 200 yards distant.

From then on Read seemed to ease the pace and gradually Hailwood closed, until on the 18th lap he assumed second place – now a long way behind Bob. The latter himself then eased the pace, to take a comfortable victory ahead of Hailwood and Read.

350cc Mallory Park – 25 laps – 33.75 miles

1st	R. McIntyre (AJS)	
2nd	S.M.B. Hailwood (AJS)	
3rd	P.W. Read (Norton)	
4th	P. Driver (Norton)	
5th	J.L. Payne (Norton)	
6th	P.H. Tait (Norton)	

Anticipating the fall of the flag to perfection, Phil Read stormed into an early lead in the 500cc final with Bob (Norton) in hot pursuit. After one lap, the pair were side by side and then Bob pulled ahead. After three circuits the order was: McIntyre, Read, Driver, Rob Fitton, Payne and Roy Ingram; Hailwood was back in a lonely 14th!

After 10 laps Bob had stretched his lead to a quarter of a lap and his pal Alastair King had come right through the field to take second place. Hailwood was also making progress and had assumed third position before his Norton tightened up and he fell at the hairpin.

Bob was by this time totally in command and on the last lap toured round to win by a wide margin, with Alastair King second and Ginger Payne taking third by a narrow margin from Phil Read and Paddy Driver. And so Bob McIntyre proved – provided his machinery remained in tune – that he was still the 'Master of Mallory'. It had been a couple of performances to savour, for both fans and rider alike. He also set the fastest laps in both races with speeds of 86.48mph and 87.73mph.

500cc Mallory Park – 25 laps – 33.75 miles
1st	R. McIntyre	(Norton)
2nd	A. King	(Norton)
3rd	J.L. Payne	(Norton)
4th	P.W. Read	(Norton)
5th	P. Driver	(Norton)
6th	F. Neville	(Matchless)

Bianchi reliability at last

Six days after his Mallory double, Bob was in action at Assen, home of the Dutch TT. And at last the Bianchi twin didn't break. This allowed what *Motor Cycle News* claimed was 'a race as thrilling as any ever witnessed by a road racing crowd.' And it was Bob who set the pace on the Bianchi twin, with Gary Hocking (MV Agusta) in hot pursuit. Amazingly, many commentators actually considered the Bianchi 'a shade faster' than Hocking's four-cylinder machine.

It was a truly thrilling struggle from two of the world's finest riders, neither wanting to give an inch. Traditionally the Dutch TT had fine weather and so it proved in 1961: 'The sun's shining brilliantly from an almost cloudless sky and there's a still breeze to keep the crowd cool and to flutter the long line of flags that top the pits.' (*MCN*). And what a crowd, as one newspaper reported:

The multitude here makes the spectators that flock the Isle of Man look like a mere trickle. The magnificent vantage points that surround this circuit are absolutely packed and an hour ago the traffic jams leading to the course were over four miles long... well over 150,000 will have paid to see the racing today.

This was, of course, the circuit where Bob suffered the crash which ultimately ruined his chances of winning the world title with Gilera back in 1957. That probably accounted for the fact that although he led for 13 of the 20 laps, he ultimately missed out on the victory.

For 19 of the 20-lap distance Hocking and Bob seemed so equally matched that it would have been a brave man who would have put his money on which would win. This is how *Motor Cycle News* described the final lap of the 4.64-mile circuit:

It looked certain that master tactician Bob McIntyre – one of the coolest brains in road racing – would win when he started the last lap thirty yards ahead of Hocking. Round the back of the circuit, crammed with over one hundred and fifty thousand sunburnt spectators, McIntyre increased his lead to fifty yards, but then in a fantastic piece of riding on one of the most acute bends on the four and a half mile circuit, Hocking made up the deficit and forced his way into the lead! Using the outstanding acceleration of the Bianchi to the full, McIntyre struck back and actually pulled alongside the MV but Hocking refused to give way and as the machines almost touched McIntyre had to close the throttle. In that fraction of a second the race was lost and won. In a day of scintillating racing, all lap records were shattered.

Bob was to recall later: 'It was certainly one of my most exciting races.'

350cc Dutch TT – 20 laps – 95.69 miles
1st	G. Hocking	(MV Agusta)
2nd	R. McIntyre	(Bianchi)
3rd	F. Stastny	(Jawa)
4th	E. Brambilla	(Bianchi)
5th	P.W. Read	(Norton)
6th	F.G. Perris	(Norton)

After the race Bob commented: 'My Bianchi was slightly the quicker machine but his MV had better handling.'

Bob also came second (behind Mike Hailwood) on the Honda four in the 250cc event. He then finished third in the 500cc race, behind Hocking (MV) and Hailwood (Norton).

The 350 and 500cc races were over 20 laps each, and the 250cc over 17 laps. Bob thus completed a total of 272.71 racing miles in a single day. Bob had also ridden three entirely different machines that day: a 250cc four, a 350cc twin and a 500cc single. The only thing they had in common was having two wheels and double overhead cam engines. It proved that the Scot could adapt to machines of a differing nature and still extract a top three finish in each class.

The Belgian Grand Prix

Unfortunately, the following week's Belgian GP at Spa Francorchamps didn't include a 350cc class – a great shame as it robbed spectators of a repeat Hocking–McIntyre duel. On Sunday 2 July, Bob was entered in the 250cc and 500cc races. In the former he was forced to retire with mechanical problems.

On his 500cc Potts Norton he repeated his third position of eight days before – behind the same pair, Hocking and Hailwood. This also meant that he was now lying third in the class points table: Hocking 32, Hailwood 29, McIntyre 14.

Six days later, on Saturday 8 July, fate once again took a hand – as it had done in previous years – when Bob, this time partnered by Alastair King, rode the Lawton & Wilson 692cc Royal Enfield Constellation in the annual Thruxton 500-miler (full story in Chapter 7). And once again things were not to go as planned, Bob being cast off the machine when a connecting rod broke! This was to be Bob's final attempt at glory in the event.

The Sachsenring

The Sachsenring, in the eastern zone of Germany, was one of the most famous of all pre-war racing circuits. It was also the place where Bob McIntyre's illustrious Scottish road-racing forebear Jimmie Guthrie met his death in 1937. After the Soviet annexation of this part of Germany following the end of World War Two, the 'Iron Curtain' had kept the Sachsenring out of the Grand Prix calendar since the World Championship series was instigated in 1949.

But all this changed for 1961, when the 5.2-mile circuit, which had been completely resurfaced and modified to bring it up to World Championship standard demanded by the FIM, was awarded the status of East German Grand Prix – counting towards the FIM world series.

Situated in the centre of the industrial province of Saxony, near the ancient twin towns of Hohenstein and Ernstthal, the Sachsenring could still be

Official Programme Is.

CADWELL PARK
Solo & Sidecar Road Races
August Monday 1961
A.C.U. National Permit No. 372

Opening Of The New 2¼ Mile International Circuit

The Journal With All The News And Pictures
THURSDAY 9d

MOTOR CYCLING
with SCOOTER WEEKLY

considered a true road course. During practice both Gary Hocking (MV) and Frantisek Stastny (Jawa) had been faster than Bob's Bianchi – as had Stastny's teammate Gustav Havel. Those four riders occupied the front rows of the grid ahead of Ernesto Brambilla (Bianchi), Jack Findlay and Rudi Thalhammer (both Nortons).

As the lights flicked to green, away the field went, headed by Stastny, Hocking, Brambilla, Havel and Thalhammer. McIntyre's Bianchi was slow to pick up and he was out of sight in the middle of the pack. But Bob Mac was not in the mood to hang about and he set off after the leaders – displacing Havel and Brambilla as he went. Eventually he claimed third and that was as far as he got, coming home behind Hocking and Stastny.

350cc East German GP – 18 laps – 97.62 miles

1st	G. Hocking	(MV Agusta)
2nd	F. Stastny	(Jawa)
3rd	R. McIntyre	(Bianchi)
4th	G. Havel	(Jawa)
5th	E. Brambilla	(Bianchi)
6th	B. Schneider	(Norton)

After suffering a mystery misfire Bob could only finish 8th in the 250cc race.

Incidentally, over 250,000 spectators watched the action at the Sachsenring – East German fans having been starved of such an event for years. Although Bob took his 500cc Norton all the way from Scotland to the Sachsenring he didn't ride it. On arrival it transpired that the organisers thought he had contracted for two starts – 250 and 350cc. Bob said he had, but he had also entered a 500cc, and how much more would they pay him to start in the big class? The organisers said they wouldn't pay anything and that was that, for Bob certainly wasn't going to wear his Norton out for nothing.

In the 350 class Bob found that while the Bianchi had handled all right on the smooth surface of Assen it was a very different case at the Sachsenring, where some of the going was extremely bumpy.

British Championships

Eight days after the Sachsenring came the annual British Championships meeting at Oulton Park on Monday 7 August. But unlike previous years, when he won the 350 and 500cc British titles, Bob did not have much success at one of his favourite circuits.

In the 250cc Championship race Bob was a non-starter (he had been down to ride an Aermacchi). In the 500cc class he didn't last long, sliding off on the second lap. He was also a non-starter in the Les Graham Memorial Race, his Norton being out of action due to the earlier accident.

His only success came in the 350 Championship race. This was described by *Motor Cycle News* as: 'A thriller all the way.' First Derek Minter (Norton) led, then John Hartle (Norton), but after five laps Minter was back in front, yards ahead of Hartle, Phil Read (Norton), Bob (AJS) and Mike Hailwood (AJS).

Then Hailwood stopped at the pits with carburettor trouble and Minter put in a spurt to draw away from his pursuers, led by Hartle. After a few more laps it appeared as though Minter had the race sewn up, but it was not to be and on the penultimate lap his Norton seized and Hartle pressed on to win, with Bob getting the better of Read to take second place, only seven seconds behind the winner.

350cc British Championship Oulton Park – 30 laps – 82.83 miles

1st	J. Hartle (Norton)
2nd	R. McIntyre (AJS)
3rd	P.W. Read (Norton)
4th	F. Neville (AJS)
5th	A. King (Norton)
6th	A. Shepherd (AJS)

Making history in Ulster

As covered in detail in Chapter 9, Bob had one of his greatest rides during the 1961 250cc Ulster GP at Dundrod on the Reg Armstrong-entered Honda four – and in the process set a faster race speed than the existing quickest held by John Surtees's 500cc MV Agusta in 1959! In the 350cc race, however, he was destined to retire on his works Bianchi – with a broken gearbox layshaft. A sister machine ridden by Alastair King finished runner-up, behind race winner Gary Hocking (MV Agusta).

More records tumbled at the international Leinster 200 held at Dunboyne, southern Ireland, on Saturday 19 August. Most of them went to Bob

350cc British Championships at Oulton Park, Monday 7 August 1961. Bob (AJS) is about to proceed to the start line for the 30-lap, 82.83-mile race (135.25km). The Scot was to finish second, to John Hartle (Norton).

Showing everyone except Derek Minter the way home in the 350cc British Championship race, Oulton Park, 7 August 1961.

Irish legend Stanley Woods with Bob at the Leinster 200 meeting, Saturday 19 August 1961. Our hero was destined to win all three races, the 250cc and the 350cc on Honda fours and the 500cc on his trusty Norton.

McIntyre, who won all three scratch races. The first 15-lap event (60 miles) was open to all machines up to 350cc, and Bob took advantage of this rule to ride the Armstrong-entered two-fifty Honda four in direct competition with 350cc machines for the first time. He won from John Hartle and Alastair King (Nortons).

The 250cc race was something of a 'walkover' (*MCN*), the only opposition coming from Dickie Carter riding Reg Armstrong's ex-works NSU Rennmax twin.

With Hartle and King in opposition, it was supposed that the 80-mile 500cc race would be another close-fought contest, like the 350cc. But Bob went into an instant lead and steadily drew ahead. As *Motor Cycle News* reported: 'The flying Scot made a new lap record of 94.74mph as against the old figure of 90mph made by Ralph Rensen two years ago.'

After racing in the Leinster 200, Bob and Alastair King spent a few days on holiday in Ireland, but they couldn't keep away from speed sports – getting involved in a meeting held at Shannon Airport to raise funds for disabled people. However, their mounts were not motorcycles, but donkeys! And the pair were well and truly beaten by Irish rugby international Mike English and Reg Armstrong.

In the 'Championship Race' in which contestants had to run 100 yards carrying a gallon of champagne without spilling it, Bob showed up better – he tied for second place with Mike English, behind the winner, the Mayor of Limerick!

The Italian Grand Prix

Then it was off to Monza in Italy for the Italian Grand Prix. And what a line-up for the 350cc race. On MV Agusta fours, Gary Hocking and Mike Hailwood (the latter having his first competitive ride for the Italian factory) were racing against no fewer than four Bianchi twins: Bob, plus Brambilla and new boys Alan Shepherd and Paddy Driver. Then there was Silvio Grassetti on a Benelli, the two Jawas of Stastny and Havel, plus a host of top privateers including Jack Findlay, Bertie Schneider and Hugh Anderson.

At the finish it was MVs first and second (Hocking then Hailwood); Havel (Jawa) and the only Bianchi to finish, Alan Shepherd. Bob's

machine once again succumbed to mechanical problems. Then, in the 250cc race, Bob crashed out while leading in a battle which had involved no fewer than *five* of the Japanese Hondas (Bob, plus Hailwood, Redman, Phillis and Hartle). The Scot had also recorded the quickest practice times. Unfortunately, Bob suffered a broken collarbone in the crash, which meant he could not race the five-hundred Norton.

On the Monday after his Monza accident, Bob underwent an operation to pin his broken collarbone and he was reported as 'resting in Italy.' At this time he said he hoped to ride in the Swedish GP at Kristianstad – the 10th round of the 1961 World Championships – the following Sunday. This was wishful thinking and at Kristianstad Alastair King told Mick Woollett that Bob had been unable to travel. When Alastair had left Italy himself, Bob had had the stitches removed and was 'recuperating at Rapallo' (on the Italian Riviera), where he was hoping to do 'some water skiing before driving home.' If his shoulder stood up to the tests of water sports and driving, Bob intended racing at Mallory Park (on Sunday 24 September), Alastair telling Mick:

Dancing with wife Joyce at the Nixe Palace, Mallorca, 31 October 1961.

'He's very, very keen to go to Mallory and if possible he'll be there.'

Again Bob's hopes were dashed. The injured shoulder didn't stand up to even the test of water sports on the Italian Riviera – the pin holding his collarbone came out and Bob had to return to the hospital in Milan where the surgery had been carried out. Although he was subsequently able to return to Scotland, his racing for the year was over. Much later, at the end of October, it was reported that his shoulder was: 'Still stiff, but making good progress.' And as for his future plans, he said he would: 'definitely be racing AJS and Norton machinery in British events the following season, but no contracts with Bianchi or Honda have been finalised.'

Although he didn't know it at that time, Bob had had his last race on a Bianchi; instead, as is revealed in the next chapter, his future lay with the giant Japanese Honda concern – and Joe Potts.

Chapter 9

Honda

BOB McIntyre's initial contract with the Japanese Honda organisation came in 1959, when the company sent a team to the Isle of Man TT for the first time. As Bob said later:

I was asked to go to their headquarters at the Nursery Hotel, Onchan, to write a newspaper article. They let me have a run on a 125cc machine [one of the CB92 overhead cam, twin cylinder Sports roadsters, with a pressed steel frame and leading link front forks] *It had the performance of an average 350cc.*

An Aintree debut

In mid-September 1960 came the news that Bob was being given a run out with Honda and had been entered by the Japanese firm at Aintree, near Liverpool, home of the famous Grand National horse race. A rumour had gone round Scarborough's Oliver's Mount circuit, which had just hosted its annual international Gold Cup meeting, to the effect that Bob had already signed a contract to ride works Hondas the following year. In fact this was false. As *Motor Cycle News's* Mick Woollett more correctly commented in the newspaper's Wednesday 21 September 1960 issue: 'If Bob is impressed by the Hondas at Aintree then that rumour could well become fact.'

Bob's contract with the Italian Gilera concern was finally due to expire at the end of the year and, so far, he had heard nothing from them to suggest that they intended to re-sign him to ride their machines in 1961. This news seemed to finally kill any fleeting hopes that Gilera intended to make a comeback to the sport. So who, asked *MCN*, would be 'at Aintree to challenge the new combination of McIntyre and Honda?' Well, there was a star-studded entry including Mike Hailwood, Tom Phillis, Johnny Grace (on works Bultacos) and John Hartle, to name but a few.

For the first time for many years, a motorcycle meeting attracted large crowds to watch the Aintree International. Organised by the North Western

ACU and sponsored by the *Daily Herald* newspaper it was held on Saturday 24 September 1960. The weather conditions also helped – it was a perfect autumn day with plenty of sunshine and no rain. As *The Motor Cycle* reported: 'The 250cc race saw an old hand aboard a new bike – McIntyre having his first outing on a four-cylinder Honda.' And it was an impressive outing, too.

The 250cc race was held directly after lunch. From the start Mike Hailwood (FB Mondial) took the lead, but at the end of the lap McIntyre was right on his tail and the pair were way ahead of John Dixon (Adler). Hailwood held a slender lead but he couldn't get away from the four-cylinder bike and as they completed three laps Bob took the lead. For the rest of the race the two battled furiously. But the Honda was home first, by 20 yards, with a new class lap record of 82.17mph to its credit. Not only had Bob Mac won the race, but it was the first outright victory by a 250cc Honda in a European race. And when one considers that the combination of Hailwood and the FB Mondial had already beaten Jim Redman on a Honda four at Brands Hatch the previous weekend, it was a doubly successful debut for the Scot.

250cc Aintree – 5 laps

1st   R. McIntyre (Honda)

2nd   S.M.B. Hailwood (FB Mondial)

3rd   J.W. Dixon (Adler)

4th   P.M. Tait (Aermacchi)

5th   J. Murgatroyd (NSU)

6th   D.F. Shorey (NSU)

Paddock Gossip

In the 28 September issue of *Motor Cycle News* the 'Paddock Gossip' column was dominated by McIntyre's Honda debut:

Well, Bob McIntyre rode the 250cc Honda at Aintree – scoop news in last week's MCN – and he won the race after a tremendous battle with Mike Hailwood on the Mondial. There was no 125cc Honda available for Bob so he didn't make his debut in the smallest international class. Bob was impressed by the four-cylinder Honda, which certainly went very fast on the straights but it was obvious to those spectating on the corners that the handling still leaves a lot to be desired.

The machine Bob rode was the one Gilberto Milani had taken to fifth place

Bob about to push start the works 250cc Honda four into life at Aintree, September 1960.

One of the Honda 250 fours of the type raced by Bob McIntyre in 1961 and 1962.

Honda 250 Four

Honda's first four-cylinder model, the RC160, made its debut at the Mount Asama circuit during a race meeting which took in three days, 22, 23 and 24 August 1959. And what a debut it was too. At the end of the 16-lap race, these machines filled five of the top six places!

Sharing the same 44x41mm bore and stroke dimensions as the 125cc twin which had made its European debut in the Isle of Man TT (winning the team prize) a couple of months earlier, the double overhead camshaft four had a displacement of 249.2cc and ran on a compression ratio of 10.5:1. It produced 35bhp at a heady 14,000rpm. On optimum gearing, this related to a maximum speed of around 130mph.

Unlike the twin of the same era, which had inclined cylinders, the RC160 had upright cylinders. Drive to the camshafts was on the offside and, unlike the 125cc twin of 1959, the four relied on shaft and bevel gears. In fact, Soichiro Honda used this system, having been impressed by its use in the German NSU racers of the mid-1950s, following his visit to Europe in the summer of 1954. A particularly interesting feature was that the RC160 was the first Honda engine to employ four-valves-per-cylinder technology.

Many of this first four-cylinder Honda's design features were also found on the 1959 125 twin, including the leading link front fork assembly. However, because of the four's superior performance, it had not simply been a case of 'make do', but instead virtually everything was re-engineered to take account of the extra speed of the heavier four.

The RC160 was never raced in Europe; however, it was a significant engineering achievement and was to lead directly to Honda's 250cc Grand

Prix entry the following year, in 1960. This later design, coded RC161, was an entirely new motorcycle and except for features such as the 44x41mm bore and stroke, dohc, four-valves-per-cylinder and horizontally-split crankcases, owed nothing to the RC160.

For 1960 Honda planned new, much improved machinery. Gone were the upright cylinders, bevel camshaft drive and leading link front forks. In their place came inclined cylinders, central gear drive (the 125 twin retained the bevel cam for that year) and telescopic front forks. The RC161 four produced 38bhp at 13,500rpm – and could be pushed up to an incredible 17,000rpm before bursting. Throughout the season development continued, resulting in improved race results. Honda had tried signing Bob McIntyre for 1960, but did not finally succeed until 1961.

The 1961 machines were considerably different from the 1960 models. Although the bore and stroke was again unchanged, the cylinders of the new RC162 four were less steeply inclined, although they still tilted forward at an angle of 30 degrees. The engine had also been modified from wet to dry-sump lubrication and was claimed to produce over 40bhp at 14,000rpm. It also featured an entirely new tubular frame, which the press claimed was modelled on MV lines, although in Honda's case it dispensed with front down-tubes. The new four also incorporated a new ignition system, employing one coil for each pair of cylinders and producing sparks on the compression and exhaust strokes; some bikes were also equipped with a Kokusan Denki magneto. Honda sources quoted maximum speed as being 145mph.

1961 saw Honda win both the 125cc (Tom Phillis) and 250cc (Mike Hailwood) World Championship titles. Bob McIntyre also led the 250cc Isle of Man TT until the final lap when he struck mechanical trouble, but did have the satisfaction of setting a new class lap record of 99.58mph.

Perhaps, understandably, there was little change to the championship winning 125 and 250cc machines (coded RC145 and RC163 respectively) for 1962, but Honda expanded their presence by announcing that they

A 1961 model RC162 two-fifty four – the cylinders were inclined forward at 30 degrees.

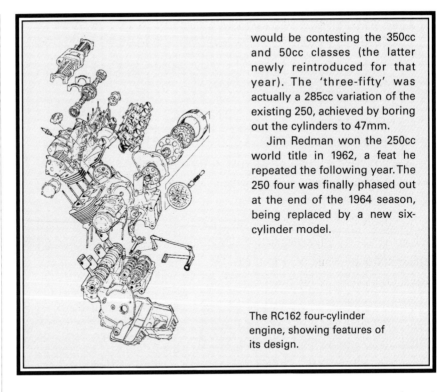

would be contesting the 350cc and 50cc classes (the latter newly reintroduced for that year). The 'three-fifty' was actually a 285cc variation of the existing 250, achieved by boring out the cylinders to 47mm.

Jim Redman won the 250cc world title in 1962, a feat he repeated the following year. The 250 four was finally phased out at the end of the 1964 season, being replaced by a new six-cylinder model.

The RC162 four-cylinder engine, showing features of its design.

at the recent Italian GP at Monza. Jim Redman brought it to Britain and raced it himself at Brands Hatch – and then Jim took it to Aintree for Bob to ride.

Actually, there were no Honda personnel at Aintree – mechanics or management – to see the McIntyre victory. As one reporter commented: 'It says a lot for the Japanese model that it only required routine maintenance after Monza and Brands Hatch.' Bob's mechanic Jim (Pim) Fleming was responsible for the machine while it was in the Scot's care, then Redman took the Honda back to Rhodesia with him, where he planned to race it in African events before returning to Europe in 1961.

So what was the possibility of McIntyre and Honda becoming a permanent fixture? Several observers thought that there was a good chance of him riding the machines in the World Championships in future. *MCN* commented: 'What a wonderful boost for road racing it would be if the popular Scot did re-enter the championship on the Japanese challenger.'

But of course, other European riders had their eyes on Honda – notably Mike Hailwood, Derek Minter and John Hartle. And not only were there a number of Japanese riders, but there were also the existing contracted foreign riders Tom Phillis and Redman himself.

This is how Bob described his Honda ride:

As *The Motor Cycle* reported: 'The 250cc race at Aintree saw an old hand aboard a new bike – McIntyre having his first outing on a four-cylinder Honda.' And it was a winning debut too, with Bob taking victory from Mike Hailwood (FB Mondial).

I had never ridden in the Lightweight class before. I had always been interested in the bigger machines and at 11½ stone I regard myself as a bit heavy even for a 250cc machine. But the Honda is a big 250 – more like a 500. I took up the offer with pleasure.

The closed season

As explained in the previous chapter, the closed season of 1960/61 was a long one for Bob McIntyre; for months he had no news about what he might be riding – except the Potts AJS and Norton singles. And there was certainly no news whatsoever from Honda.

Eventually Bianchi, rather than the Japanese firm, showed an interest, with Bob going out to Italy twice before actually signing on the dotted line for the Italian marque in mid-March 1961. This contract tied Bob up to race the Bianchi twin-cylinder machine in the 350cc World Championship series.

Then a month later, on Monday evening 11 April, news broke that Bob was to campaign a two-fifty Honda machine. This was not a full works effort; instead he was to be entered by Reg Armstrong, the former AJS, Norton and Gilera star who was the Honda importer for southern Ireland. In case the reader should think that this was somewhat strange, this was quite common practice with Honda. For example, in 1961, not only was Bob McIntyre contracted in this way, but Mike Hailwood and John Hartle (via the British importers, Maico UK) also were, while in 1962 Derek Minter had a similar agreement.

A week after the news that Bob was to ride a Honda had come through, the Japanese company announced that a maintenance base was to be opened in Hanover, Germany, to service all the various works models being raced in Europe.

At that time there were four Japanese-contracted riders: Kunimitsu Takahashi, Moto Kitano, Sadao Shimazaki and Naomi Taniguchi – plus Jim Redman and Tom Phillis. The 'satellite' team members, as described earlier, were Bob McIntyre, Mike Hailwood and John Hartle. With so many riders, not all would be able to ride at every round of the 250cc World Championship series that year. In 1961 there were 11 venues: Barcelona, Hockenheim, Clermont-Ferrand, Isle of Man, Assen, Spa Francorchamps, the Sachsenring, Dundrod, Monza, Kristianstad and Buenos Aires.

Bob therefore missed the first three rounds of the title hunt, only coming in at the TT, the fourth round. But what an impact he made!

His first Isle of Man practice session on the Honda was, as *The Motor Cycle* described: 'Understandably, leisurely. But he was obviously highly chuffed with this first spin – it's not often he gets off a strange model with a

Bob became a Honda rider for 1961, entered by Irishman Reg Armstrong. He is shown here during practice week for that year's Isle of Man TT.

big grin.' It wasn't long before Bob was getting to grips with his new mount, one commentator reporting:

What a belting the two-fifty lap record received last Monday evening! Knocking an incredible 22.8s off Ubbiali's 1960 record time, Bob McIntyre showed the true potential of the Honda four on the Mountain course. Indeed, there is even talk now that we may yet see this year a 100mph lap by the formidable McIntyre-Honda duo.

Just for the record, Bob Mac's figures for the evening session on Monday 5 June 1961 were: 23 minutes 22 seconds, a speed of 96.88mph. McIntyre's brilliance during the practice week on the Honda (do not forget he was also out on the 350cc Bianchi twin and the 500cc Potts Norton) simply astounded everyone. For example, *The Motor Cycle* reported: 'The achievements which had set everyone talking were Bob McIntyre's incredible 96.88mph on his third outing on a two-fifty Honda four – which knocked over 20s off the record.'

Following his showing in practice, expectations were high for Bob to get round even faster in the race, this taking place on Monday 12 June 1961.

A sensational race

It was to prove a truly sensational race. This is how *The Motor Cycle* described the scene prior to the start: 'Above the grandstand the bright flags fluttered bravely and, though the skies had dulled, the hills of the Island backcloth stood out clearly as the cacophony of the warm-up ceased at last.'

Bob McIntyre was to be the first man away (with race number 3). Down went the starter flag to send Bob on his way, the howl of the Honda four raising the echoes on his descent of Bray Hill. *The Motor Cycle* again:

Even before the grid area was clear the scoreboard clocks had come to life to signal the leaders past Ballacraine. Ahead lay the twisty, wooded tunnel of Glen Helen, the climb to Cronk-y-Voddee, the drop to Kirkmichael – where spectators saw Bob Mac scream past, out on his own and with the whole Island to play with.

Bob airborne on the Armstrong entered works Honda in the 1961 Lightweight TT.

Forcing on during the 1961 Lightweight event. After blitzing the opposition Bob was forced out through lack of oil near the end of the race, after pushing the class lap record up to almost 100mph.

Behind him came a star-studded field including the MV twin of Gary Hocking, the Suzuki squad of Hugh Anderson, Paddy Driver and Alastair King, the Yamahas of Fumio Ito and teammates Oishi and Sunako, the Moto Morini of Tarquinio Provini, the Aermacchi of Alberto Pagani, and Gilberto Milani, and no fewer than *nine* (including Bob) Honda fours. Actually, 10 had been entered but John Hartle was a non-starter. Honda riders included Mike

Hailwood, Tom Phillis and Jim Redman. The works MZs had decided not to race. There had been a record entry for the 1961 Lightweight (250cc) TT, with a huge variety of privately entered bikes including GMS, Ariel, NSU, Ducati, Moto Guzzi, REG, BSA, Velocette, Norton, AJS, Puch and FB Mondial.

From a standing start, Bob McIntyre 'ripped off a lap which blew the existing figures to fragments; on the second lap he cracked the existing *three-fifty* record and was mighty close to crashing through the 'ton' barrier.' Quite simply, on that June day in 1961 nobody else could get near Bob's times.

With two of his five laps completed, Bob at breakneck speed forced on, while the timekeepers looked at their watches and rubbed their eyes in disbelief. That second lap had taken just 22 minutes 44 seconds and the record lap had soared to 99.58mph – faster than John Surtees's best on the *three-fifty* MV Agusta; incredible.

Bob, however, was now in serious trouble. On left-hand corners the Honda had given its rider a warning twitch or two and, on looking down, he had seen oil spraying onto the wall of the rear tyre. There was also the added hazard of a light drizzle on some parts of the circuit.

The third lap times came up and Bob had certainly slowed, though not by much; his lap speed stood at 99.26mph; his race average at 99.23mph. Oversize tanks on the Hondas permitted a non-stop race. But as *The Motor Cycle* race report said: 'As though by clockwork, McIntyre pressed on, but though his engine sounded in as fine fettle as ever, he gave a definite thumbs-down sign as he passed through to start his final lap.' Certainly Hailwood was gaining ground, but he was still a massive 33.8 seconds astern and without abnormal luck, could never hope to demolish such an advantage in the single lap which remained.

Then the final part of the drama unfolded. This is how *The Motor Cycle* described what happened on that fateful last lap:

> *At corner after corner, programmes were waved to encourage Mac while the scoreboard pointers charted his way to victory. Safely through Ballacraine, where rain now spattered the roadway; safely over the awkward humped Ballaugh Bridge. But Mac really meant that thumbs-down signal, and for the second time in the race the Sulby Bridge crowds consulted their watches and peered along the road for a man late on schedule. And it was Mike (Hailwood) who came into sight, heeling his four over to take the bridge turn, then cranking away out of view around the left-hander at Ginger Hall; Mike, screaming on his way to score a double-in-a-day (he had earlier won the 125cc event*

Jim Redman

Jim Redman was one of the first Western riders to be signed for the Honda Grand Prix team – and as such was a teammate of Bob McIntyre's in 1961 and 1962.

Originally from England, but soon resident in Rhodesia (now Zimbabwe), Jim was born on 8 November 1931, and in many ways was the ultimate professional racing motorcyclist. Having first returned to the UK during the late 1950s, to race a Ducati 125 Grand Prix and a brace of Manx Nortons, Redman was to display the cool, calculated approach which was to characterise his career. Crashes were infrequent, Jim believing that 'you have to finish a race to win it!' Certainly this is a formula needed to win season-long championship titles – finish every race in the highest possible position.

Honda needed just such a man, and Jim became, in effect, the Honda

Bob and Jim Redman shared several battles during the 1962 season as members of the full Honda works teams, but became good friends.

Grand Prix team captain. His chance to join Honda as a full-time member of the team had come after the death of Australian Bob Brown (Bob McIntyre's teammate at Gilera during his historic 1957 double TT victories) at Solitude in 1960, although Redman had already ridden one of the Japanese 125 twins during the Ulster GP, coming home third behind race winner Carlo Ubbiali (MV) and Honda teammate Tom Phillis. But that year (Honda's first full year in Europe) the Japanese marque was not the dominant force it was in later years, with Ubbiali and MV taking both the 125 and 250cc titles.

In 1961, Jim Redman's first GP victory came aboard one of the revised fours at the Belgian GP, followed later that year by another win, this time at the Italian round. He finished the season third in the 250cc class and fourth in the 125cc, already showing championship potential. During 1962 he won six of the 10 rounds counting towards the 250cc championship, thus winning the title; he also finished runner-up (behind Luigi Taveri) in the 125cc class. But the real surprise was his second title that year in the 350cc category on a larger four-cylinder model.

Jim repeated his title success in 1963, although in the 250cc series he was given a stern contest all season by Tarquinio Provini's dohc Moto Morini single. In 1964 his main challenger was Phil Read, who had joined the Yamaha team at the end of 1963. Read ultimately came out on top, gaining five victories to Redman's three in the 11-round series. However, Jim retained his 350cc crown, winning all eight rounds on the larger four.

Then came 1965 and the arrival of new boy Giacomo Agostini at MV Agusta. But even Ago and teammate Mike Hailwood could not prevent Jim Redman taking his sixth – and as it happened – last world title on board a combination of the existing 349cc four and new 297cc six-cylinder Hondas.

At the beginning of 1966, Jim Redman took the new four-cylinder Honda to victory in the first round of the 500cc World Championship at Hockenheim, in West Germany, with Agostini runner-up. In the Isle of Man it was Hailwood first, Ago second. The third round in the Dutch TT at Assen saw Jim once again victorious, with the Italian again runner-up. Then came that fateful day in July 1966, when during the 500cc Belgian GP at Spa Francorchamps, Jim crashed, breaking an arm, and subsequently announced his retirement from the sport. He then returned home to Bulawayo – and became the Yamaha importer for Rhodesia. In recent years Jim Redman has become a familiar figure, like many other stars of yesteryear, riding at historic events all around the world.

on a Honda twin). But luck comes in two forms, good and bad. An engine cannot run without oil, and McIntyre's Honda had seized at Quarry Bends. He was ready for it and had stretched for the clutch lever immediately.

In the author's mind, even though Bob McIntyre was a realist and true professional, losing victory in this way, half way round the final lap and only a few miles from victory, must have been a truly heartbreaking experience. But he was never heard to complain of his misfortune. Simply writing this has saddened me – even though the event was over 44 years ago, as I compile this book in the summer of 2005.

This is how Bob summed up the experience, early the following year:

My first race with the Honda (1961) was the Lightweight TT when I led until the last lap, only to have the machine seize due to an oil leak. If it had been necessary, I believe I could have pushed my record 99.58mph lap up to 100mph. Yet it was only in 1957 that the first 100mph lap was recorded – and then I used a Gilera twice the size of the Honda. That is a measure of the advances made in the Lightweight classes. On the straight the Honda can clock 145mph; only 10mph less than an MV 500.

As readers can see, there was no hint of frustration, bitterness or any other negative thought on what might have been.

In fact, Bob was full of praise for Honda, also commenting:

It was a rude shock for those who had regarded the Japanese as copyists turning out in little sweatshops shoddy replicas of famous-name cigarette lighters, toys and cameras made in Britain and Germany. There is no copying about their motorcycles, there is nothing shoddy. They are magnificent pieces of engineering. Engineers had tried to make four-cylinder 250cc machines before, but the results had been unsatisfactory. The Japanese succeeded – using a complex system of four-valves-per-cylinder. They achieved some 14,500 engine revolutions per minute compared with ten or eleven thousand of other 250cc machines. This gave them several more brake horsepower.

The Dutch TT

After the Isle of Man, the Dutch TT at Assen on Saturday 24 June was Bob's next Honda outing. For this the Japanese firm fitted a new engine.

Held in superb weather, over 110,000 enthusiasts packed the circuit to see five races (125, 250, 350, 500cc and sidecars), in which every class witnessed race and lap records shattered. The 250cc race got the meeting under way, and as *The Motor Cycle* said: 'Some curtain-raiser, that two-fifty race. Anxious to repeat his Island double, young Mike (Hailwood) screamed off like a demon, with Bob Mac on Reg Armstrong's Honda equally determined.'

Unfortunately for Bob his machine was to suffer a misfire, which meant that from the third lap Hailwood was able to consolidate his lead. So at the finish it was Hailwood, McIntyre and Redman in that order.

250cc Dutch TT – 17 laps – 81.38 miles

1st   S.M.B. Hailwood (Honda)

2nd   R. McIntyre (Honda)

3rd   J.A. Redman (Honda)

4th   S. Grassetti (Benelli)

5th   F. Stastny (Jawa)

6th   F. Ito (Yamaha)

One commentator described the next meeting in the following terms: 'A scorcher in every sense. Last Sunday's Belgian Grand Prix over the ultra-fast 8.76-mile Spa Francorchamps circuit in the Ardennes will long be remembered for the near-tropical heat and the fierce pace set by the leaders.'

For five of the nine laps, Phillis, Redman and McIntyre fought a massive battle for the lead – until the latter's machine began to misfire badly, leaving Redman to take the victory from Phillis, with Hailwood third.

The East German GP

Five weeks later, on Sunday 30 July, the GP circus moved behind the Iron Curtain to the Sachsenring, East Germany. But right from the start of the 250cc race, Bob's four fired on only three cylinders and he lay last of the five Hondas up front. On lap three the Scot pulled to the roadside and unhooked each plug lead in turn to try to cure the misfire – the dodge didn't work – and he had dropped to ninth before he rejoined the fray. But as *The Motor Cycle* reported:

> *The delay stung him and for the next ten laps the vast crowd (totalling some half a million) was treated to a display of vintage McIntyre. First Gustav Havel and his Jawa got the chop. Then the MZs of Werner Musiol and Walter Brahme were passed by the stuttering three. Alan Shepherd on the leading MZ was the next victim; and even Phillis, who's Honda was running on four but seemed overgeared, was powerless to halt Mac's progress. And Takahashi (who was ultimately to finish third) might have suffered a similar indignity if he had not got 36s in hand with only five laps to go. But Mac defied him to improve his advantage. Until the penultimate lap, at least, when a nasty clunk in the engine really crippled the ailing Honda and Mac limped in eighth – lapped.*

Once again machine gremlins had prevented the Scot from showing his best, but in typical fashion he had battled on against the odds.

Back in luck

Dundrod, Bob's favourite circuit, was also to be the scene of his greatest Honda success in 1961 – a stunning victory in the 250cc Ulster Grand Prix on Saturday 12 August. His average speed for the 12-lap, 88.29-mile race was faster than both the 350 and 500cc victories by Gary Hocking (MV Agusta) – 95.44mph – compared with 92.90 and 90.49mph! And with a new class lap record of 96.94mph, McIntyre's performance was better than Hocking's new 350cc lap record of 95.55mph.

No other rider was in the same orbit as Bob that day. As *The Motor Cycle* described:

Tom Phillis shown in 1961. Bob joined Tom and Jim Redman as full members of the works Honda squad the following year.

Even Hailwood (Honda) was powerless to prevent the Scot from stretching his lead by a few seconds every lap. And just consider what Bob might have achieved in the 1961 250cc World Championships if his bike had performed as well as it did that day in August. But unfortunately, at every other race counting towards the championship it either blew up, or was stricken by some other problem, thus preventing McIntyre giving of his best.

This victory, his first classic win since 1957, was also a popular one for his countless fans, both inside and outside Scotland.

Bob and Alastair King discuss matters at Oulton Park, August 1961.

Dundrod, Bob's favourite circuit, was the scene of his greatest Honda success in 1961, a stunning victory in the 250cc Ulster GP. He completed the 12-lap, 88.29-mile race (142km) in just over 54 minutes.

Oulton Park, August 1961.
Bob with his privately
entered works two-fifty
Honda four.

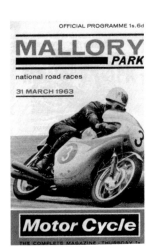

250cc Ulster GP – 12 laps – 88.29 miles

1st	R. McIntyre (Honda)
2nd	S.M.B. Hailwood (Honda)
3rd	J.A. Redman (Honda)
4th	T. Phillis (Honda)
5th	A. Shepherd (MZ)
6th	K. Takahashi (Honda)

Mac Scoops the Lot

On his private five-hundred Norton and the works two-fifty Honda four, Bob had nothing less than a field day exactly one week after his 250cc Ulster GP victory. The meeting was the Leinster 200 in southern Ireland. He won all three events at record speeds and made fastest lap in two.

The meeting opened with the 350cc event over 15 laps of the four-mile circuit. The event was most exciting – a two-fifty to do battle with bikes with an additional 100cc. Piloting the Reg Armstrong Honda, Bob, plus John Hartle and Alastair King (Nortons), put on a show which had the large crowd on its toes throughout.

Tom Phillis leading Bob during the 1961 250cc Ulster Grand Prix, both mounted on Honda fours.

McIntyre led the two Nortons for the first three laps; then King went ahead, only to lose the lead to Hartle a lap later. After that no one could predict just who might be in front – and there was never more than a second between first and third! Behind them New Zealander John Farnsworth (AJS), Irishman Len Ireland and future Honda star Ralph Bryans (Norton) had their own private battle.

1961 Ulster Grand Prix 250cc winner Bob McIntyre. The Scot also set the fastest lap at 96.94mph.

Mike Hailwood pictured at Aberdare Park, 15 August 1959.

Mike Hailwood

Many consider S.M.B. (Stanley Michael Bailey) Hailwood to have been the greatest motorcycle racer of all time. He was born in Oxford on 2 April 1940, the son of a self-made millionaire motorcycle dealer. His father, Stan, had competed pre-war on two, three and four wheels, before going on to build up the largest grouping of dealerships seen up to that time in Great Britain.

Mike began his racing career aboard an MV Agusta 125 single overhead camshaft production racer loaned to him by family friend Bill Webster (also a close friend of Count Domenico Agusta). This debut occurred on Easter Monday 22 April 1957, at Oulton Park in Cheshire, only a few miles from Webster's base.

Unlike Bob McIntyre's early racing days, there is absolutely no doubt that Stan Hailwood went about buying success for his son, with the best bikes, the best tuners and a huge media hype. However, in fairness, Mike did not really need this vast support, as he had natural talent in abundance. An example of Stan Hailwood's methods is displayed by a story concerning the NSU Sportmax Mike rode during the early part of his career. In 1955, John Surtees had raced the new German bike thanks to his employers Vincent (who were the British NSU distributors). John was given a bike, plus a spare engine. Then, towards the end of 1957, John received a phone call from Stan asking: 'Can we borrow the NSU for Mike to use in South Africa this winter?' John agreed, and the machine went to the Hailwood équipe. Again John was approached and agreed to lend the spare engine. Now Stan had both bike and engine – and John was never to see either again, because Stan conveniently became an NSU dealer. The 'deal' with the new London-based importers meant that King's of Oxford would only become agents if Stan could keep the racer and the engine – even though it had been given to Surtees.

In many ways, Mike Hailwood was embarrassed by his father's wheeler dealings, and as soon as he could, he became self-sufficient – his race results giving him freedom from his father's overpowering attention. In fact, Mike nicknamed his father 'Stan the Wallet'. But this was not before Stan had bought bikes such as a 125 Paton, a 125 Grand Prix Ducati, various Desmo Ducati twins and singles for the 125, 250 and 350cc classes, a couple of ex-works FB Mondial 250 singles, a squadron of Manx Nortons and an AJS 7R. In 1958, Mike was able to score a trio of British ACU Star titles (125, 250 and 350cc).

Mike's first Grand Prix victory came aboard a 125 Ducati Desmo single during the 1959 Ulster – the man he beat that day was none other than his future teammate at MV Agusta, Gary Hocking (riding an MZ). That year he also won all four ACU Stars – adding the 500cc to the classes he had retained for a second year. He repeated this feat the following year and it is one which no man before or since has equalled.

For 1961, Mike rode 125 and 250cc works Hondas, plus a 350cc AJS 7R and a 500cc Manx Norton. He gained his first world title, the 250cc, on the four-cylinder Honda, took the 125 and 250cc Isle of Man TTs and the Senior

Hailwood with his ex-works FB Mondial dohc, Lightweight (250cc) TT, 1959.

race on his Norton. On the latter machine (tuned by Bill Lacey) Mike averaged over 100mph for the six-lap, 226-mile race.

At the end of 1961 he signed for MV Agusta – going on to win the 500cc world title four years in a row (1962–65). In 1964, Mike set a new one-hour world speed record (at Daytona), thus breaking the existing record set by Bob McIntyre on a 350cc Gilera four at Monza in November 1957. Not only did the MV have an additional 150cc engine capacity, but Mike went to considerable lengths to explain why he had made his successful attempt – and to give credit to Bob for what Mike called a 'fantastic achievement' by his late friend.

In 1966 Mike rejoined Honda, winning both the 250 and 350cc classes on the new six-cylinder models, equalling this feat the following year before switching his attention to four wheels. But even he could not tame the wayward 500cc four-cylinder Honda, with MV (ridden by Giacomo Agostini) retaining the title.

For more than a decade Mike largely stayed away from bikes (except for a couple of outings on BSA and Yamaha machines) before making a historic comeback TT victory on a Ducati V-twin in 1978. The following year, 1979, he rode a Suzuki to a final TT victory. Then he retired once more, becoming a partner in the Hailwood & Gould business (with fellow World

Mike, 499cc Norton, Race of the Year, Mallory Park, September 1961.

Champion Rod Gould). By a twist of fate, the premises they used had formerly been the home of the Birmingham branch of King's of Oxford (part of father Stan's dealership chain).

Mike died tragically (with his young daughter Michelle) while driving home in his Rover car after collecting a fish and chip supper on 14 March 1982.

The previous class lap record had been held by Hartle, set in 1960 at 88mph. However, by the end of the race Bob had upped this to 91.25mph – and on a two-fifty!

Next came the 60-mile 250cc race, but in an entry which had dwindled from 18 to 10, the Honda-mounted star had virtually no opposition save the ex-works NSU twin of Dickie Carter (also entered by Reg Armstrong). In the 500cc event, Bob took his Potts Norton to his third victory of the day, ahead of Tommy Robb (Matchless).

350cc Leinster 200 – 15 laps – 60 miles

1st   R. McIntyre (250 Honda)
2nd   J. Hartle (Norton)
3rd   A. King (Norton)
4th   J. Farnsworth (AJS)
5th   E. Oliver (AJS)
6th   W.M. McCosh (AJS)

For the first time since his factory's entry into Grand Prix racing during 1959, factory boss Soichiro Honda visited Europe. And although he saw his machines fill the first three places in the 250cc class at the Italian GP at Monza – and clock the fastest-ever lap in the class – Bob McIntyre's name was not among the finishers. Instead he was on his way to hospital with a badly broken collarbone after crashing heavily in an accident caused by a broken oil pipe. This incident and the aftermath are described fully in the previous chapter. Unfortunately there were complications to the healing process, which effectively meant that Bob was not to race again that year.

Back on Honda for 1962?

The big question during the closed season leading up to the 1962 season was, would Bob McIntyre be Honda mounted again? The answer to this puzzle came partly on Thursday 8 February when Bob and Reg Armstrong arrived at Heathrow Airport, London, from Tokyo. The two had been to the Honda factory to discuss plans for the next season's racing.

In their 15 February 1962 issue *The Motor Cycle* had this to say:

Honda are expected to make their customary large-scale invasion of Europe for the classic races, bringing machines, riders and technicians

Bob pictured in Japan during early February 1962, about to test the latest Honda four-cylinder model (the 285 four) prior to signing a full works contract with the Japanese company. Soichiro Honda is pictured second left.

Back in the Potts workshop with one of his Norton engines about to go on the Heenon & Froude dyno.

in vast numbers. And though no official announcement has been made following Bob's and Reg's visit, it would surprise nobody to see Armstrong shouldering the responsibilities of team management with Mac as the team's spearhead.

Additionally, Alastair King, Bob's Potts teammate and great friend, told Charlie Rous of *Motor Cycle News* that both he and Bob would be 'off shortly for words with the Bianchi people.' Then, when Bob and Reg had returned, both told Rous (like *The Motor Cycle* report) that they had 'fixed nothing – but there are definite possibilities.' The negotiations just hadn't reached 'the final stage yet.'

Similarly, there had been considerable talk (from the press) that Derek Minter would be aboard a Honda in the 250cc class, under the sponsorship of Maico Ltd, who marketed Honda machines in the UK at that time. But as Charlie Rous pointed out: 'Once again there is nothing fixed, it's just a case of wait and see.'

On 26 February, speaking from his Dublin home, Reg Armstrong told *Motor Cycle News*: 'I don't feel I should comment on this at the moment. All the details will not be settled for at least another two weeks.' This was in response to continued speculation about Honda's intentions by certain sections of the media.

In their 14 March issue, *Motor Cycle News* ran the following story:

A cable exclusively to MCN received on Monday 12 March from the boss of the Tokyo factory, informed us that they will be fielding teams in all the world classic events this year in the 50cc, 125cc and 250cc classes, and will be entering one or two riders in the 350cc category. In company with Bob McIntyre, already confirmed as number-one runner, the factory is arranging with its riders from last year, and that means 125cc World Champion, Tom Phillis, plus Rhodesian Jim Redman, and let's not forget that rising-sun-of-a-gun, Kunimitsu Takahashi.

In addition to Bob and the other riders mentioned, a new name, Tommy Robb, came up. Robb, who in 1961 rode works Matchless machines, had not come into anyone's reckoning before. But with Reg Armstrong confirmed as team manager, this should not have come as such a big surprise, as Reg knew Tommy very well – and was known to value his riding abilities.

Also, it had now, separately, been confirmed that Derek Minter would be riding one of the four-cylinder machines for the British importer. As for Mike Hailwood, the reigning 250cc World Champion, he was now contracted to the Italian MV Agusta team.

The jinx strikes again

The jinx that had dogged Bob Mac's career over the years was to strike during his very first competitive ride for Honda as a full works team member. As *Motor Cycle News*, dated 4 April 1962, reported:

> *A tremendous crowd saw excitement, suspense, failure – in fact just about everything that goes to make a cracking race meeting at Mallory Park, on Sunday (1 April). But most staggering of all was the cruel blow that struck Bob McIntyre, who crashed in practice on the 280cc (285cc actually) works Honda four!*

It happened when Tom Thorpe fell on the exit from the hairpin. Dave Degens, riding Geoff Duke's 350 Norton Special, and Bob on the larger-engined Honda were immediately behind him. Degens managed to scrape past, but Bob cannoned into the fallen machine, which catapulted him over the handlebars to land on the road on his back. Luckily both riders escaped serious injuries. The Honda, however, was extensively damaged and was thus eliminated from the meeting.

It should be pointed out that the arrival of the new, larger-engined Honda four had put paid to the original plans by Bob and Alastair King to discuss continuing to ride the Bianchi 350cc twin. The proposed visit to Italy never took place. Bob was contracted to Honda for classes up to and including 350cc, but he was still at liberty to ride for Joe Potts in the 500cc division. The choice of machinery for the big class was either a Manx Norton or the newly constructed Matchless Special (see Chapter 8).

Later, a medical report on Bob after his Mallory Park incident said: 'He is no more damaged than severely bruised.' A doctor examined him after the meeting – and this was his finding. A Honda spokesman informed the press that: 'Bob McIntyre hopes to be fit to ride at Silverstone (on Saturday 7 April).' The company were 'doing all they can to straighten out the damaged machine.'

Two of Honda Motor Company's top brass were among the most disappointed men at Mallory on that fateful day, when Bob spilled on the larger four. They were M. Inada (chief of the technical section) of the firm's export division and I. Matumoto of the service section. Their comment: 'very unfortunate. These things happen.' Later the same week it was confirmed that Ulsterman Tommy Robb had signed a contract to ride Honda works bikes in the 1962 World Championship series; the first of which was the Spanish Grand Prix at Barcelona on Sunday 6 May, in company with Tom Phillis, Jim Redman, Kunimitsu Takahashi and, of course, Bob McIntyre.

Even if Bob himself was fit to ride at Silverstone – it was the 30th Hutchinson 100 meeting – his 285cc Honda most certainly was not. So all Bob rode that day was his Matchless Special; coming in runner-up behind Mike Hailwood in the 15-lap 500cc event.

The Easter weekend

Next came the Easter weekend, but Bob didn't race at Brands Hatch on Friday 20 April or Snetterton on Sunday 22 April. His only appearance came at the international meeting staged at Oulton Park on Monday 23 April. The last race of the day – and what *MCN* called the 'race of the day' – was watched by 52,000 spectators, who all stayed because this was the one they had come to see: Bob McIntyre riding his first race on the 285cc Honda four, rebuilt since his unfortunate practice spill at Mallory Park three weeks earlier. And Bob didn't disappoint his many fans.

After lying second in the early stages of the first lap, he dropped right back, but then forced his way through the pack and at the end of the 14th lap snatched the lead from Alan Shepherd (AJS). As *MCN* explained: 'But that was only the half of it! Throughout the race there had been a terrific battle between Phil Read (Norton) and Alastair King (AJS) for second place – until Mac howled past them.'

At the same time the crowd's eyes were also fixed upon Derek Minter (Norton) who, though last away, was emulating McIntyre's stepladder act, and eventually finished fourth.

After passing Shepherd, Bob slowly drew away, setting the fastest lap in the process at 87.19mph, and he began his final lap with a four-second lead. Then

Leading Alan Shepherd
(Matchless G50) at Oulton
Park on Easter Monday, 23
April 1961. Bob was riding
his recently completed
Matchless Special and he
won!

came drama as the dreaded McIntyre jinx struck again. This time he suffered a puncture, which, as *Motor Cycle News* said: 'brought his 285cc Honda to a ragged halt.' The report continued: 'Tragic, because Mac had made a bad start and had fought his way to the front. Due to an obscure ignition fault his machine was misfiring at high rpm.'

The McIntyre-Shepherd battle had in fact been a direct follow on from the pair's 'epic battle' (*MCN*) during the 500cc race earlier in the afternoon in which Bob, riding his home-built Matchless Special, set a new course lap record of 90.36mph.

Very seldom were the two more than a few feet apart, and the lead changed constantly. However, as *Motor Cycle News* said: 'Towards the end, McIntyre established his superiority.' Both riders finished over half a minute ahead of Derek Minter on the works development Norton Dominator twin which, although appearing extremely fast, appeared to lack the superlative qualities of its single-cylinder brother.

Another rider that Bob beat in the 500cc race at Oulton Park on Monday 23 April 1961 was the up-and-coming Phil Read (Norton).

500cc Oulton Park – 19 laps – 51.3 miles

1st	R. McIntyre (Matchless Special)
2nd	A. Shepherd (Matchless)
3rd	D. Minter (Norton)
4th	P.W. Read (Norton)
5th	A. King (Norton)
6th	F. Fisher (Norton)

Englishman Dan Shorey, riding an air-cooled Bultaco 196cc single-cylinder two-stroke, finished fourth, fourth and sixth in the first three rounds of the 1962 250cc World Championship series. Bob referred to the Spanish bike as 'that bloody thing!' when he joked with Dan on the start line of the French GP.

McIntyre the magnificent!

In the 2 May 1962 issue of *Motor Cycle News*, the headline on the back page read: 'Mallory – and it's McIntyre the magnificent!' Alan Shepherd again provided the opposition to the Flying Scot, in both the 350 and 500cc races. In the larger capacity event Bob overtook Shepherd on the seventh lap and went on to win from Shepherd, Minter and Read. An identical result to Oulton!

In the 350cc final Bob, on the 285cc Honda, was so far ahead of everyone else (including Shepherd) that as one commentator said: 'The only thing he had to chase was his own shadow.' And at long last he had not only finished a race on the 285cc Honda, but also tasted victory into the bargain. This, together with his 500cc win, made that Sunday, 29 April, a rather special day for Mr McIntyre.

Only seven days later, on Sunday 6 May 1962, Bob was racing a two-fifty works Honda four in the Spanish Grand Prix – the 12th such event organised by the *Real Moto Club de Catalana* and staged on a sun-drenched Montjuich Park, Barcelona, road circuit.

The 250cc race was the 'big' event of the day (the other events being the 50cc, 125cc and sidecars). Tom Phillis, Jim Redman and Bob McIntyre, all on Hondas, shared the front row, with the Italian Silvio Grassetti on a four-cylinder Benelli. The race pattern quickly settled down to the three Honda riders circulating closely together, with the lone Benelli fourth. But if the Honda stars thought they were in for an easy race, they were to be proved wrong, as the Benelli offered what appeared to be a viable challenge. In fact, Grassetti managed to get in front of Bob before retiring at his pits.

The war of attrition on all the machinery taking part had taken its toll, and four laps from the end only six riders were still circulating, with the three

Hondas followed by Dan Shorey's 196cc Bultaco. And, as a guide to just how the field had strung out behind the Japanese four-cylinder bikes, as the leaders started their 29th lap, Alberto Pagani (Aermacchi) was on his 26th lap, and he was in fifth position! Jim Redman went on to win, with Bob second, Tom Phillis third and Shorey fourth. But, unknown to anyone except Bob at the time, the Scot's gearbox had been playing up.

250cc Spanish GP – 33 laps – 78.23 miles

1st	J.A. Redman (Honda)
2nd	R. McIntyre (Honda)
3rd	T. Phillis (Honda)
4th	D.F. Shorey (Bultaco)
5th	A. Pagani (Aermacchi)
6th	M. Toussaint (Benelli)

The French Grand Prix

After Spain, the Grand Prix circus travelled north to Clermont-Ferrand in central France. As *The Motor Cycle* race report dated 17 May reveals: 'One extreme to another – from the blistering sunshine of Barcelona a week earlier to the windswept, bitterly cold heights of Clermont-Ferrand for the French Grand Prix, second classic of the 1962 season.'

As in Spain, the French round only held races for 50cc, 125cc, 250cc and sidecar. So Bob was restricted to a single outing – whereas his Honda teammates had at least two rides.

Without Silvio Grassetti and his Benelli four, and with the withdrawal of the Suzuki twins (after various practice troubles), the two-fifty race was obviously going to be a Honda benefit. The only question was, who would win? Once again the order was Redman, McIntyre and Phillis. The press generally labelled it rather boring – *MCN*'s headline read: 'French Farce!'

250cc French Grand Prix – 16 laps – 80.08 miles

1st	J.A. Redman (Honda)
2nd	R. McIntyre (Honda)
3rd	T. Phillis (Honda)
4th	D.F. Shorey (Bultaco)
5th	R. Beltoise (Morini)
6th	B. Savage (FB Mondial)

Home wins for Bob Mac

Scorning the lure of more lucrative meetings, Bob Mac brought his works

Bob took the factory 285 Honda four to Beveridge Park on 19 May 1962. He is seen here with the bike in the paddock at the Scottish parkland circuit.

285cc Honda four to Beveridge Park, Kirkcaldy, on Saturday 19 May 1962 and as *The Motor Cycle* said: 'Showed his 'ain folk' just what this screaming Japanese device was capable of.'

There was a crowd estimated to have been around 8,000 and although rain during practising caused some accidents, the actual racing was held in brilliant sunshine. Altogether 187 riders lined up for the racing; nearly a further 100 had been refused an entry.

There is absolutely no doubt that Bob stole the limelight that day, not only winning both his heat and final on the Honda in the 350cc race, but also repeating these results on his Potts Norton in the 1000cc class. During the prize-giving at the conclusion of the meeting, Bob received a standing ovation from the crowd. He didn't know it at the time, but when he finally left Beveridge Park later that evening he would never again see the Parkland venue where he had witnessed his first road race all those years earlier, and enjoyed taking part in many other races over the succeeding years.

Next stop was the Isle of Man. *Motor Cycle News* of Wednesday 30 May 1962 reported:

Bob McIntyre set the ball rolling on the 1962 TT races on Saturday morning (26 May) in a style more dazzling than the brilliant sun which graced the Island at dawn for the opening practice period... Indeed, it must have come as an omen from the East for the flying Scot whipped his Japanese Honda 250cc around the 37.73-mile circuit in 23 mins 10.6 secs; at the magnificent speed of 97.68mph.

Bob flat out on the Honda four in the 350cc race, Beveridge Park, Kirkcaldy, 19 May 1962. He won both the 350cc and 500cc races and set the fastest lap in each. In the bigger class he rode his Matchless Special.

This was an incredible opening performance – especially when one takes into account the fact that he cut the Honda's engine on the run down the Glencrutchery Road from Governor's Bridge, thus slowing to a stop at the pits! The Japanese rider Moto Kitano was second fastest with a speed of 88.16mph, while Jim Redman was third, clocking 82.68mph.

The latest Honda fours were equipped with new extra-large fuel tanks of no less than 8 imperial gallons, intended to provide for a non-stop run over the six-lap distance for both 250s and the 285s in the Junior race.

1962 Isle of Man TT, riding the 285 Honda in practice. After leading the 250cc race he retired (oil leak), in the 350cc he retired (ignition), while in the 500cc Bob was a non-starter.

Geoff Duke's opinion

In giving his view upon who would win the Lightweight (250cc) TT, Geoff Duke, writing in *Motor Cycle News*, voiced the opinion that Honda had scared off MV and Morini. So as he said: 'It would therefore appear that the only remaining question is – which Honda man will win'. He went on to say: 'On sheer ability, backed up by last year's performance, Bob McIntyre is my automatic choice, but from the Spanish and French GP results it would appear that Jim Redman is their chosen man for 1962!

Another feature of the 1962 TT races was that Bob was using a new triangular sectioned rear tyre which had been developed by the Birmingham-based Dunlop concern after extensive research and practical tests. Use of the tyre followed successful testing at Mallory Park, much of it carried out by Bob himself.

No 285cc fours were present during the early part of TT practice, but by Wednesday morning Bob was out on the bigger fours in the Junior (350cc) session – going round in 23 mins 6 secs, a speed of exactly 98mph (the fastest of the riders taking part). He also retained his position at the head of the Lightweight (250cc) class.

Drama all the way

It was drama all the way in the 250cc race, which took place on Monday 4 June 1962. Derek Minter, entered on a 1961 Honda four, but fitted with one of the latest '62 type engines, eventually won, but only after he had had the shock of starting number 1 on the grid and seeing Bob McIntyre roar past him, having wiped off a 30-second deficit with the first lap less than half over. But Bob, after setting up a 99.06mph first lap from a standing start (only 0.52 of a second outside his previous year's record) then found his Honda four running on only two cylinders and he retired at Baaregarroo second time around. Much controversy followed Minter's victory. It was widely rumoured that he had displeased the Honda factory so much that they ignored him from then on. For the record, only eight machines actually finished – three Hondas, Minter plus Redman and Phillis, Arthur Wheeler (Moto Guzzi), Alberto Pagani (Aermacchi), Dan Shorey (Bultaco), Fred Hardy (REG twin) and D. Guy on a Triumph Tiger Cub modified to 242cc.

So for the second year running Bob McIntyre had been forced to retire his two-fifty Honda while leading the race – and setting the fastest lap. What cruel, cruel luck.

Again Geoff Duke tipped Bob to win, this time the Junior (350cc) on his 285cc four. And once again the Scot was to be ruled out by machine trouble – he retired on lap three, when in third place behind the MV Agustas of Gary Hocking and Mike Hailwood (who went on to finish first and second respectively). Bob's engine expired at Keppel Gate. And to everyone's deep sorrow teammate Tom Phillis, on the other 285, crashed fatally at Laurel Bank on the second lap.

To cap a thoroughly miserable week, Bob was a non-starter in the Senior TT, when his 285cc Honda was pronounced as: 'still hopelessly bug-ridden after the Junior failure and not even checked in'.

Mallory Park Post-TT

The annual Mallory Park Post-TT meeting on Sunday 10 June saw Bob have to resort to his trusty Matchless Special, which, confronted by the four-cylinder MVs of Hailwood and Hocking (first and second respectively), had to concede; even though its constructor rode his brilliant best. *Motor Cycle News* commented in their issue of 13 June 1962: 'Third man was Bob McIntyre, who rode in his usual immaculate style.'

No Hondas were available for Bob to ride; Jim Redman won both the 125 and 250cc races on the Japanese machines.

500cc Mallory Park Post TT – 20 laps – 27 miles

1st	S.M.B. Hailwood (MV Agusta)
2nd	G. Hocking (MV Agusta)
3rd	R. McIntyre (Matchless Special)
4th	H. Anderson (Matchless)
5th	A. King (Norton)
6th	D.F. Degens (Matchless)

At the Dutch TT, the 285cc Honda four once again expired. This time, right from the start, the engine 'spewed out oil' (*The Motor Cycle*). So, after only a few minutes, Bob was forced to drop away from teammate Redman. The latter went on to win. In fact, Redman also won the 250cc race and one began to feel that just maybe the best machines were being reserved for the Rhodesian. But at least in this latter race Bob's machine did keep going, allowing him to finish runner-up in front of the super-fast Moto Morini single of Tarquinio Provini.

250cc Dutch TT – 17 laps – 81.2 miles

1st   J. Redman (Honda)

2nd   R. McIntyre (Honda)

3rd   T. Provini (Morini)

4th   C. Swart (Honda)

5th   F. Perris (Suzuki)

6th   A. Wheeler (Moto Guzzi)

Belgian Grand Prix

The glorious sunshine and a scorching battle between Jim Redman and Bob McIntyre in the 250cc race were the highlights of the 1962 Belgian Grand Prix at Spa Francorchamps, on Sunday 8 July.

In the end Bob won by what *Motor Cycle News* described as: 'a street'. However, for much of the nine-lap, 78.85-mile race it was a hard-fought battle with championship leader and Honda teammate Jim Redman. In the end it was Redman's turn to strike bike trouble, and Bob went on to record his first GP victory since the previous August when he had won the 250cc Ulster GP.

This is how former World Champion Geoff Duke saw the battle:

Bob working on one of the Hondas at a British short-circuit meeting. Pim Fleming (in white overalls) looks on.

I was a very impressed spectator at the Eau Rouge Bridge during the '250' event. This is a downhill left-hander, followed immediately by a long climbing banked curve. The fabulous performance of the two leaders, Bob McIntyre and Jim Redman, as they changed positions from lap to lap, certainly kept the crowd on their toes and made up for the smaller number of starters. Bob had a shade better

*line from the beginning, and was most consistent, leaving his peeling
off point very late, and on one occasion at least swept past Jim by the
top of the rise.*

Luigi Taveri on the other four had to concede some seven seconds a lap to the
two leaders. Allan Robinson, reporting for *Motor Cycle News,* had this to
say: 'McIntyre rode like a champion to win his first classic of the season, and
there was no suggestion of anyone riding to team orders.'

Towards the end of the race, Redman's engine went sour and he was almost
caught by Taveri – Jim's oil tank had split at Stavelot and he was forced to
limp the last few miles. The fastest lap of the race was set by Bob at
114.5mph.

Pim Fleming, Bob and Jim
Redman.

250cc Belgian GP – 9 laps – 78.85 miles

1st   R. McIntyre (Honda)

2nd   J. Redman (Honda)

3rd   L. Taveri (Honda)

4th   G. Beer (Adler)

5th   A. Wheeler (Moto Guzzi)

6th   P. Vervroegen (Aermacchi)

West German Grand Prix

The *Motor Cycle News* headline shouted:

> *Terrific Redman-McIntyre duel in Germany… the 250cc race was clearly the most dramatic of the four on the 11.4 kilometre (7.08-mile) Solitude circuit, twisting through the wooded hills near Stuttgart. The thrilling duel between Redman and McIntyre had the crowd of over 300,000 on their toes throughout. Frequently during the 11 laps, McIntyre inched ahead on the climbs with Redman regaining the lead on the straights. Side by side the two Hondas screamed down the final 200-metre straight, with Redman winning by half a length.*

250cc West German GP – 11 laps – 78.1 miles

1st   J. Redman (Honda)

2nd   R. McIntyre (Honda)

3rd   T. Tonaka (Honda)

4th   G. Beer (Honda)

5th   A. Wheeler (Moto Guzzi)

6th   M. Schneider (NSU)

Bob flew back to Britain in an Austrian Airlines Vickers Viscount, with Honda teammate Tommy Robb, and the two enjoyed a meal together of steak and mushrooms, with fresh peaches and coffee afterwards.

After the West German Grand Prix, the 250cc World Championship points placings stood as follows:

1	J. Redman (Honda)	8 – 8 – 6 – 8 – 6 – 8 = 44
2	R. McIntyre (Honda)	6 – 6 – 0 – 6 – 8 – 6 = 32
3	T. Phillis (Honda)	4 – 4 – 4 – 0 – 0 – 0 = 12
4	D. Minter (Honda)	0 – 0 – 8 – 0 – 0 – 0 = 8
5	A. Wheeler (Moto Guzzi)	0 – 0 – 3 – 1 – 2 – 2 = 8
6	G. Beer (Adler/Honda)	0 – 0 – 0 – 0 – 3 – 3 = 6

A new arrival

Only three days after the West German Grand Prix, Bob's wife Joyce gave birth to a baby daughter, Eleanor Campbell McIntyre, weighing 8lb and born on Wednesday 18 July 1962.

And so to that fateful day, at Oulton Park on Bank Holiday Monday, 6 August 1962, at the scene of the annual British Championship meeting at the 2.7-mile Cheshire circuit. Bob was entered in the 250, 350 and 500cc Championship races, plus the Les Graham Memorial Trophy Race – on Honda and Matchless machines. However, actually, he was a non-starter in the 250 (no bike), while in the larger class his Matchless entry was in fact a Norton on the day.

Race number four was the British Junior championship. This was scheduled to start at 2pm and would run over 30 laps (82.83 miles). Riding under No.6, Bob's mount was the 285cc Honda four. In typical McIntyre style, Bob fought his way into the lead from the back of the grid, but after establishing a new lap record of 88.59mph the 'evil jinx' (*The Motor Cycle*) returned on lap eight. As Bob was to explain to reporters back in the pits: 'The engine just stopped.' From then on the issue of who would be the 1962 350cc British champion was between Mike Hailwood (AJS), Derek Minter

With the Honda team at the 1962 West German GP at Solitude, 15 July. Bob can be seen with team manager Reg Armstrong, centrally at rear of bikes. This was to be his last meeting before the fateful day at Oulton Park three weeks later.

and Phil Read (Norton). And once Bob Mac had retired, the duel between these three went to Minter.

'Bright and sunny' had been the weather forecast, but there were streaming wet roads and heavy rain to greet race five, the British Senior Championship race, which was scheduled for 3.50pm and was to be over 30 laps.

As a spectator that day I well remember the clouds of spray and water lying around the circuit. The early leaders included Read and Minter (Norton) and New Zealander Hugh Anderson (Matchless). Both Bob and Mike Hailwood were well down the field. But Bob, in his usual fashion, not only fought his way up to second place, but also started closing on Minter. However, on lap 19 he crashed heavily on Clay Hill and was rushed to hospital (Chester Royal Infirmary) with, it was reported: 'Serious head, arm and other injuries' (*The Motor Cycle*). Many spectators on that day, including myself, simply did not know what had happened. We certainly did not realise the serious nature of the accident. *Motor Cycle News* reported that: 'His Matchless [this was incorrect as he was riding a Manx Norton] appeared to seize, and he was thrown.'

Bob in 1962 – the concentration and commitment he put into every race is evident in this shot.

First clue to cause

In *Motor Cycle News* dated 15 August 1962, the first details of what had caused Bob's crash were given courtesy of his great friend Alastair King: 'Inspecting the course, Alastair found a skid mark 100 yards long near the point where Bob crashed and said he thought that his gearbox must have seized.'

By then Bob's wife and his mother and father had moved temporarily to a furnished house in Chester to be nearer the Chester Royal Infirmary. This had been arranged by fellow racer Bill Smith. *MCN* went on to say: 'Early on Tuesday morning (14 August) Bob McIntyre was fighting for his life.' The report went on: 'His condition had deteriorated and he was critically ill.' Alastair King withdrew his entries from the Ulster GP to be on hand to help the McIntyre family.

In fact, the very day *Motor Cycle News* was published, Bob passed away – Wednesday 15 August 1962. The Flying Scot was dead. And as I write these words almost 43 years to the very day later, a lump has come to my throat and tears bubble up in my eyes – just as they did all those years ago. I was stunned, as the rest of the motorcycling world was. We had all lost a very special man.

Among the 500 mourners at the funeral on Saturday 19 August were relatives and friends, but every facet of motorcycling was represented – riders past and present, organisers, mechanics, clubmen, the Auto Cycle Union, trade, industry and the press.

The Motor Cycle (23 August 1962) set the scene:

A sunny calm befitting Bob McIntyre's imperturbable nature settled on Daldowie Crematorium, Glasgow last Saturday midday. In pleasant surroundings several hundred admirers filled the chapel seats, floor space and precincts in a last homage to one of the best loved and most talented of all racers.

The crematorium service was conducted by the Reverend James McKay, Pastor of Scotstoun (Bob's birthplace), Glasgow. Among those present at the service were: Dave Fisher and P.A. Moffat of the SACU, Ken Shierson (ACU), Tom Milton, Les Weir and Fred Petty (all from the *Scottish Clubman* magazine), James Kay (*Motor Cycle News*), Alastair King, Charlie Bruce, Bill Robertson, Jim Rae, Jim Buchan, Jack Adam, Glen Anderson, Ewan Haldane, Bill Smith (the sales manager of AMC), Sam and Les Cooper and a large number of club members from Glasgow and the rest of Scotland (including Mercury and Kirkcaldy clubs). And of course Joe Potts and Jim (Pim) Fleming.

From south of the border came an equally large number, including: Geoff Duke, John Hartle, Derek Minter, Jim Redman, Syd Lawton, Eric Bowers, Rex Foster and Terry Shepherd. Trade representatives included: Roberto Persi (Gilera), Bill Hannah (Liverpool), Bill Fitton (Kings Glasgow), Jack Williams (AMC), Dickie Davies (Dunlop), Jimmy Simpson (Castrol), Lew Ellis (Shell/BP), Vic Doyle (Renolds chains), Reg Armstrong (Honda) and Bob Walsham (Avon Tyres).

Bob McIntyre during his last race, the 500cc British Championship event at Oulton Park, 6 August 1962. He is seen here on the approach to Clay Hill on his Potts Norton machine, almost the exact spot where he was later to crash. The terribly wet conditions are evident in this photograph.

And there were others. One of these, and one who remained a solitary figure after everyone else had departed – after paying silent tribute – was one of Bob's old workmates from long before he became a legend in his own lifetime. This was Ian Mackay, who in 1962 was working with Albion Motors in Scotstoun. Ian and Bob had both been engineering apprentices at Robb Brothers in Partick during 1947. Then, both aged 18, they had shared a friendship which had lasted the test of time.

Later that day a private service took place at the McIntyre home in Ballater Drive, Bearsden.

The tributes

Very rarely has there been such an outburst of feeling for a fallen comrade. Tributes came from all round the world, from a vast and varied number of people. Here are just a few of them:

Joe Potts: 'My eight years' racing association with Bob was the most exhilarating of my life. His unassuming manner, quiet grin and intense keenness were tremendously endearing. He loved the sport deeply and was a sportsman in the finest British tradition. Bob never rode for gain but for the love of speed. With his tragic end we have lost a great champion and a great friend.'

John Hartle: 'Bob's determined struggles in the face of long odds and bad luck earned him the esteem always accorded to a fighter. He was the safest rider to be in a close scrap with; others could well emulate his considerate riding.'

Geoff Duke: 'Though it took a little while to get to know him, Bob was then a wonderful friend and teammate. He would help anyone, and it was a privilege to be with him. I held him in the highest esteem as a man and considered him the world's finest rider. Racing has lost its last real personality.'

Roberto Persi (Gilera team manager in 1957): 'I shall miss not only a brilliant rider but also a good friend. The mechanics loved him and always did their best for him. Bob was very cooperative and always humble.'

Jim (Pim) Fleming: 'Perfection was his only standard. Many an argument it caused but he was adamant – absolutely everything had to be spot-on. As he demanded the best, so he gave his best. There was no rider to touch him.'

Charlie Bruce: 'This is the end of an era. In his first day's racing Bob qualified as a Scottish expert. In the workshop he was full of bright ideas. Both as a rider and man Bob was an inspiration – the only one of his kind.'

Alastair King (who also announced his own retirement from racing): 'Since Bob and I met at our first race meeting 11 years ago our friendship grew in strength until he became a part of my life. I greatly admired his efforts and

OFFICIAL PROGRAMME 2s.

OULTON *PARK*

THE AUTO-CYCLE UNION **INTERNATIONAL** ROAD RACE **MEETING FOR THE 1962** BRITISH CHAMPIONSHIPS

GET DOWN TO IT EVERY THURSDAY WITH

Motor Cycle

THE COMPLETE MAGAZINE. 1s.

achievements. A brilliant rider, he left a lasting impression of strength and the joy of life. His death is like the end of a monarch's reign. I am proud and grateful he was my friend.'

There were also hundreds of letters from racing enthusiasts. I have selected a couple to illustrate just how fondly Bob the rider and Bob the man were viewed by the general public:

'I can hardly believe yet that Bob Mac has gone. I will remember him as someone who upheld everything that is fine in our sport, and he gave everything that he had to the racing game. For many of us, the spectacle of motorcycle road racing will not be quite the same. We will miss the determined McIntyre jaw line, the weatherworn Mercury badge on his helmet, and the thrill of seeing him press on with the utmost determination in adverse conditions. A school teacher is reported to have said: "Bobby McIntyre, you're a terrible dunce. You'll never make your mark in the world." Yet he made his own special mark, probably beyond his own early dreams, and was admired and respected by all whose privilege it was to have met him. Bob McIntyre was a very gallant gentleman.' **A. Small, Dundee.**

'To me, Bob McIntyre lived and died as the greatest of them all; his individual efforts made him so. Though I have been riding motorcycles for only three years and spectating at race events for two and a half, I realized Bob's greatness from the start. He was a rider-tuner, no easy life, but he certainly made up for it on the track, and it seems it was usually the machinery that packed up first. My blood ran cold when he hurtled past the pits on that two-eight-five Honda, that fateful Monday. I feel proud to say that I have stood within his shadow, and I treasure (and always will) his autograph.' **K. Biddlestowe, Bilston, Staffs.**

Vic Willoughby's appreciation

But probably the greatest tribute of all was written by Vic Willoughby, himself a former racer and much respected journalist, who, at the time worked for *The Motor Cycle*. Here are a few extracts from what I still consider a moving and superbly written personal tribute, which appeared in all 20,000 copies of *The Motor Cycle* printed for Scotland, and more issues distributed to various other parts of the UK.

> *It was training time for the 1952 TT. Carburation on my Velocette was completely haywire and unresponsive to routine adjustments. I*

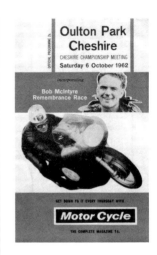

had no transport. One lunchtime a BSA box-float drew up at my digs. The driver, a soft-spoken, serious-looking young Scot, had heard of my plight. In the fewest possible words he offered to take the Velo and me up to the Mountain Mile for tests. That quiet generosity to a stranger was typical of Bob McIntyre, then on his first Island visit and probably unknown to everyone but Sam Cooper, his sponsor before he came under Joe Potts' wing.

Vic concluded his lengthy appreciation by saying:

A life of adventure was as compulsive to Bob as flying is to a bird. Challenge and conquest were food and drink to his spirit. It is hard to realize that his slow, broad smile, grim jawline and masterly riding – so integral a part of the racing scene these last ten years – are gone. Nine days after his August Monday crash in vile weather at Oulton Park, his tragic death dealt road racing one of its most stunning blows and left a gap that none can fill. Though we mourn, we can be proud that the sport he graced and those who were privileged to enjoy his friendship are richer people for his impact.

When I spoke to Vic Willoughby during the late 1980s, I realised that, over a quarter of a century after these words had been written, he was just as passionate about Bob as he had been back in 1962. This, I feel, really sums up the aura of Bob McIntyre. He was the genuine article and all those who had been able to gain his confidence and trust were left with a lasting feeling of the true greatness this humble, but fiercely determined Scot exuded. What more fitting tribute could there possibly be?

Alastair King announced his retirement from racing following Bob's death. Alastair rode his 500cc Norton for the last time at Oulton Park on a demonstration lap in October 1962, together with Geoff Duke (Gilera) and Georg Meier (BMW). As Alastair said of Bob 'A brilliant rider, he left a lasting impression of strength and the joy of life. His death is like the end of a monarch's reign.'

Tim Miller and ...

Ian Ambler with the trophies they won at the 2004 Bob McIntyre Memorial meeting.

Baby Eleanor McIntyre.

Chapter 10

A Place in History

THE first thing one has to say of Bob McIntyre is that he was the greatest road racer never to have been crowned World Champion. In fact, in my opinion, many who have actually achieved this feat have not measured up to Bob's skill, ability, dedication and, above all, real fighting spirit.

Spirit and determination were at the very heart of the Flying Scot's make-up. He simply would never accept defeat. And perhaps here was one of the reasons Bob never became a World Champion. However, just why he never achieved this goal is multi-faceted. You have to finish races to win titles and Bob was often forced to retire through mechanical failure. So was this inadequate preparation? Well, as he was a skilled engineer this is very unlikely. As his mechanic Jim (Pim) Fleming was to recall, Bob was 'thorough to the point of argument if things were not right', Pim admitting that often the two argued on this point. And in any case, the works bikes he rode, particularly Bianchi and Honda, broke too. So was it that he simply rode the bikes too hard? Well, again Bob was someone who understood engines and why they were equipped with rev counters! So, again this theory is somewhat flawed. Yes, he did ride the wheels off his mounts – but not to the point of being foolhardy by overrevving in extremes. Also, although he did have his share of crashes, these were not on any higher a ratio than other top liners. In fact Bob probably had fewer accidents; certainly compared to the likes of John Hartle.

This leaves the element of luck – which in Bob McIntyre's case was often of the bad variety. There were countless times during his 12-year long racing career when his machine would fail – often near the very end of the race. For example, from 18 TT starts between 1952 and 1962, he retired 11 times and finished only seven events!

Another factor was that Bob McIntyre was an entirely self-made man.

Unlike, say, Giacomo Agostini or Mike Hailwood, there were no well-off parents. Nor, as in John Surtees's case, was there a father figure to lend support and dish out knowledge. No, Bob fought his way up from the very bottom. This, combined with his grim determination, fantastic natural ability as a rider and engineer, and perhaps most of all his honesty, made him the peoples' champion. And his fan base was not just restricted to his Scottish homeland, but spread all over Great Britain and Ireland. However, he was largely unknown in Europe and further afield. And this was associated with the fact that he had to earn his living from racing. So, he could not afford to travel all over Europe. Not only that, but, as he was the first to admit, he didn't really enjoy foreign travel, being never happier than when he was with friends and family.

Bob McIntyre was also a man of few words – he certainly did not waste them on idle chatter or self-promotion. He very much believed in letting his riding do the talking. Yes, others, certainly in the modern era, can often talk a good race. But Mr McIntyre got on his bike and made people sit up and take notice.

George Wilson, Associate Editor of *The Motor Cycle*, writing in the programme of the Bob McIntyre Memorial meeting at Oulton Park on 6 October 1962, summed Bob up in the following way:

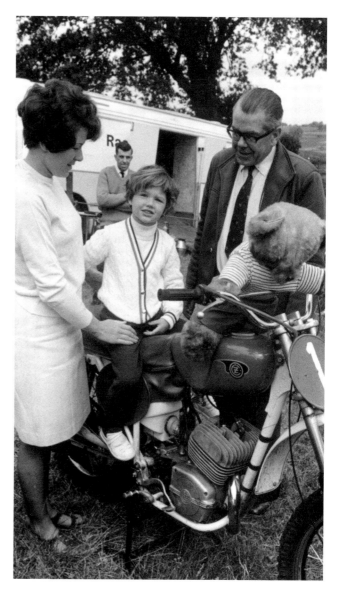

Early 1970s. Eleanor, now 10 years of age, with her mother and Lew Ellis, who together with his wife Kath was to remain a good friend to the McIntyre family after Bob's untimely passing.

Slow, soft-spoken, Bob was every inch a man's man. He was a lover of truth; he had a hatred of factual inaccuracy. And to the making and choosing of friends Bob applied the same ice-cold logic and judgement he displayed in the saddle. Yet friends of Bob had a friend in the fullest sense.

Bob also had a wonderful smile – when he was happy, it showed!

Although Bob raced for a total of 12 years (mid-1950 until mid-1962), he

The first Bob McIntyre
Memorial meeting took
place at Knockhill in 1985.
This photograph was
taken at the 1987 event.
Left to right: Luigi Taveri,
Tommy Robb, Eleanor and
Ralph Bryans.

The author's friend Tommy
Robb and Bill Cadger, who
together with wife Agnes
has done so much to keep
Bob McIntyre's memory
alive, at the 'Bob Mac' at
Knockhill, 21 June 1992.

The Bob McIntyre
Memorial Classic Races

East Fortune

Saturday/Sunday
19/20 June 2004

VEHICLE PASS

THIS PASS MUST BE DISPLAYED

only racked up a total of some 400 races (excluding heats), compared to Mike
Hailwood whose total exceeds 700 (again excluding heats). Also, Mike rode
no fewer than 18 different makes of bike; Bob's total was only eight:
Aermacchi, AJS, Bianchi, BSA, Honda, Gilera, Norton and NSU.

    The respect, admiration, and even love displayed by fellow competitors,
spectators, friends and family came to the fore after his fatal accident at
Oulton Park in August 1962. Not only were the tributes many and genuine in

their appreciation of the man, but there have also been the events which have transpired since, beginning with the race meetings in his honour at Oulton Park and Gask in the weeks following his funeral. At Oulton Park, not only did Geoff Duke do a demonstration lap on one of the 1957 'dustbin' faired Gilera fours, but the 1939 Senior TT winner, Georg Meier, also came over from Germany as a mark of respect and rode his supercharged factory BMW. And don't forget Bob never rode a BMW – but it just shows the respect in which he

Eleanor receiving the induction plaque when Bob was inducted into the Scottish Sports Hall of Fame, St Andrew's Day, 2002. On Eleanor's right is Scottish first minister Jack McConnell.

Guests at the Bob McIntyre Memorial Meeting

1985	Mrs Margaret King (Alastair King's wife), Jock Weddell
1986	Syd Lawton
1987	Mrs Elizabeth McIntyre (Bob's mother), Eleanor McIntyre (Bob's daughter)
1988	Ralph Bryans
1989	Alan Shepherd
1990	Percy Tait
1991	Bill Lomas
1992	Luigi Taveri, Ralph Bryans, Tommy Robb, Alan Shepherd, Eleanor Quigley
1993	Robin Sherry
1994	Mick Grant
1995	Derek Minter
1996	Geoff Duke
1997	Derek Minter
1998	Adam Brownlie
1999	Bill Swallow
2000	Jim Redman
2001	Jim Curry
2002	Donnie McLeod
2003	Jack Martin
2004	Dave Kay and Gilera 4 (event sponsors)
2005	Dave Kay, Mick Walker, Eleanor Quigley

The Bob McIntyre meeting has been held at Knockhill (1985–1998) and East Fortune (1999–2005).

George Plenderleith pictured at East Fortune in June 2005. George was a well-known Scottish racer in his own right during the 1950s and 1960s. He purchased the ex-McIntyre 250 Norton c.1959. He confirmed to the author just how difficult a bike it was to ride.

The Gilera 500 four-cylinder replica built by the Kay family. The three generations are shown here. Left to right: Pat Sefton (rider), Mark Kay, Mitchell Kay and the 'Old Man' Dave Kay. Bob McIntyre Memorial, East Fortune, 18/19 June 2005.

Kirkcaldy & District Motor Club

Kirkcaldy and District Motor Club was formed in 1922, with the first event being held on 20 May of that year. In 1925, the Club joined the Scottish Auto Cycle Union. In 1933, Kirkcaldy and District Motor Club members won the Senior and Junior Manx Grand Prix Team Awards at the Isle of Man with members J.K. Swanston, J.H. Blythe and T. McEwan.

After World War Two, in 1948, the Club organised the first Scottish Road races at Beveridge Park in Kirkcaldy. This meeting was titled the Kirkcaldy Grand Prix. In 1949, the second Scottish Road Races were run and broadcast live on BBC radio with Graham Walker, father of Murray, doing the commentary. There was a live broadcast every year until at least 1964.

In 1951 Bob McIntyre made his debut, and this started a decade of duels with Alastair King. In 1952 the Club hosted a combined car and motorcycle race within Beveridge Park, with Ken Tyrell winning and notable entries including Joe Potts and Ninian Sanderson. Also that year, the Club organised a motorcycle only race meeting at the old World War Two airfield of Crail, with Bob McIntyre dominating events.

In the 1960s, the Club organised scrambling meetings at Kilrie (outside Kirkcaldy) which were broadcast live on the BBC's sports programme, *Grandstand*. At the 1962 Scottish Road Races, Bob McIntyre entered the works 285cc Honda four-cylinder machine and again cleaned up. In 1967, the BBC was back in Kirkcaldy, this time to broadcast live the Scottish Road Races from Beveridge Park.

In 1974, the Club heralded a new dawn in motorcycling in Fife by holding a race meeting at the newly opened Knockhill racing circuit near Dunfermline. Four years later Club member Jock Taylor went on to win the Isle of Man Sidecar TT with Kenny Arthur in the chair. In 1980 Jock, with passenger Benga Johansson, reached the pinnacle of sidecar racing by winning the Sidecar World Championship. In 1981 a notable newcomer entered the Scottish Road Races, Niall MacKenzie on a Yamaha 350LC.

In 1982 the Club was informed of the tragic news that Jock had been killed in a racing accident at the Finnish Grand Prix in Imatra. A memorial now stands in Beveridge Park in honour of him and other Club members.

In 1984 the Club introduced the highly successful Battle of the Twins to Scotland, with Jack Gow putting one over World F2 Champion Tony Rutter. 1988 witnessed the historic 40th and final running of the Scottish Road Races at Beveridge Park. It was decided that due to the speed of the modern machinery, and the narrowness of the tree-lined circuit, that racing would have to move to a more purpose-built circuit, with better facilities and safer racing for all concerned. The Club also ran that year's Celtic match races (Isle of Man, Ireland, Scotland, Wales and Cornwall) at Knockhill.

Next, in 1989, Club member Steve Hislop won three TT races in the week at the Isle of Man. Steve repeated this feat in 1991. Also during the TT he broke the outright lap record for the 37.73-mile Mountain course, taking the speed to over 123mph and the average race speed to 121mph riding a 750 Honda in the TT Formula 1.

In 1992 the Club returned to the old World War Two airfield at Crail in the East Neuk of Fife to organise race meetings. In 1993 the Club was given the honour of organising and officiating at a round of the British Championships at Knockhill. With the officials at the ACU being impressed by the Club's organisational skills, they were then asked in 1994 to organise and officiate at the first Supercup at the Knockhill circuit. In 1996 the Club again organised the Celtic match races at Knockhill, between Scotland, Ireland, Isle of Man and Wales.

1998 saw the 50th anniversary of the Scottish Road Races, Golden Jubilee celebrations being held in Beveridge Park, Kirkcaldy, with static displays of machines from years gone by and also parade laps by some of the riders who raced in the park throughout the years including Alan Duffus, Dennis Gallagher, Stewart Cole, George Paterson and Charlie Wright. Also in that year, Club member John Crawford won the British Supersport 600 Championship.

In 1999, the Club was asked to organise road racing events at Knockhill as part of the circuit's 25th anniversary. Also that year in the Isle of Man TT races, Club member Jim Moodie brought the official lap record back to Scotland and John Crawford retained his British 600 Supersport title.

In the new century, the Club held an anniversary film show, celebrity panel and reunion in the Adam Smith Centre in Kirkcaldy. The Club also organised the road racing events for the SACU millennium meeting held at Knockhill. In July Club member Jim Moodie won the British Supersport 600 championship, racing in the first half of the season on a Honda then moving across to a Yamaha.

In 2002, the Club was asked to run the final round of the European Sidecar Championship at Knockhill Race Circuit in the annual Jock Taylor Memorial meeting, and in 2004 the Eastern Airways Sidecar Championship was incorporated into the meeting.

The Club hopes to have the same success in the future with Club members, and also the chance to organise and officiate at some of the greatest motorcycling events in Scotland.

KIRKCALDY AND DISTRICT MOTOR CLUB LTD.

present the

40th
Scottish Road Races

BEVERIDGE PARK, KIRKCALDY
(By Kind Permission of Kirkcaldy District Council)

SATURDAY, 18th JUNE, 1988
First Race 12.30 p.m.

Official Programme   70p

Machines raced by Bob McIntyre at KDMC events:

1951	BSA Gold Star
1952	BSA Gold Star, AJS 7R
1953	AJS 7R, Matchless G45
1955–58	250cc, 350cc, 500cc Nortons
1959–61	350cc, 500cc Potts Nortons; Aermacchi (1961)
1962	285cc Honda, 500cc Norton

Bob McIntyre raced 11 years at KDMC events and won a total of 39 races.

Eleanor with husband David and children, June 2005.

Final Beveridge Park programme, 1988.

THE BOB McINTYRE MEMORIAL CLASSIC RACES

East Fortune Raceway
NATIONAL RESTRICTED EVENT

19th and 20th June 2004

ORGANISED BY
THE SCOTTISH CLASSIC RACING MOTORCYCLE CLUB
(SCRMC LTD) LIMITED

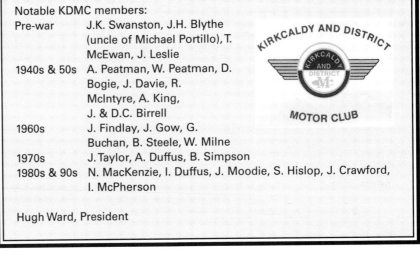

Notable KDMC members:

Pre-war	J.K. Swanston, J.H. Blythe (uncle of Michael Portillo), T. McEwan, J. Leslie
1940s & 50s	A. Peatman, W. Peatman, D. Bogie, J. Davie, R. McIntyre, A. King, J. & D.C. Birrell
1960s	J. Findlay, J. Gow, G. Buchan, B. Steele, W. Milne
1970s	J. Taylor, A. Duffus, B. Simpson
1980s & 90s	N. MacKenzie, I. Duffus, J. Moodie, S. Hislop, J. Crawford, I. McPherson

Hugh Ward, President

The author's friend Jimmy Mitchell with the model of Bob's 1957 Senior TT-winning Gilera, made by Ian Welsh of Edinburgh.

was held. At the same event, Alastair King demonstrated the 500cc Matchless with the lightweight frame developed by Bob. And when Alastair came back into the Oulton pits that day, he hung his leathers up for good. Sadly, Bob's fatal crash weighed heavily on Alastair and he was later killed in a car crash during the 1970s. After Bob's demise, Alastair's life was simply not the same.

The very same lightweight Matchless Special which Bob had constructed passed into the hands of the Australian Continental Circus rider Jack Findlay – and Jack took the bike to runner-up spot in the 1968 500cc World Championships, behind the works MV Agusta of Giacomo Agostini; it being entered as the 'McIntyre Matchless'. Today this motorcycle is owned and raced in classic events by Northampton dealer Mick Hemmings. Thus Bob's engineering skills continue to be remembered.

And another sign of how the Bob McIntyre name has lived on came in 1985, when the SCMRC (Scottish Classic Motorcycle Racing Club) held the first of its annual Bob McIntyre Memorial Races. Staged at the Knockhill circuit in Fife, this has stood the test of time and the 20th anniversary meeting was held at East Fortune on 19/20 June 2004.

Bob's daughter, Eleanor, has often been a guest at the meeting, and it was the author's pleasure to meet her, together with her husband, David, and children, Mark (12) and Alysse (8), at the 2005 event. And I feel absolutely convinced that Bob would be proud of Eleanor and her family. Unfortunately, as Eleanor was Bob's only child and his brother David (who migrated to Australia and worked as a mechanic in an opal mine) never married, the McIntyre name will not be carried on in the next generation.

But I am equally sure that the legend of Bob McIntyre, the Flying Scot, will live on – the greatest motorcycle racer never to win a world title.

Appendices
Bob McIntyre Motorcycle Road Racing Results

1950

Position	Class	Machine	Circuit	Date
1	350cc (heat)	BSA	Ballado	23 July
1	350cc (final)	BSA	Ballado	23 July
1	500cc (heat)	BSA 350cc	Ballado	23 July
Retired (crashed)	500cc (final)	BSA 350cc	Ballado	23 July
1	350cc	BSA	Kinneill Hillclimb	August
2	500cc	BSA 350cc	Kinneill Hillclimb	August

1951

Position	Class	Machine	Circuit	Date
1	350cc	BSA	Winfield	April FL
1	500cc	BSA	Winfield	April FL
2	350cc (heat)	BSA	Beveridge Park	7 July
2	350cc (final)	BSA	Beveridge Park	7 July
1	500cc (heat)	BSA 350cc	Beveridge Park	7 July
Retired	500cc (final)	BSA 350cc	Beveridge Park	7 July
1	350cc	BSA	Kinneill	August
3	500cc	BSA 350cc	Kinneill	August

1952

Position	Class	Machine	Circuit	Date
1	350cc	BSA	Winfield	April FL
2	500cc	BSA 350cc	Winfield	April
2	500cc	BSA	Beveridge Park	20 April
2	Junior Clubman's TT	BSA 350cc	Isle of Man	June FL
1	350cc	AJS	Beveridge Park	5 July FL
1	500cc	AJS 350cc	Beveridge Park	5 July FL
1	Junior Manx GP	AJS	Isle of Man	September FL
2	Senior Manx GP	AJS 350cc	Isle of Man	September
1	350cc	AJS	Crail	21 September FL
1	Unlimited	AJS 350cc	Crail	21 September FL
Retired (crash)	350cc	AJS	Silverstone	27 September

1953

Position	Class	Machine	Circuit	Date
5	350cc	AJS	Silverstone	6 April
3	350cc	AJS	Silverstone	18 April
1	350cc	AJS	North West 200	9 May FL
1	Handicap	AJS	North West 200	9 May FL
Retired (engine)	350cc Junior TT	AJS	Isle of Man	9 June
1	350cc	AJS	Beveridge Park	9 July FL
1	500cc	Matchless	Beveridge Park	9 July FL
1	350cc	AJS	Charterhall	23 July FL
1	Scottish Championship Mediumweight	Matchless 500cc	Charterhall	23 July FL

Position	Class	Machine	Circuit	Date
1	Scottish Championship Heavyweight	Matchless 500cc	Charterhall	23 July FL
1	Club Team Race	Matchless 500cc	Charterhall	23 July FL
2	Junior	AJS 350cc	Blandford	3 August
Unplaced	Avon Trophy	Matchless 500cc	Blandford	3 August
2	350cc Ulster GP	AJS	Dundrod	13 August
Retired (broken exhaust valve)	500cc Ulster GP	Matchless	Dundrod	13 August
1	350cc	AJS	Aberdare Park	29 August
2	500cc	Matchless	Aberdare Park	29 August
1	350cc	AJS	Snetterton	4 September
Retired (firing on one cylinder)	500cc	Matchless	Snetterton	4 September
5	350cc	AJS	Scarborough	18/19 September
Unplaced	500cc	Matchless	Scarborough	18/19 September
1	500cc	Norton	Charterhall	20 September
2	350cc	AJS	Silverstone	26 September
Unplaced	500cc	Matchless	Silverstone	26 September
1	350cc	AJS	Oulton Park	17 October
1	1000cc (heat)	Matchless 500cc	Oulton Park	17 October

1954

Position	Class	Machine	Circuit	Date
2	350cc	AJS	Silverstone	10 April
6	500cc	AJS	Silverstone	10 April
2	350cc	AJS	Blandford	19 April
1	500cc	Matchless	Blandford	19 April FL
Retired (engine)	Invitation	Matchless 500cc	Blandford	19 April
2	500cc	Matchless	North West 200	15 May
Retired (engine)	350cc Junior TT	AJS	Isle of Man	14 June
14	500cc Senior TT	AJS	Isle of Man	18 June
Retired	500cc Ulster GP	AJS	Dundrod	24 June
3	350cc Ulster GP	AJS	Dundrod	26 June
6	350cc Belgian GP	AJS	Spa Francorchamps	4 July
4	500cc Belgian GP	AJS	Spa Francorchamps	4 July
3	350cc	AJS	Thruxton	1 August
3	500cc	Matchless	Thruxton	1 August
1	350cc	AJS	Silverstone	7 August FL
3	350cc Championship	AJS	Silverstone	7 August
2	500cc	AJS	Silverstone	7 August
6	350cc Swiss GP	AJS	Berne	21 August
Retired (electrics/water)	500cc Swiss GP	AJS	Berne	21 August
2	350cc	AJS	Scarborough	17 September
3	500cc	AJS	Scarborough	18 September
1	350cc	AJS	Aintree	25 September FL
6	1000cc	AJS	Aintree	25 September
3	Handicap	AJS 350cc	Aintree	25 September

1955

Position	Class	Machine	Circuit	Date
3	350cc	Norton	Brough	3 April
1	Brough 25	Norton 500cc	Brough	3 April FL
Non-starter	350cc	Norton	Snetterton	10 April
2	500cc	Norton	Snetterton	10 April
1	1000cc	Norton 500cc	Oulton Park	11 April FL

Position	Class	Machine	Circuit	Date
3	500cc	Norton	Silverstone	23 April
2	350cc	Norton	Aintree	30 April
1	1000cc	Norton 500cc	Aintree	30 April FL
1	Handicap	Norton 500cc	Aintree	30 April FL
Retired (oiled plug)	350cc	Norton	Oulton Park	7 May
2	1000cc	Norton 500cc	Oulton Park	7 May
1	350cc	Norton	Errol	8 May FL
1	1000cc	Norton 500cc	Errol	8 May FL
2	350cc	Norton	Aberdare Park	14 May
2	500cc	Norton	Aberdare Park	14 May
2	1000cc	Norton 500cc	Aberdare Park	14 May
3	350cc	Norton	Brands Hatch	15 May
4	500cc	Norton	Brands Hatch	15 May
3	Handicap	Norton 500cc	Brands Hatch	15 May
1	350cc	Norton	Errol	22 May FL
1	1000cc	Norton 500cc	Errol	22 May FL
2	Junior TT	Norton 350cc	Isle of Man	6 June
5	Senior TT	Norton 500cc	Isle of Man	10 June
1	350cc	Norton	Aberdare Park	18 June FL
1	Invitation	Norton 500cc	Aberdare Park	18 June FL
1	350cc	Norton	Beveridge Park	2 July FL
1	500cc	Norton	Beveridge Park	2 July FL
1	350cc	Norton	Oulton Park	30 July FL
1	1000cc	Norton 500cc	Oulton Park	30 July FL
1	Les Graham Trophy Race	Norton 500cc	Oulton Park	30 July FL
4	350cc	Norton	Thruxton	1 August
5	500cc	Norton	Thruxton	1 August
2	350cc	Norton	Errol	21 August
1	1000cc	Norton 500cc	Errol	21 August FL
1	350cc	Norton	Snetterton	10 September
2	500cc	Norton	Snetterton	10 September
3	350cc	Norton	Scarborough	16 September
Unplaced	500cc	Norton	Scarborough	17 September
6	350cc	Norton	Aintree	24 September
5	500cc	Norton	Aintree	24 September
2	350cc	Norton	Brough	25 September
Retired in heat	500cc	Norton	Brough	25 September
2	350cc	Norton	Silverstone	1 October FL
2	500cc	Norton	Silverstone	1 October
2	350cc Championship	Norton	Silverstone	1 October
4	500cc Championship	Norton	Silverstone	1 October
2	350cc	Norton	Brands Hatch	2 October
3	1000cc Invitation	BSA	Brands Hatch	2 October

1956

Position	Class	Machine	Circuit	Date
1	250cc	Norton	Brough	30 March FL
1	350cc	Norton	Brough	30 March FL
1	Brough 25	Norton 500cc	Brough	30 March FL
1	250cc	Norton	Oulton Park	2 April FL
1	350cc	Norton	Oulton Park	2 April FL
1	500cc	Norton	Oulton Park	2 April FL
2	250cc	Norton	Snetterton	8 April
1	350cc	Norton	Snetterton	8 April FL

Position	Class	Machine	Circuit	Date
2	500cc	Norton	Snetterton	8 April
Retired (waterlogged ignition)	350cc (heat)	Norton	Silverstone	14 April
2	1000cc	Norton 500cc	Silverstone	14 April
1	250cc	Norton	Errol	22 April FL
1	350cc	Norton	Errol	22 April FL
1	500cc	Norton	Errol	22 April FL
1	250cc	Norton	Charterhall	28 April FL
Retired	350cc	Norton	Charterhall	28 April
1	1000cc	Norton 500cc	Charterhall	28 April FL
Retired (split fuel tank)	500cc	Norton	North West 200	12 May FL
1	250cc	Norton	Errol	13 May FL
2	350cc	Norton 250cc	Errol	13 May
1	1000cc	Norton 500cc	Errol	13 May FL
1	250cc	Norton	Oulton Park	21 May FL
1	350cc	Norton	Oulton Park	21 May FL
2	500cc	Norton	Oulton Park	21 May
Retired (oil leak)	Junior TT	Norton 350cc	Isle of Man	4 June
Retired (sheared pannier tank bolt)	Senior TT	Norton 500cc	Isle of Man	8 June
Retired (crashed)	9-Hour race	BSA Gold Star 500cc (shared with Alastair King)	Thruxton	23 June
1	Southern 100 350cc	Norton	Billown	12 July FL
4	Southern 100 500cc	Norton	Billown	12 July FL
1	250cc	Norton	Beveridge Park	14 July FL
1	350cc	Norton	Beveridge Park	14 July FL
1	500cc	Norton	Beveridge Park	14 July FL
Retired (drive chain)	250cc	Norton	Aintree	28 July
1	350cc	Norton	Aintree	28 July FL
1	500cc	Norton	Aintree	28 July
3	Handicap	Norton 500cc	Aintree	28 July
1	250cc	Norton	Oulton Park	4 August FL
2	350cc	Norton	Oulton Park	4 August
Retired (broken footrest)	1000cc	Norton 500cc	Oulton Park	4 August
3	Handicap	Norton 500cc	Oulton Park	4 August
1	250cc	Norton	Snetterton	5 August FL
1	350cc	Norton	Snetterton	5 August FL
1	500cc	Norton	Snetterton	5 August FL
1	British Ch'ship 250cc	Norton	Thruxton	6 August FL
2	British Ch'ship 350cc	Norton	Thruxton	6 August
1	British Ch'ship 500cc	Norton	Thruxton	6 August
1	250cc	Norton	Errol	12 August FL
Retired (engine)	350cc	Norton	Errol	12 August
Retired (gearbox)	500cc	Norton	Errol	12 August
1	350cc	Norton	Scarborough	15 September FL
2	500cc	Norton	Scarborough	15 September
1	250cc	Norton	Cadwell Park	16 September FL
3	350cc	Norton	Cadwell Park	16 September
2	1000cc	Norton 500cc	Cadwell Park	16 September
2	250cc	Norton	Silverstone	22 September
2	350cc	Norton	Silverstone	22 September
1	500cc	Norton	Silverstone	22 September FL
3	250cc Championship	Norton	Silverstone	22 September
2	350cc Championship	Norton	Silverstone	22 September FL
2	500cc Championship	Norton	Silverstone	22 September
2	250cc	Norton	Brands Hatch	23 September
2	350cc	Norton	Brands Hatch	23 September

Position	Class	Machine	Circuit	Date
2	1000cc	Norton 500cc	Brands Hatch	23 September
2	Slazenger Trophy	Norton 500cc	Brands Hatch	23 September
1	250cc	Norton	Aberdare Park	29 September FL
1	350cc	Norton	Aberdare Park	29 September FL
1	500cc	Norton	Aberdare Park	29 September FL
1	250cc	Norton	Crystal Palace	6 October FL
1	350cc	Norton	Crystal Palace	6 October
1	500cc	Norton	Crystal Palace	6 October

1957

Position	Class	Machine	Circuit	Date
3	350cc	Gilera	Imola	22 April
Retired (mechanical problems)	500cc	Gilera	Imola	22 April
Non-starter	250cc	Norton	Errol	12 May FL
2	350cc	Norton	Errol	12 May FL
1	Unlimited	Norton 500cc	Errol	12 May FL
1	Handicap	Norton 500cc	Errol	12 May FL
Retired (crash)	350cc German GP	Gilera	Hockenheim	19 May FL
2	500cc German GP	Gilera	Hockenheim	19 May FL
1	350cc Junior TT	Gilera	Isle of Man	3 June FL
1	500cc Senior TT	Gilera	Isle of Man	7 June FL
4	250cc	Norton	Oulton Park	10 June
1	500cc	Norton	Oulton Park	10 June FL
1	350cc	Norton	Scarborough	15 June
1	500cc	Norton	Scarborough	15 June
1	250cc	Norton	Errol	23 June
1	350cc	Norton	Errol	23 June
1	500cc	Norton	Errol	23 June
2	Unlimited	Norton	Errol	23 June
2	350cc Dutch TT	Gilera	Assen	29 June
Retired (crash)	500cc Dutch TT	Gilera	Assen	29 June
1	250cc	Norton	Crimond	27 July
2	350cc	Norton	Crimond	27 July
1	Unlimited	Norton 500cc	Crimond	27 July
Retired (engine)	350cc Ulster GP	Gilera	Dundrod	10 August
2	500cc Ulster GP	Gilera	Dundrod	10 August
1	350cc Italian GP	Gilera	Monza	1 September
Did not start (illness)	500cc Italian GP	Gilera	Monza	1 September

1958

Position	Class	Machine	Circuit	Date
Unplaced	350cc	Norton	Brands Hatch	4 April
Unplaced	500cc	Norton	Brands Hatch	4 April
Unplaced	350cc	Norton	Oulton Park	7 April
Retired (front fork problems)	500cc	Norton	Oulton Park	7 April
2	350cc	Norton	Silverstone	19 April
2	500cc	Norton	Silverstone	19 April
Retired	250cc	Norton	Beveridge Park	26 April
1	350cc	Norton	Beveridge Park	26 April
1	500cc	Norton	Beveridge Park	26 April
2	350cc	Norton	Aintree	10 May FL
2	500cc	Norton	Aintree	10 May FL
Retired (broken clutch cable)	Handicap 350cc	Norton	Aintree	10 May
Retired (dropped valve)	500cc	Norton	North West 200	17 May FL

Position	Class	Machine	Circuit	Date
Retired (engine tightened up)	350cc Junior TT	Norton	Isle of Man	2 June
Retired (stripped camshaft bevel gear)	500cc Senior TT	Norton	Isle of Man	6 June
2	350cc	Norton	Errol	14 June FL
1	500cc	Norton	Errol	14 June FL
1	Handicap	Norton	Errol	14 June FL
2	500-mile Endurance Race	Royal Enfield 700cc (shared with Derek Powell)	Thruxton	20 June FL
1	350cc	Norton	Charterhall	28 June FL
1	500cc	Norton	Charterhall	28 June FL
4	Handicap	Norton 500cc	Charterhall	28 June FL
1	350cc Southern 100	Norton	Billown	9 July FL
2	500cc Southern 100	Norton	Billown	10 July FL
1	250cc	NSU	Charterhall	27 July FL
1	350cc Race 1	Norton	Charterhall	27 July FL
1	350cc Race 2	Norton	Charterhall	27 July FL
1	500cc Race 1	Norton	Charterhall	27 July FL
1	500cc Race 2	Norton	Charterhall	27 July FL
1	350cc	Norton	Oulton Park	4 August FL
1	500cc	Norton	Oulton Park	4 August FL
1	Les Graham Trophy Race	Norton 500cc	Oulton Park	4 August FL
5	350cc Ulster GP	Norton	Dundrod	9 August
2	500cc Ulster GP	Norton	Dundrod	9 August
1	350cc	Norton	Errol	17 August
1	500cc	Norton	Errol	17 August
1	350cc	AJS	Silverstone	13 September
1	500cc	Norton	Silverstone	13 September
Retired in heat (mainshaft nut came loose)	350cc	AJS	Scarborough	19 September
4	500cc	Norton	Scarborough	20 September
2	350cc	AJS	Aintree	27 September
4	500cc	Norton	Aintree	27 September
4	Race of the Year	Norton 500cc	Mallory Park	28 September
Retired heat (failed oil pump)	350cc	AJS	Oulton Park	4 October
1	250cc	NSU	Oulton Park	4 October
2	500cc	Norton	Oulton Park	4 October

1959

Position	Class	Machine	Circuit	Date
4	350cc	Norton	Mallory Park	22 March
1	500cc	Norton	Mallory Park	22 March FL
Retired (crash)	350cc	Norton	Brands Hatch	27 March
2	1000cc Race 1	Norton 500cc	Brands Hatch	27 March
1	1000cc Race 2	Norton 500cc	Brands Hatch	27 March FL
Retired (lubrication problems)	350cc	Norton	Oulton Park	30 March
Retired (seized engine)	500cc	Norton	Oulton Park	30 March
4	350cc	AJS	Silverstone	18 April
2	500cc	Norton	Silverstone	18 April FL
1	350cc	AJS	Mallory Park	19 April
Retired (would not start)	500cc	Norton	Mallory Park	19 April
1	350cc	Norton	Beveridge Park	25 April FL
2	500cc	Norton	Beveridge Park	25 April FL
1	350cc	AJS	Charterhall	26 April FL
2	500cc	Norton	Charterhall	26 April
3	350cc	AJS	Mallory Park	3 May

Position	Class	Machine	Circuit	Date
1	500cc		Mallory Park	3 May FL
1	500cc	Norton	North West 200	9 May FL
1	350cc	Norton	Errol	10 May FL
2	500cc	Norton	Errol	10 May FL
Retired (engine stopped on last lap)	Les Graham Trophy Race	AJS 350cc	Oulton Park	16 May
1	500cc	Norton	Oulton Park	16 May FL
3	350cc	Norton	Blandford	18 May
2	500cc	Norton	Blandford	18 May
1	Formula 1 500cc	Norton	Isle of Man	30 May FL
Non-starter	250cc Lightweight TT	NSU	Isle of Man	3 June
Retired	350cc Junior TT	AJS	Isle of Man	1 June
5	500cc Senior TT	Norton	Isle of Man	6 June
1	350cc	AJS	Mallory Park	7 June
1	500cc	Norton	Mallory Park	7 June
Retired (crash)	500-mile Endurance Race	Royal Enfield 700cc (shared with Eric Hinton)	Thruxton	20 June FL
1	350cc Southern 100	AJS	Billown	1 July FL
Retired (broken valve spring)	500cc Southern 100	Norton	Billown	2 July FL
Retired (broken valve spring)	350cc Ulster GP	AJS	Dundrod	8 August
2	500cc Ulster GP	Norton	Dundrod	8 August
1	350cc	AJS	Silverstone	22 August
1	1000cc	Norton 500cc	Silverstone	22 August
1	350cc	AJS	Oulton Park	28 August FL
1	500cc	Norton	Oulton Park	28 August FL
1	Handicap	Norton 500cc	Oulton Park	28 August FL
1	350cc	Norton	Errol	6 September FL
1	500cc	Norton	Errol	6 September FL
Non-starter (crashed in heat)	350cc	AJS	Scarborough	19 September
Non-starter (crashed in 350cc heat)	500cc	Norton	Scarborough	19 September
1	350cc	AJS	Aintree	26 September FL
1	500cc	Norton	Aintree	26 September FL
Retired (clutch trouble)	Aintree Century	Norton 500cc	Aintree	26 September FL
1	350cc	AJS	Mallory Park	27 September FL
1	500cc	Norton	Mallory Park	27 September FL
1	Race of the Year	Norton 500cc	Mallory Park	27 September
Retired (recurrence of old injury)	350cc	AJS	Brands Hatch	11 October
4	500cc	Norton	Brands Hatch	11 October

1960

Position	Class	Machine	Circuit	Date
1	350cc	AJS	Silverstone	8 April FL
1	500cc	Norton	Silverstone	8 April FL
1	350cc	AJS	Oulton Park	18 April FL
2	500cc	Norton	Oulton Park	18 April
1	350cc	AJS	Charterhall	24 April FL
1	1000cc	Norton 500cc	Charterhall	24 April FL
1	350cc	AJS	Mallory Park	30 April
2	500cc	Norton	Mallory Park	30 April
1	350cc	Norton	Beveridge Park	7 May FL
1	Unlimited	Norton	Beveridge Park	7 May FL
2	350cc	AJS	North West 200	14 May FL
Retired (oil leak)	500cc	Norton	North West 200	14 May FL

Position	Class	Machine	Circuit	Date
Retired (engine tightened)	350cc	AJS	Silverstone	27 May
Retired (crash, engine seizure)	500cc	Norton	Silverstone	27 May
3	350cc Junior TT	AJS	Isle of Man	15 June
Retired (misfire)	500cc Senior TT	Norton	Isle of Man	17 June
2	350cc	Norton	Mallory Park	19 June
1	500cc	Norton	Mallory Park	19 June FL
Retired (crash)	500-mile Endurance Race	Royal Enfield 700cc (shared with Alan Rutherford)	Thruxton	25 June
2	350cc Southern 100	Norton	Billown	6 July FL
Disqualified (for refuelling during race)	500cc Southern 100	Norton	Billown	7 July
1	350cc	AJS	Mallory Park	17 July FL
2	500cc	Norton	Mallory Park	17 July FL
1	350cc British Ch'ship	AJS	Oulton Park	1 August FL
1	500cc British Ch'ship	Norton	Oulton Park	1 August
1	Les Graham Trophy Race	Norton 500cc	Oulton Park	1 August
Retired (stopped at pit)	350cc Ulster GP	AJS	Dundrod	6 August
Retired (engine vibration)	500cc Ulster GP	Norton	Dundrod	6 August
1	250cc	Honda	Aintree	24 September FL
2	350cc	AJS	Aintree	24 September
3	500cc	Norton	Aintree	24 September
Retired (crash)	Aintree Century	Norton	Aintree	24 September
1	350cc	Norton	Mallory Park	25 September FL
1	500cc	Norton	Mallory Park	25 September FL
Retired (engine)	Race of the Year	Norton	Mallory Park	25 September

1961

Position	Class	Machine	Circuit	Date
Retired	500cc	Norton	Oulton Park	3 April
Non-starter (bike lost by British Rail)	350cc	AJS	Oulton Park	3 April
5	350cc	AJS	Silverstone	8 April
2	500cc	Norton	Silverstone	8 April
2	350cc	AJS	Mallory Park	9 April
3	500cc	Norton	Mallory Park	9 April
Retired (engine)	500cc	Bianchi 350cc	Imola	16 April
1	350cc North West 200	AJS	Dundrod	6 May
1	500cc North West 200	Norton	Dundrod	6 May FL
Retired (piston failure)	350cc German GP	Bianchi	Hockenheim	14 May
Retired (after winning heat)	250cc	Aermacchi	Beveridge Park	20 May
2	350cc	AJS	Beveridge Park	20 May
1	1000cc	Norton 500cc	Beveridge Park	20 May FL
1	350cc	AJS	Charterhall	21 May FL
1	Unlimited	Norton	Charterhall	21 May FL
Retired (engine lack of oil)	250cc Lightweight TT	Honda	Isle of Man	12 June FL
Retired (broken gearbox layshaft)	350cc Junior TT	Bianchi	Isle of Man	14 June
2	500cc Senior TT	Norton	Isle of Man	16 June
1	350cc	AJS	Mallory Park	18 June FL
1	500cc	Norton	Mallory Park	18 June FL
2	250cc Dutch TT	Honda	Assen	24 June
2	350cc Dutch TT	Bianchi	Assen	24 June
3	500cc Dutch TT	Norton	Assen	24 June
Retired (misfire)	250cc Belgian GP	Honda	Spa Francorchamps	2 July
3	500cc Belgian GP	Norton	Spa Francorchamps	2 July
Retired (broken con rod)	500-mile Endurance Race	Royal Enfield 700cc (shared with (Alastair King)	Thruxton	8 July

Position	Class	Machine	Circuit	Date
8 (serious misfire)	250cc East German GP	Honda	Sachsenring	30 July
3	350cc East German GP	Bianchi	Sachsenring	30 July
Non-starter	250cc British Ch'ship	Aermacchi	Oulton Park	7 August
2	350cc British Ch'ship	AJS	Oulton Park	7 August
Retired (crash)	500cc British Ch'ship	Norton	Oulton Park	7 August
Non-starter	Les Graham Trophy Race	Norton 500cc	Oulton Park	7 August
1	250cc Ulster GP	Honda	Dundrod	12 August FL
Retired (broken gearbox layshaft)	350cc Ulster GP	Bianchi	Dundrod	12 August
1	250cc Leinster 200	Honda	Dunboyne	19 August FL
1	350cc Leinster 200	Honda 250cc	Dunboyne	19 August FL
1	500cc Leinster 200	Norton	Dunboyne	19 August FL
Retired	350cc Italian GP	Bianchi	Monza	3 September
Retired (crash caused by broken oil pipe)	250cc Italian GP	Honda	Monza	3 September

1962

Position	Class	Machine	Circuit	Date
Non-starter (crashed in practice)	350cc	Honda 285cc	Mallory Park	1 April
2	500cc	Norton	Silverstone	7 April
Retired (puncture)	350cc	Honda 285cc	Oulton Park	23 April
1	500cc	Matchless Special	Oulton Park	23 April FL
1	350cc	Honda 285cc	Mallory Park	29 April FL
1	500cc	Matchless Special	Mallory Park	29 April FL
2	250cc Spanish GP	Honda	Barcelona	6 May
2	250cc French GP	Honda	Clermont-Ferrand	13 May
1	350cc	Honda 285cc	Beveridge Park	19 May FL
1	1000cc	Matchless Special 500cc	Beveridge Park	19 May FL
Retired (oil leak)	250cc Lightweight TT	Honda	Isle of Man	4 June FL
Retired (ignition)	350cc Junior TT	Honda 285cc	Isle of Man	6 June
Non-starter	500cc Senior TT	Honda 285cc	Isle of Man	8 June
Retired (ignition)	350cc	Honda 285cc	Mallory Park	10 June FL
3	500cc	Matchless Special	Mallory Park	10 June
2	250cc Dutch TT	Honda	Assen	30 June
Retired (oil leak)	350cc Dutch TT	Honda 285cc	Assen	30 June
1	250cc Belgian GP	Honda	Spa Francorchamps	8 July FL
2	250cc W German GP	Honda	Solitude	15 July
Retired (engine)	350cc British Ch'ship	Honda 285cc	Oulton Park	6 August FL
Retired (crash)	500cc British Ch'ship	Norton	Oulton Park	6 August

Note: Results for 1950, 1951 and 1952 are not complete.

Index